Created by
Neil Gibson & Caspar Wijngaard

Story
Neil Gibson

Art
Caspar Wijngaard

Lettering
Jim Campbell

Layouts
Naila Scargill & Eric Irving

Additional Colouring (Pages 17-27)
Anja Poland

T
PUB

Published by T Publication

Credits

CEO / Creative Director: Neil Gibson
Art Director: Caspar Wijingaard
Head of Operations: Ryan O'Sullivan
Head of Marketing: Will O'Mullane
Distribution (Print): Rafael Mondragón
Distribution (Digital): Dan Watters

For Amy,
For everything.

-Caspar

To Tara,
Who finally enjoys comics.

-Neil

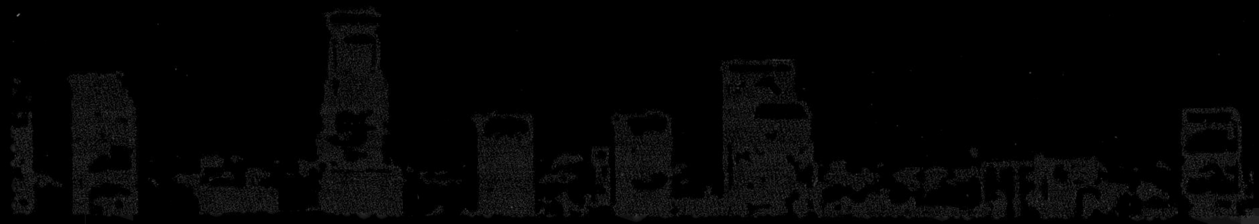

"LEAVE TABATHA ALONE."

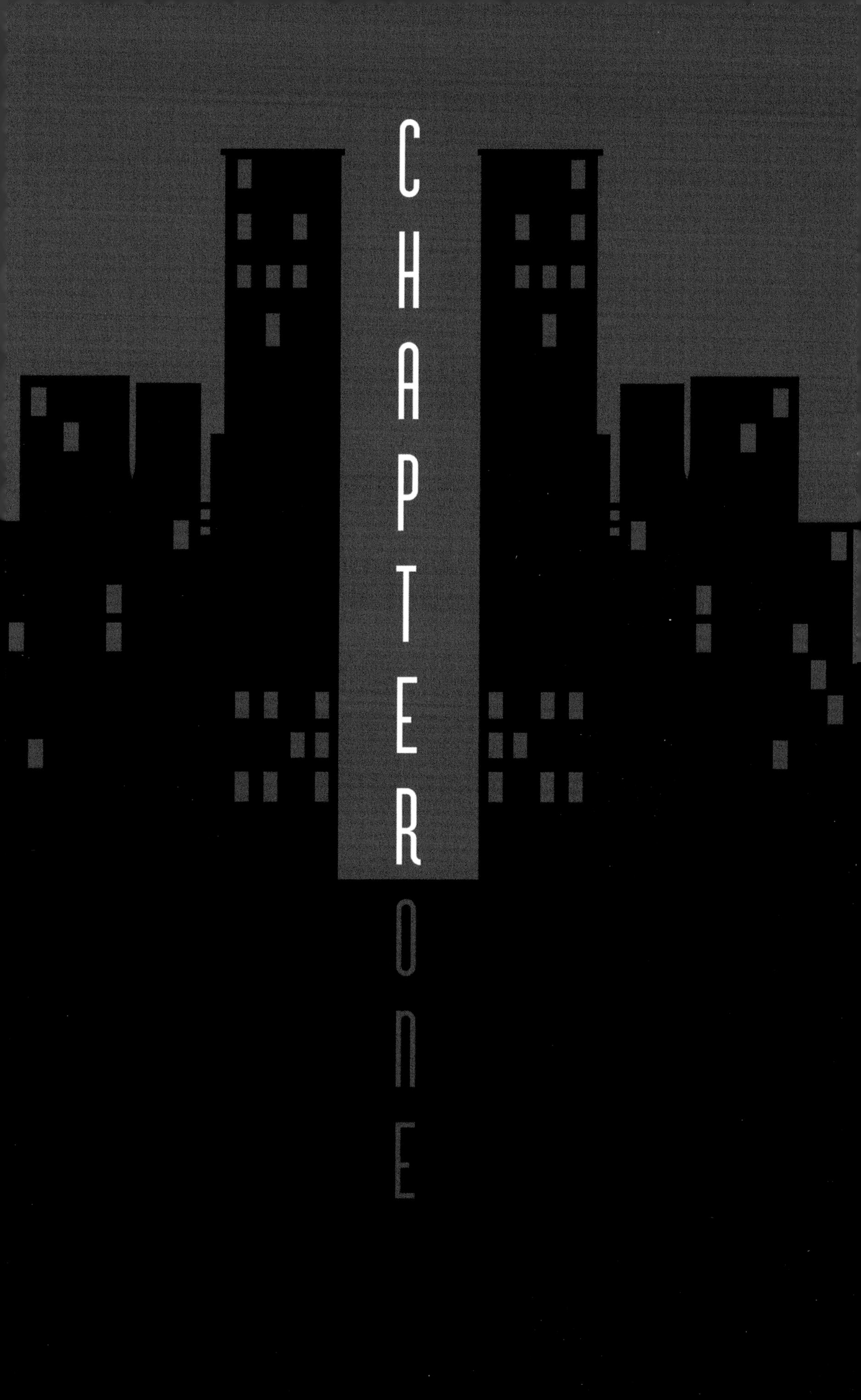

CHAPTER ONE

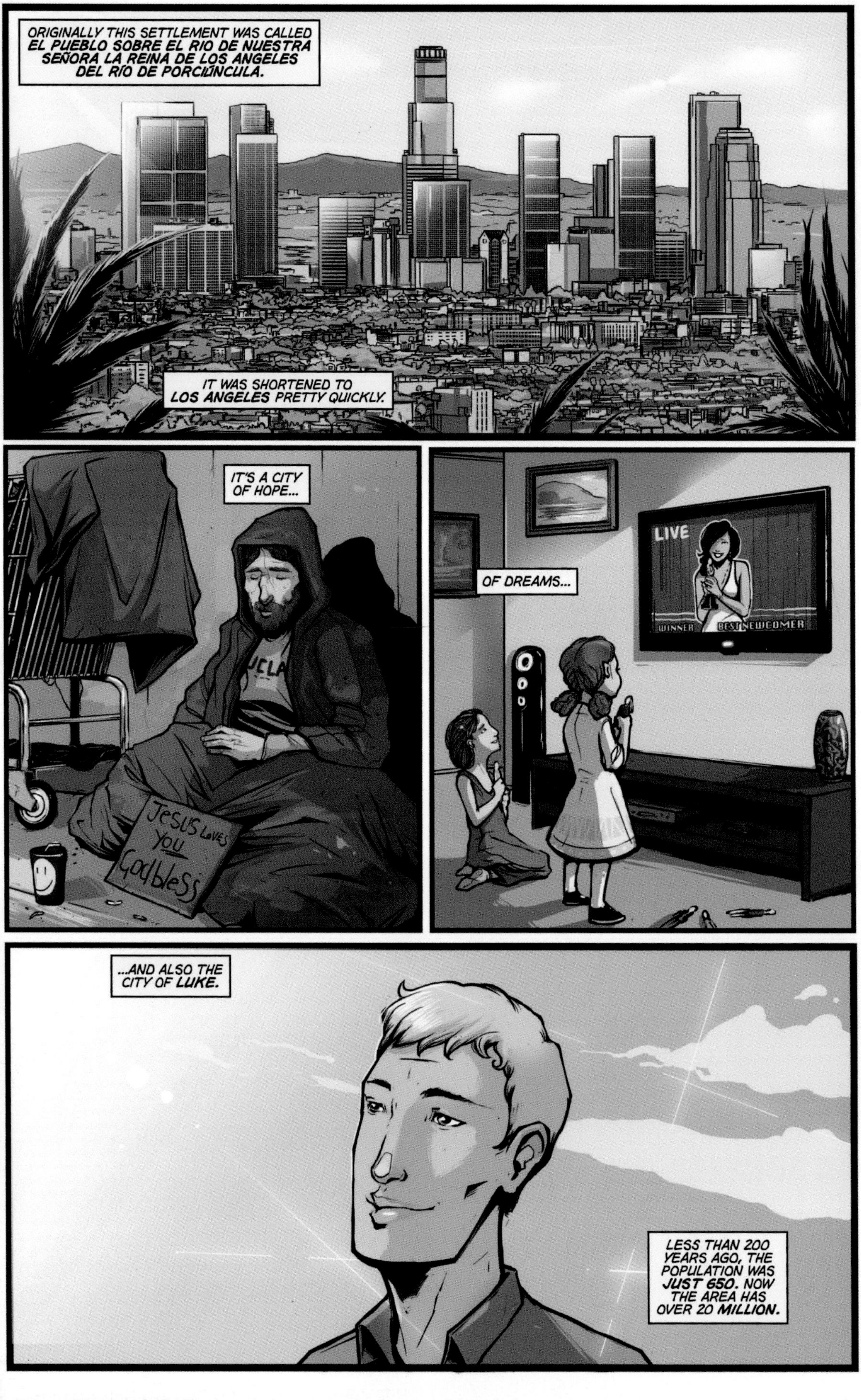
ORIGINALLY THIS SETTLEMENT WAS CALLED EL PUEBLO SOBRE EL RIO DE NUESTRA SEÑORA LA REINA DE LOS ANGELES DEL RÍO DE PORCIÚNCULA.
IT WAS SHORTENED TO LOS ANGELES PRETTY QUICKLY.
IT'S A CITY OF HOPE...
UCLA
JESUS LOVES YOU Godbless
OF DREAMS...
LIVE
WINNER
BEST NEWCOMER
...AND ALSO THE CITY OF LUKE.
LESS THAN 200 YEARS AGO, THE POPULATION WAS JUST 650. NOW THE AREA HAS OVER 20 MILLION.

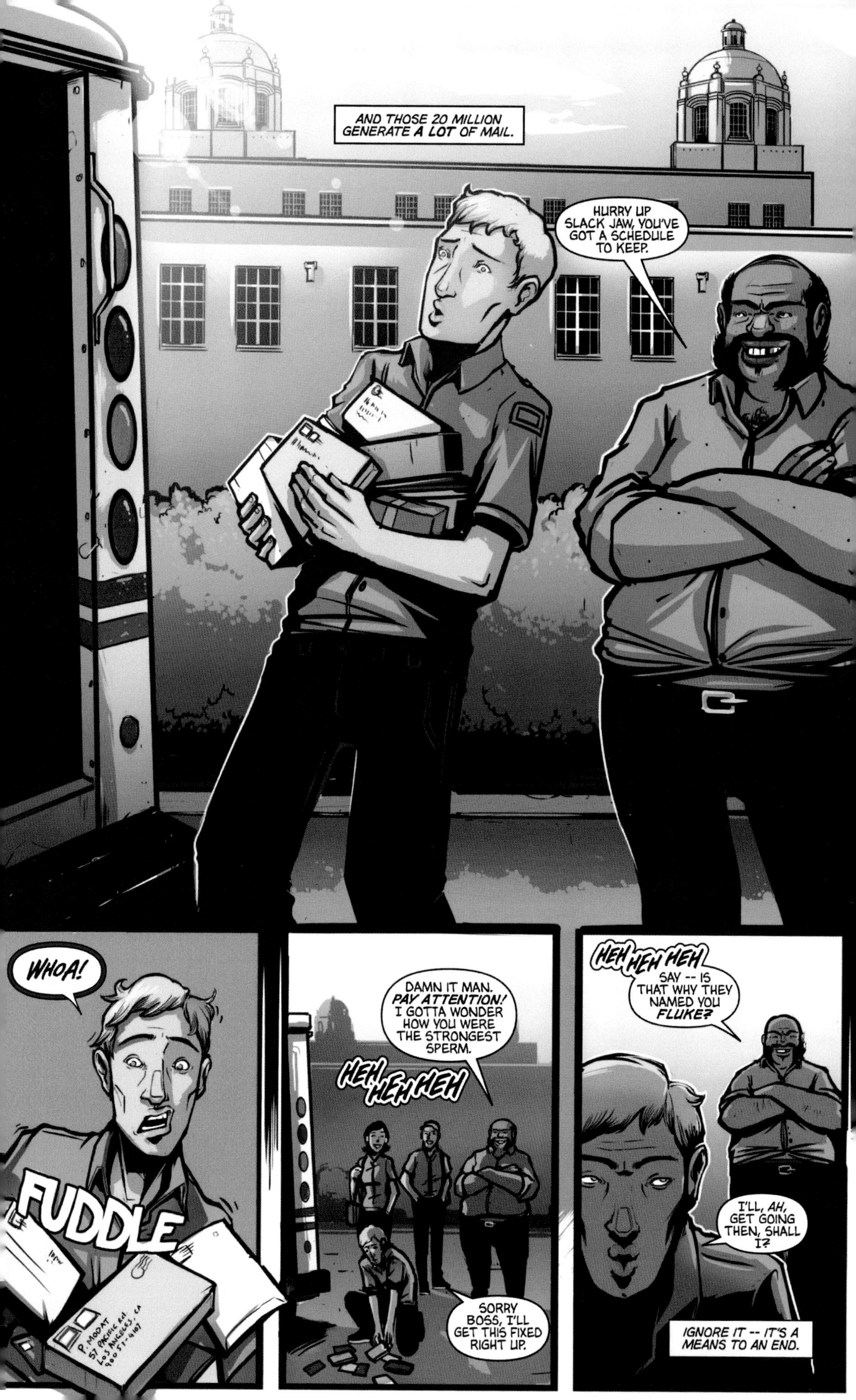
AND THOSE 20 MILLION GENERATE A LOT OF MAIL.
HURRY UP SLACK JAW, YOU'VE GOT A SCHEDULE TO KEEP.
WHOA!
FUDDLE
DAMN IT MAN. PAY ATTENTION! I GOTTA WONDER HOW YOU WERE THE STRONGEST SPERM.
HEH HEH HEH
SORRY BOSS, I'LL GET THIS FIXED RIGHT UP.
HEH HEH HEH
SAY -- IS THAT WHY THEY NAMED YOU FLUKE?
I'LL, AH, GET GOING THEN, SHALL I?
IGNORE IT -- IT'S A MEANS TO AN END.

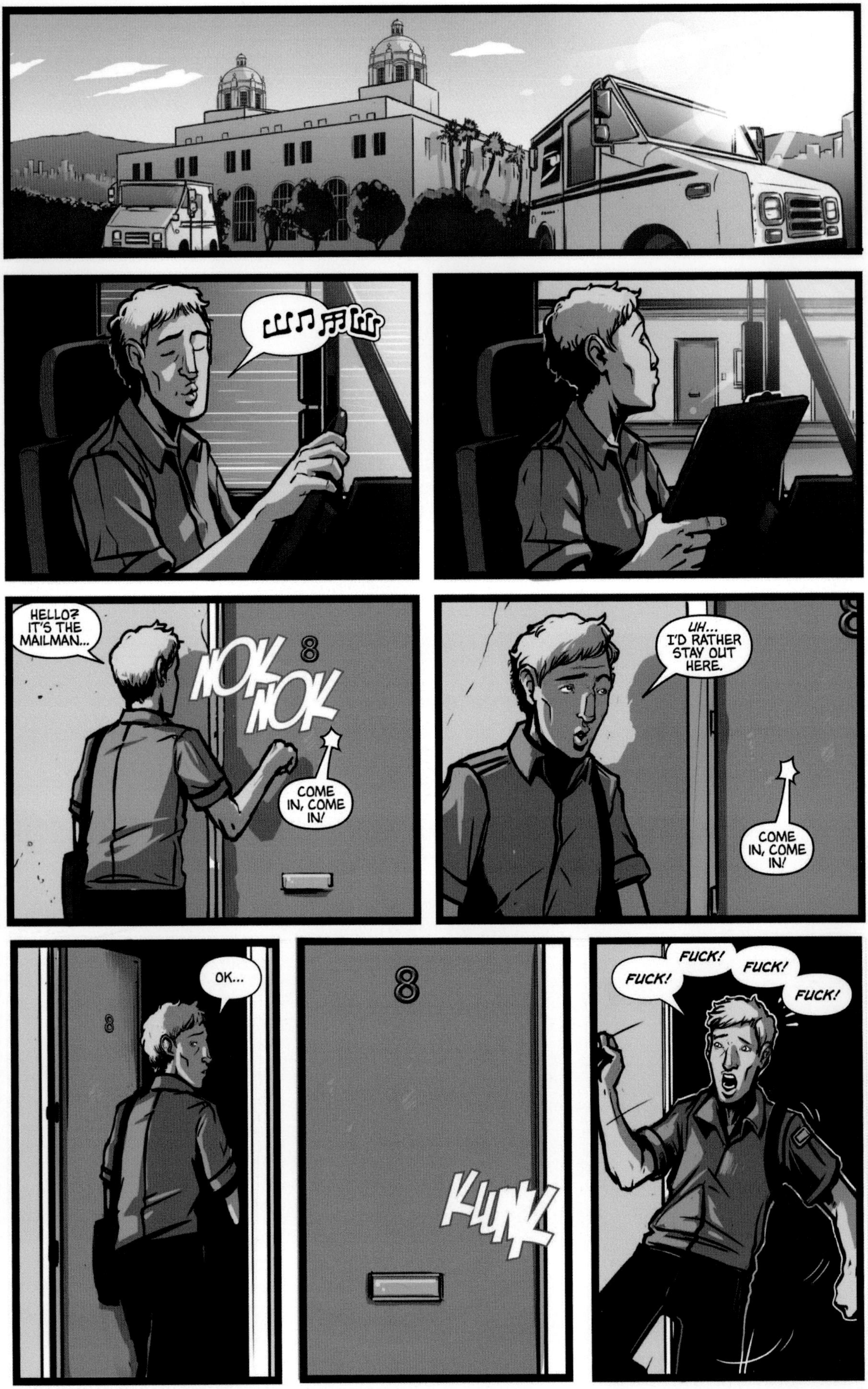

HELLO? IT'S THE MAILMAN...
NOK NOK
COME IN, COME IN!
UH... I'D RATHER STAY OUT HERE.
COME IN, COME IN!
OK...
KLUNK
FUCK!
FUCK!
FUCK!
FUCK!

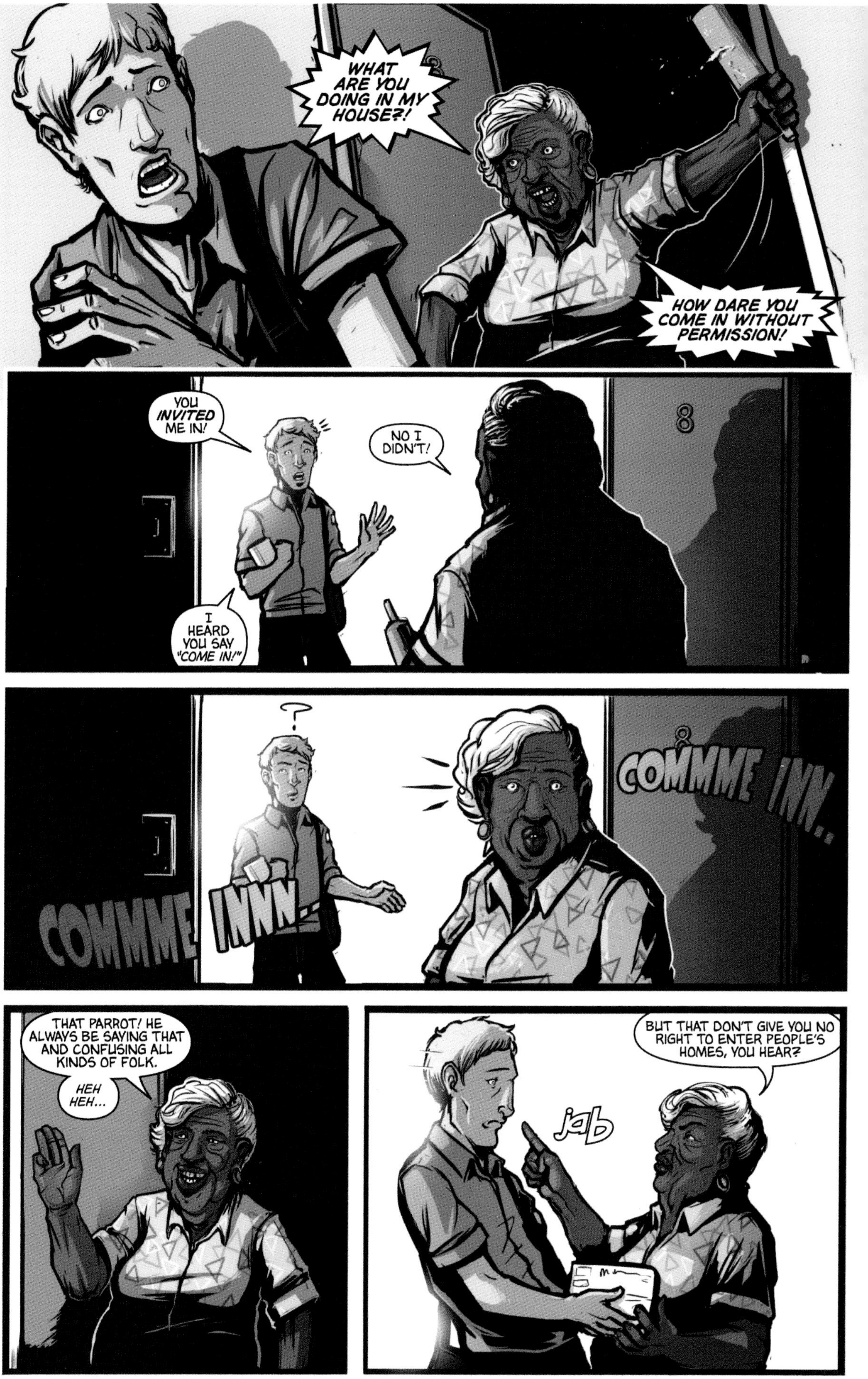
WHAT ARE YOU DOING IN MY HOUSE?!
HOW DARE YOU COME IN WITHOUT PERMISSION!
YOU INVITED ME IN!
NO I DIDN'T!
I HEARD YOU SAY "COME IN!"
COMMME INNN
COMMME INN..
THAT PARROT! HE ALWAYS BE SAYING THAT AND CONFUSING ALL KINDS OF FOLK.
HEH HEH...
BUT THAT DON'T GIVE YOU NO RIGHT TO ENTER PEOPLE'S HOMES, YOU HEAR?
jab

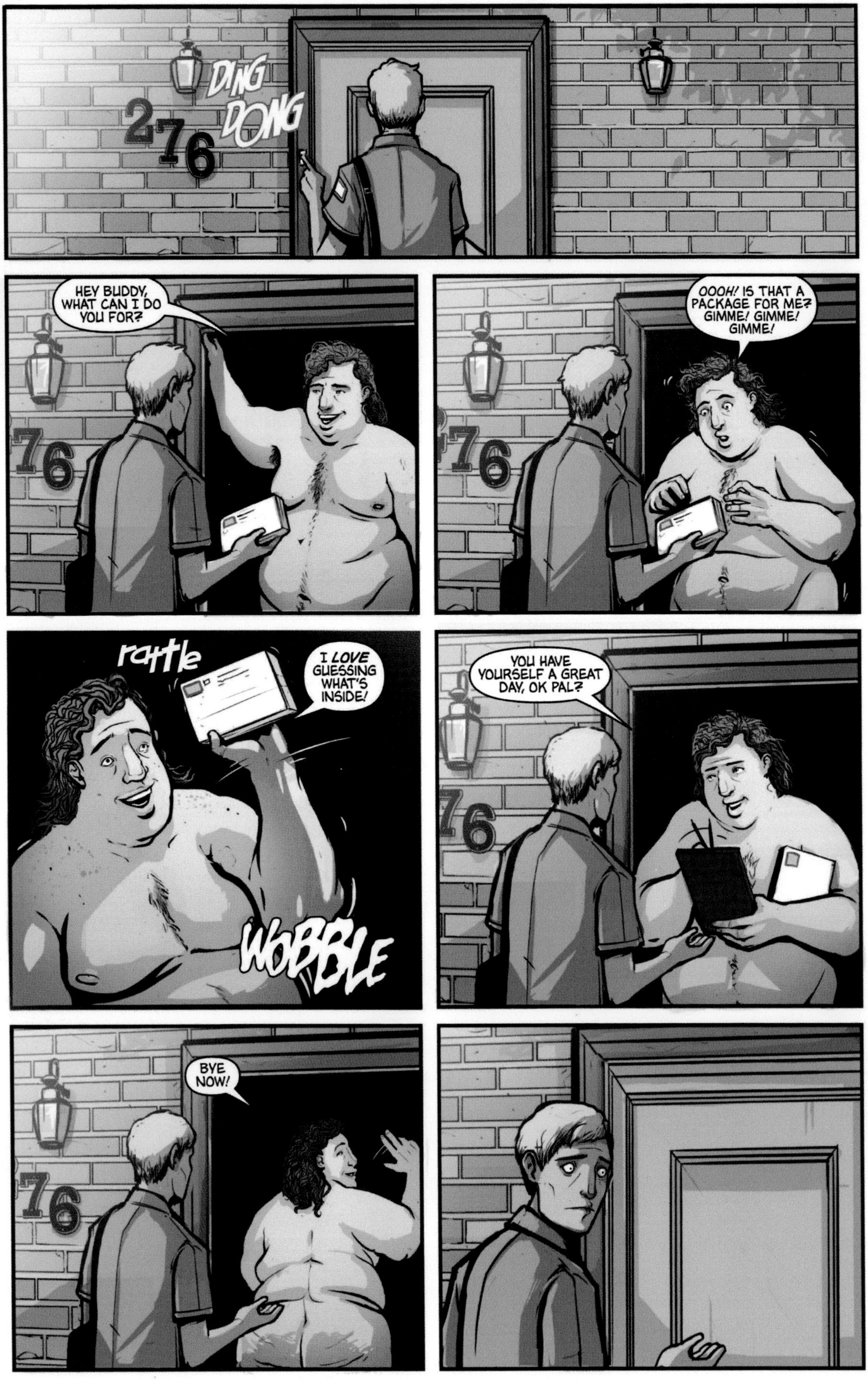
DING
DONG
276
HEY BUDDY, WHAT CAN I DO YOU FOR?
OOOH! IS THAT A PACKAGE FOR ME? GIMME! GIMME! GIMME!
rattle
I LOVE GUESSING WHAT'S INSIDE!
WOBBLE
YOU HAVE YOURSELF A GREAT DAY, OK PAL?
BYE NOW!

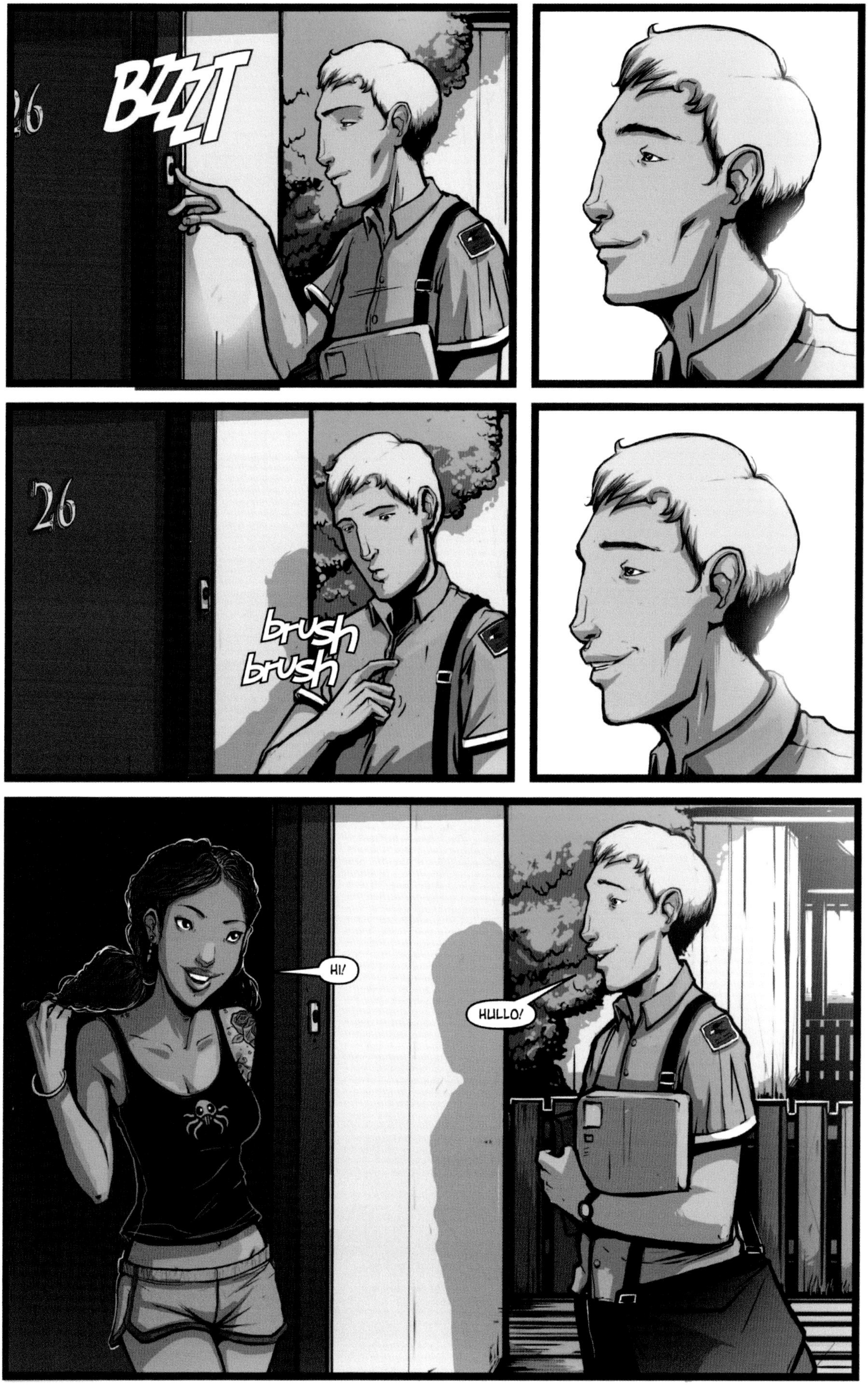
26
BZZZT
26
brush
brush
HI!
HULLO!

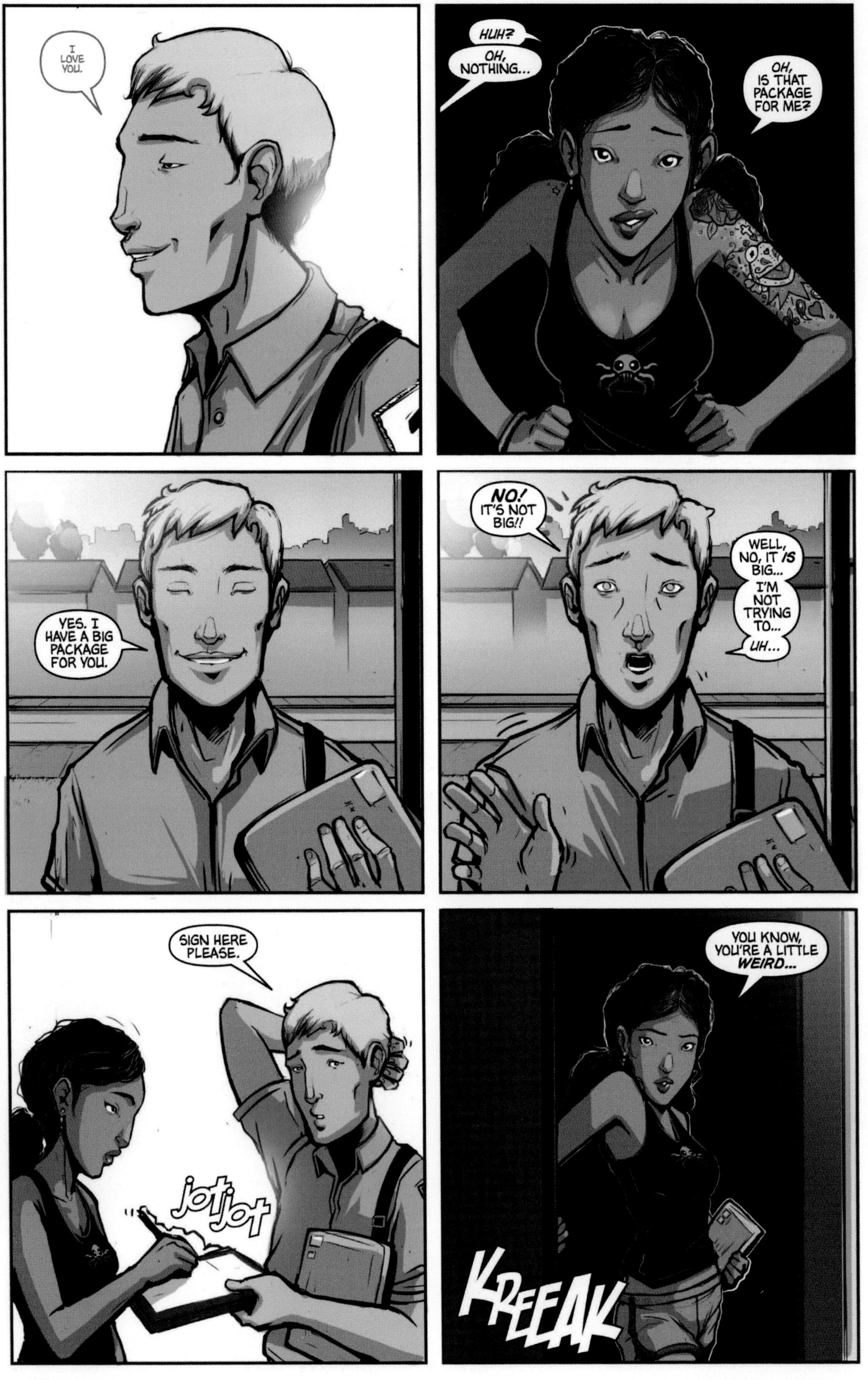
I LOVE YOU.
HUH?
OH, NOTHING...
OH, IS THAT PACKAGE FOR ME?
YES. I HAVE A BIG PACKAGE FOR YOU.
NO! IT'S NOT BIG!!
WELL, NO, IT IS BIG...
I'M NOT TRYING TO...
UH...
SIGN HERE PLEASE.
jot jot
YOU KNOW, YOU'RE A LITTLE WEIRD...
KREEAK

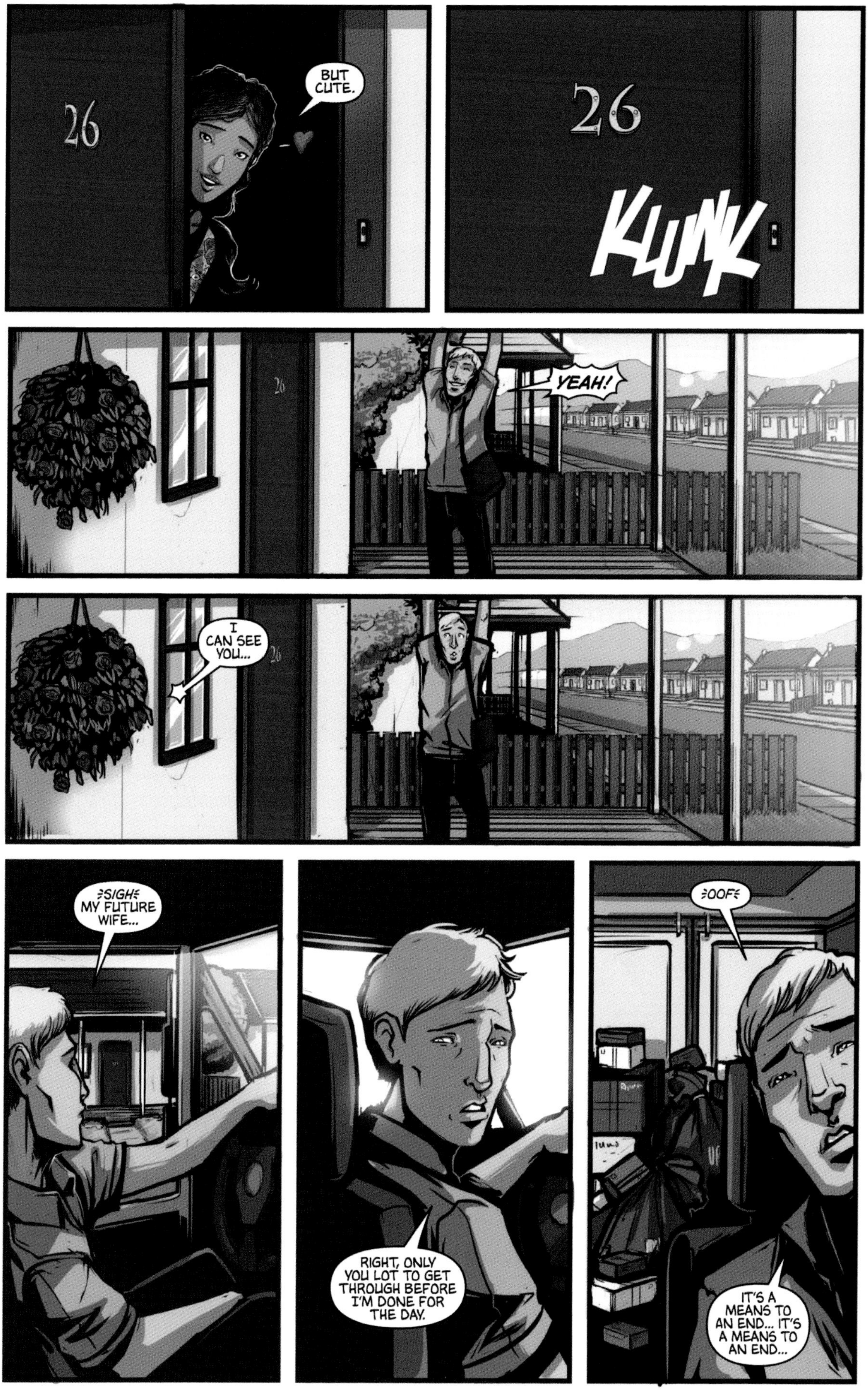
BUT CUTE.
26
26
KLUNK
26
YEAH!
26
I CAN SEE YOU...
=SIGH= MY FUTURE WIFE...
RIGHT, ONLY YOU LOT TO GET THROUGH BEFORE I'M DONE FOR THE DAY.
=OOF=
IT'S A MEANS TO AN END... IT'S A MEANS TO AN END...

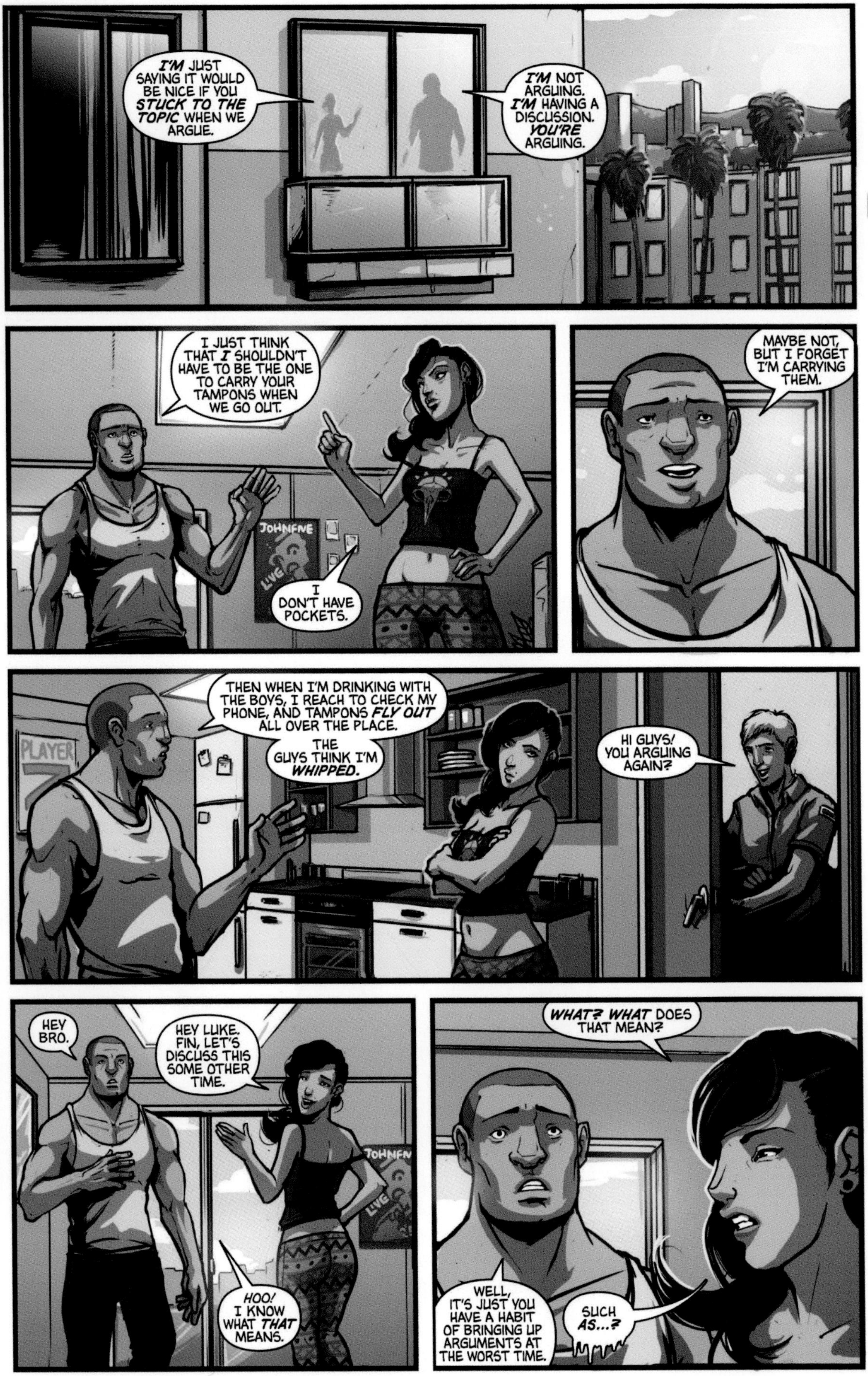
I'M JUST SAYING IT WOULD BE NICE IF YOU STUCK TO THE TOPIC WHEN WE ARGUE.
I'M NOT ARGUING. I'M HAVING A DISCUSSION. YOU'RE ARGUING.
I JUST THINK THAT I SHOULDN'T HAVE TO BE THE ONE TO CARRY YOUR TAMPONS WHEN WE GO OUT.
I DON'T HAVE POCKETS.
MAYBE NOT, BUT I FORGET I'M CARRYING THEM.
THEN WHEN I'M DRINKING WITH THE BOYS, I REACH TO CHECK MY PHONE, AND TAMPONS FLY OUT ALL OVER THE PLACE.
THE GUYS THINK I'M WHIPPED.
PLAYER
HI GUYS! YOU ARGUING AGAIN?
HEY BRO.
HEY LUKE. FIN, LET'S DISCUSS THIS SOME OTHER TIME.
HOO! I KNOW WHAT THAT MEANS.
WHAT? WHAT DOES THAT MEAN?
WELL, IT'S JUST YOU HAVE A HABIT OF BRINGING UP ARGUMENTS AT THE WORST TIME.
SUCH AS...?

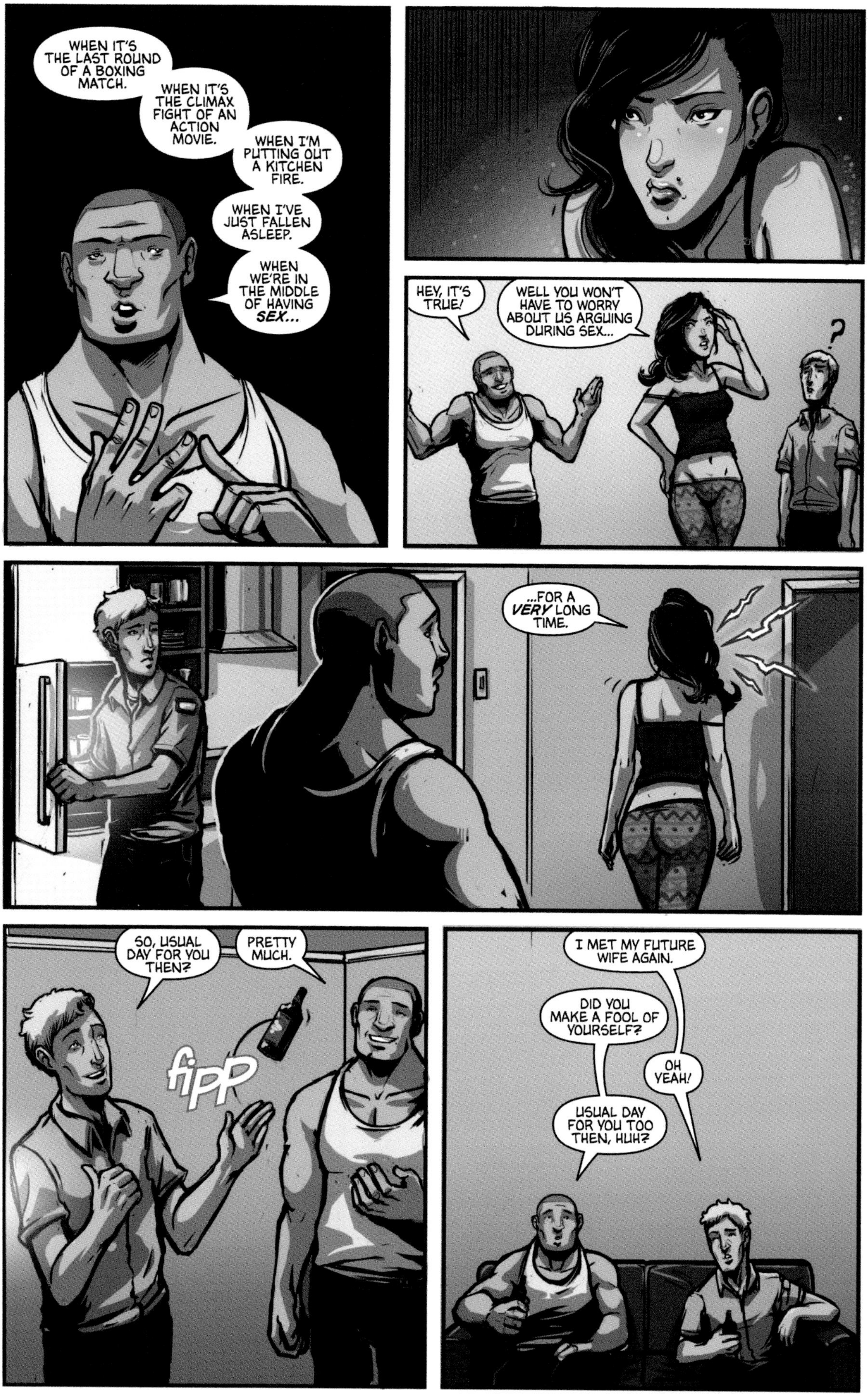

WHEN IT'S THE LAST ROUND OF A BOXING MATCH.
WHEN IT'S THE CLIMAX FIGHT OF AN ACTION MOVIE.
WHEN I'M PUTTING OUT A KITCHEN FIRE.
WHEN I'VE JUST FALLEN ASLEEP.
WHEN WE'RE IN THE MIDDLE OF HAVING **SEX...**
HEY, IT'S TRUE!
WELL YOU WON'T HAVE TO WORRY ABOUT US ARGUING DURING SEX...
?
...FOR A ***VERY*** LONG TIME.
SO, USUAL DAY FOR YOU THEN?
PRETTY MUCH.
fiPP
I MET MY FUTURE WIFE AGAIN.
DID YOU MAKE A FOOL OF YOURSELF?
OH YEAH!
USUAL DAY FOR YOU TOO THEN, HUH?

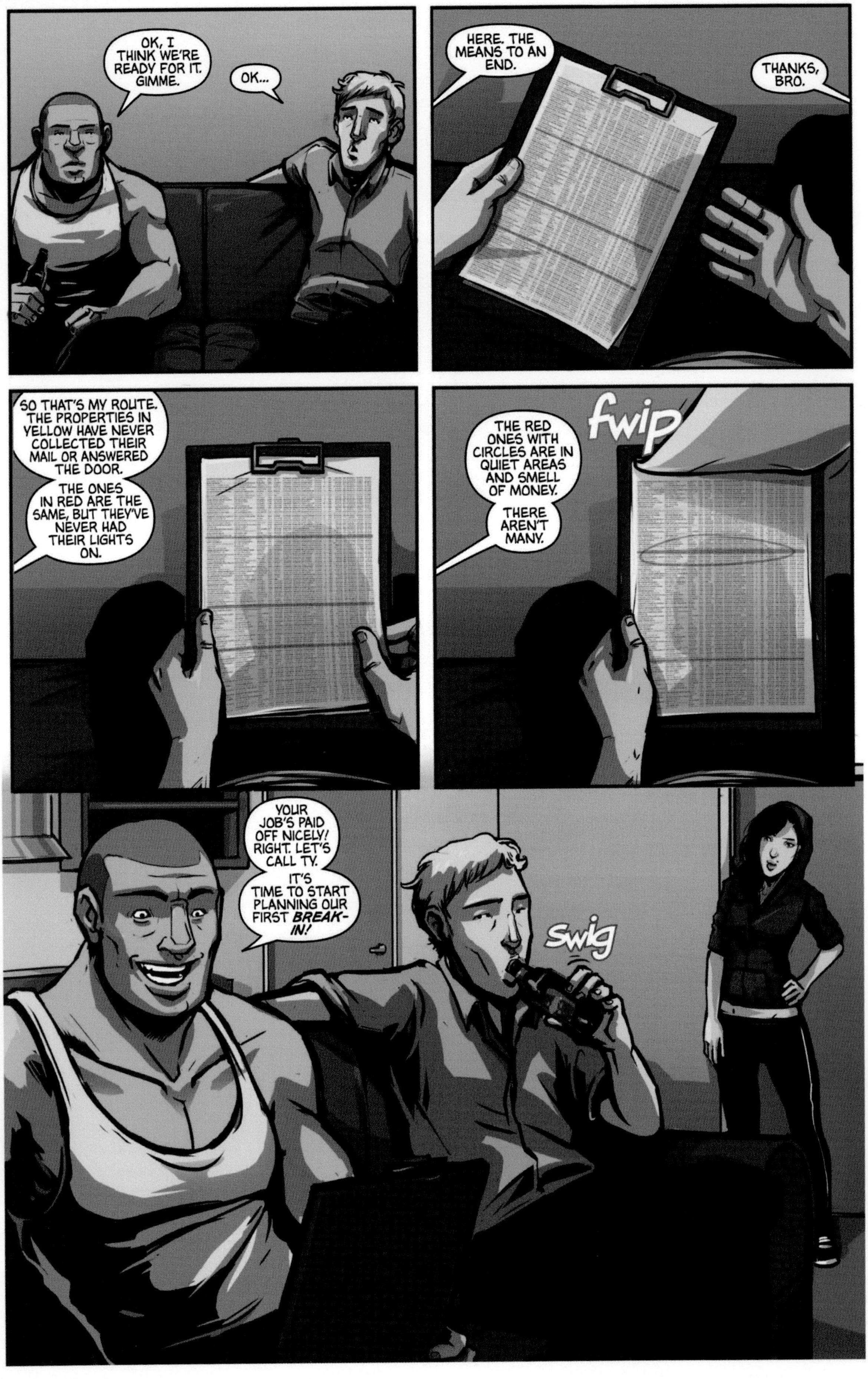
OK, I THINK WE'RE READY FOR IT. GIMME.
OK...
HERE. THE MEANS TO AN END.
THANKS, BRO.
SO THAT'S MY ROUTE. THE PROPERTIES IN YELLOW HAVE NEVER COLLECTED THEIR MAIL OR ANSWERED THE DOOR.
THE ONES IN RED ARE THE SAME, BUT THEY'VE NEVER HAD THEIR LIGHTS ON.
fwip
THE RED ONES WITH CIRCLES ARE IN QUIET AREAS AND SMELL OF MONEY.
THERE AREN'T MANY.
YOUR JOB'S PAID OFF NICELY! RIGHT. LET'S CALL TY.
IT'S TIME TO START PLANNING OUR FIRST BREAK-IN!
swig

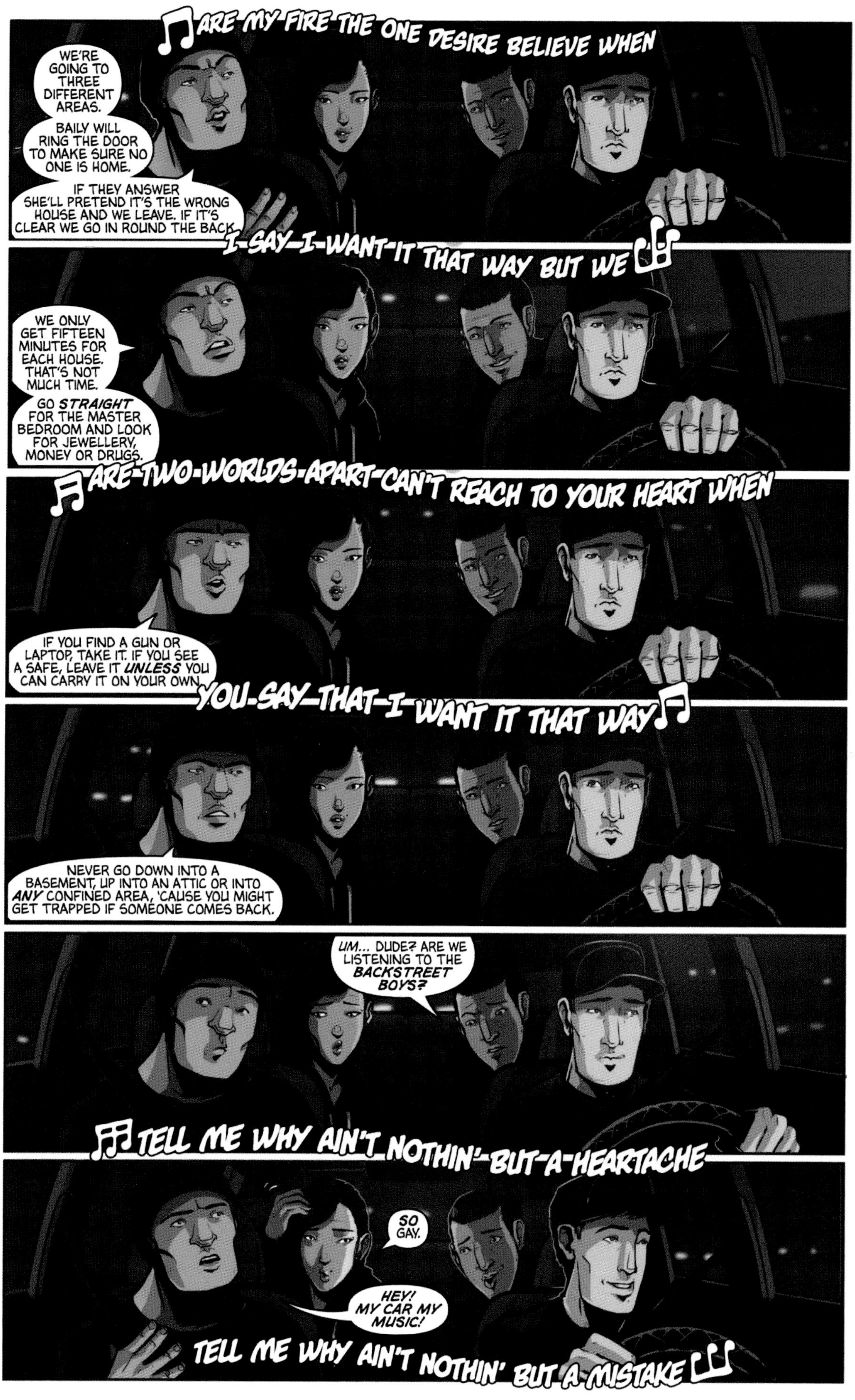
ARE MY FIRE THE ONE DESIRE BELIEVE WHEN
WE'RE GOING TO THREE DIFFERENT AREAS.
BAILY WILL RING THE DOOR TO MAKE SURE NO ONE IS HOME.
IF THEY ANSWER SHE'LL PRETEND IT'S THE WRONG HOUSE AND WE LEAVE. IF IT'S CLEAR WE GO IN ROUND THE BACK.
I SAY I WANT IT THAT WAY BUT WE
WE ONLY GET FIFTEEN MINUTES FOR EACH HOUSE. THAT'S NOT MUCH TIME.
GO STRAIGHT FOR THE MASTER BEDROOM AND LOOK FOR JEWELLERY, MONEY OR DRUGS.
ARE TWO WORLDS APART CAN'T REACH TO YOUR HEART WHEN
IF YOU FIND A GUN OR LAPTOP, TAKE IT. IF YOU SEE A SAFE, LEAVE IT UNLESS YOU CAN CARRY IT ON YOUR OWN.
YOU SAY THAT I WANT IT THAT WAY
NEVER GO DOWN INTO A BASEMENT, UP INTO AN ATTIC OR INTO ANY CONFINED AREA, 'CAUSE YOU MIGHT GET TRAPPED IF SOMEONE COMES BACK.
UM... DUDE? ARE WE LISTENING TO THE BACKSTREET BOYS?
TELL ME WHY AIN'T NOTHIN' BUT A HEARTACHE
SO GAY.
HEY! MY CAR MY MUSIC!
TELL ME WHY AIN'T NOTHIN' BUT A MISTAKE

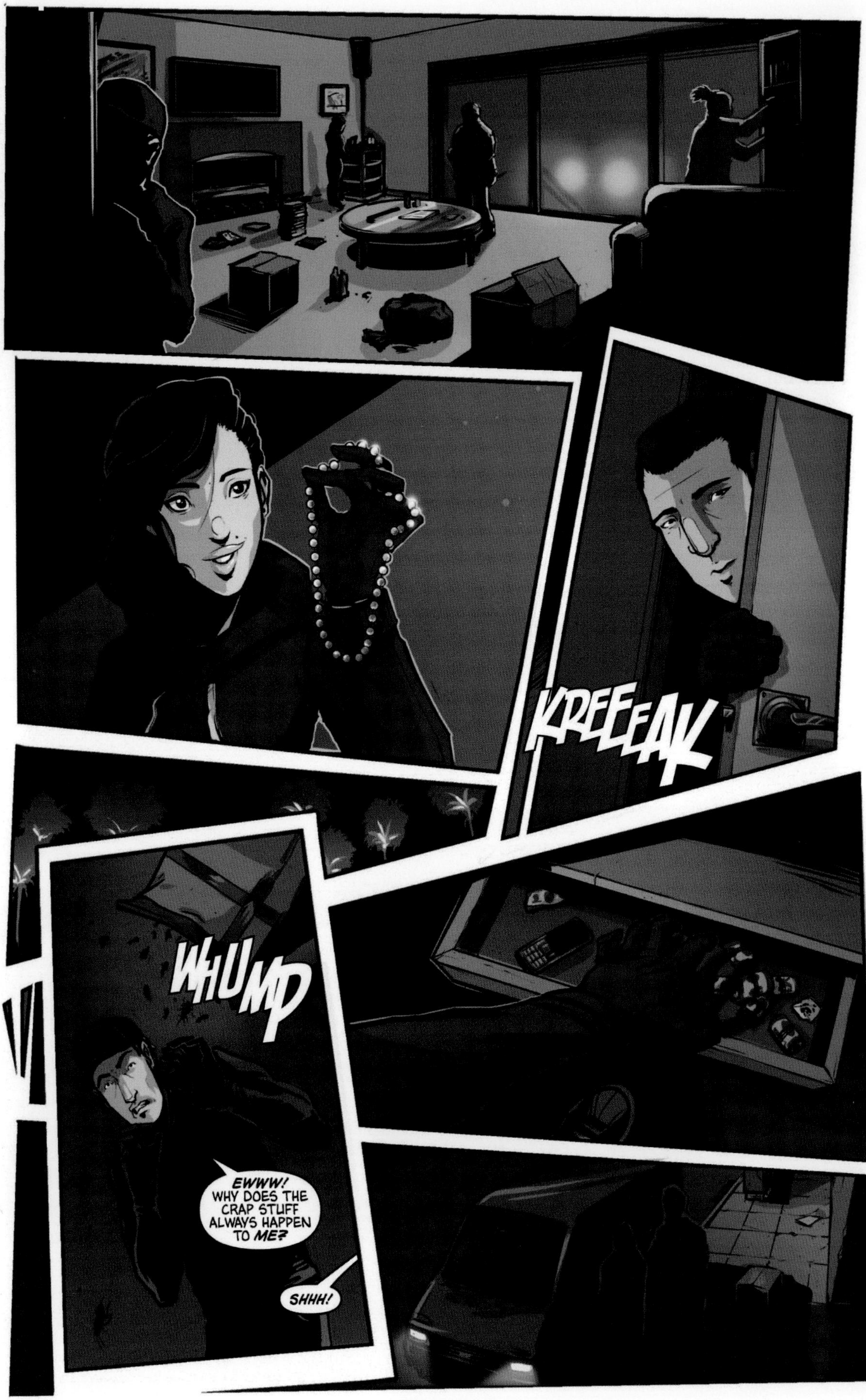
KREEEAK
WHUMP
EWWW! WHY DOES THE CRAP STUFF ALWAYS HAPPEN TO ME?
SHHH!

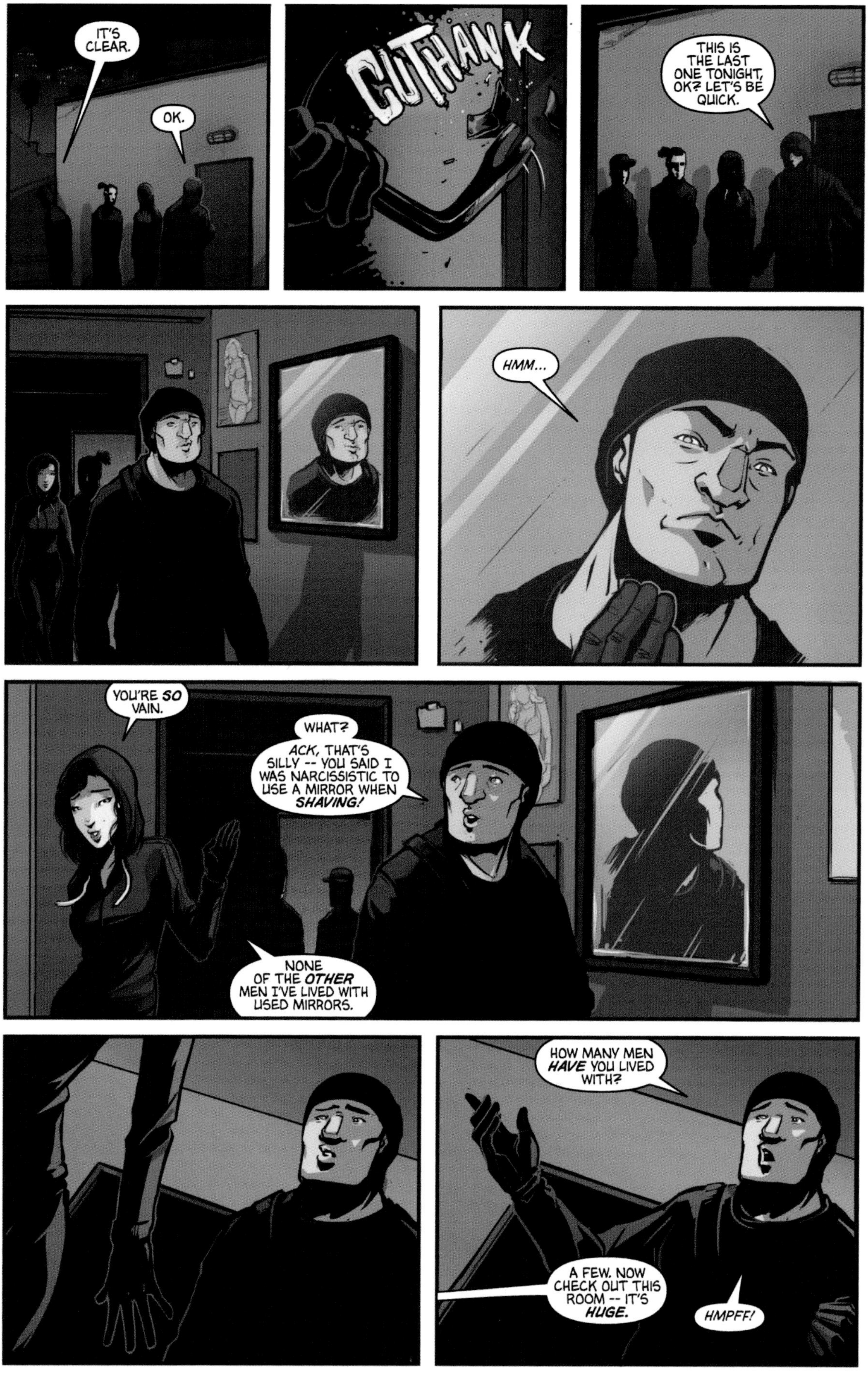
IT'S CLEAR.
OK.
CUTHANK
THIS IS THE LAST ONE TONIGHT, OK? LET'S BE QUICK.
HMM...
YOU'RE SO VAIN.
WHAT?
ACK, THAT'S SILLY -- YOU SAID I WAS NARCISSISTIC TO USE A MIRROR WHEN SHAVING!
NONE OF THE OTHER MEN I'VE LIVED WITH USED MIRRORS.
HOW MANY MEN HAVE YOU LIVED WITH?
A FEW. NOW CHECK OUT THIS ROOM -- IT'S HUGE.
HMPFF!

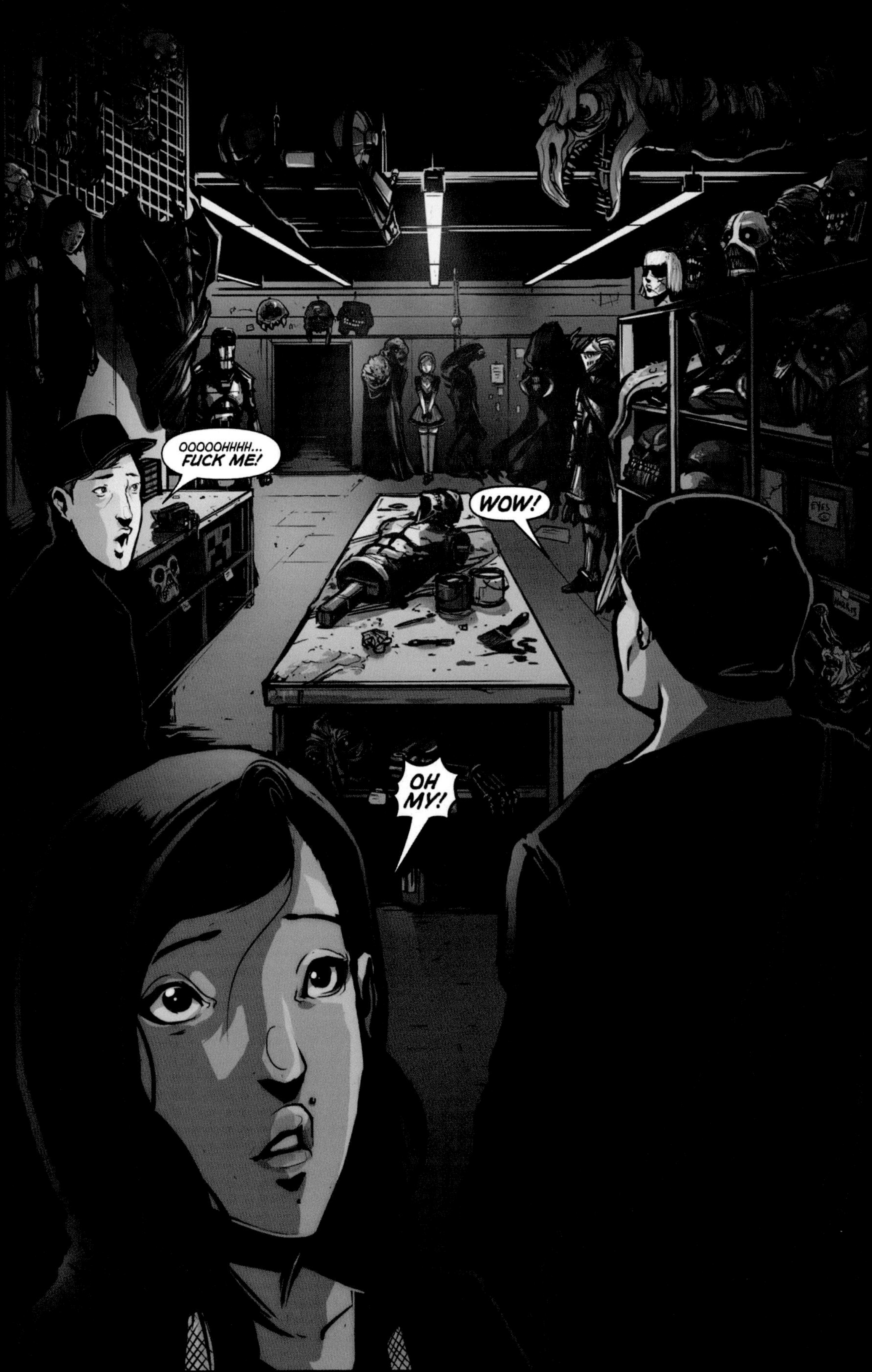
OOOOOHHHH...
FUCK ME!
WOW!
OH MY!

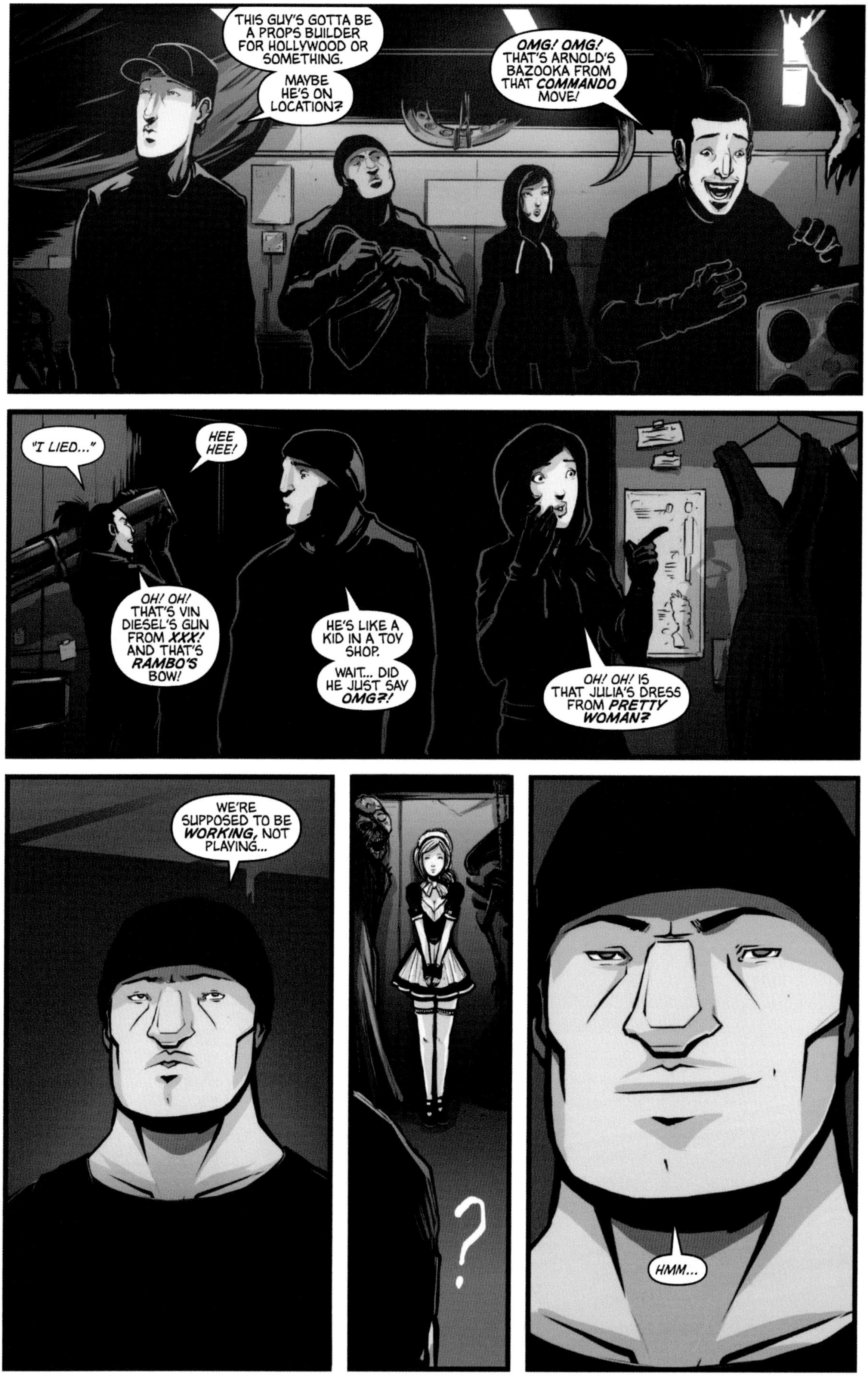
THIS GUY'S GOTTA BE A PROPS BUILDER FOR HOLLYWOOD OR SOMETHING.
MAYBE HE'S ON LOCATION?
OMG! OMG! THAT'S ARNOLD'S BAZOOKA FROM THAT COMMANDO MOVE!
"I LIED..."
HEE HEE!
OH! OH! THAT'S VIN DIESEL'S GUN FROM XXX! AND THAT'S RAMBO'S BOW!
HE'S LIKE A KID IN A TOY SHOP.
WAIT... DID HE JUST SAY OMG?!
OH! OH! IS THAT JULIA'S DRESS FROM PRETTY WOMAN?
WE'RE SUPPOSED TO BE WORKING, NOT PLAYING...
?
HMM...

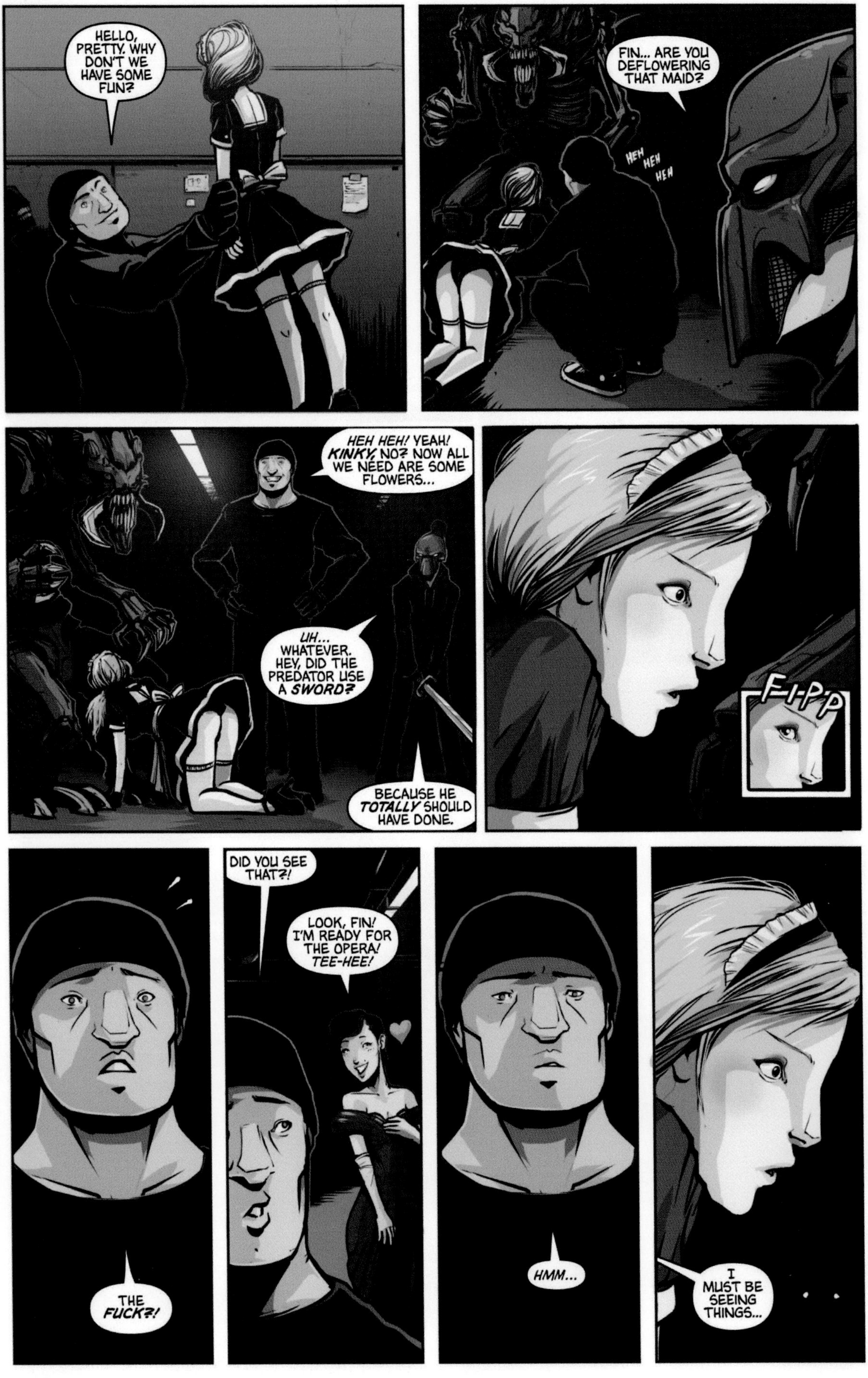
HELLO, PRETTY. WHY DON'T WE HAVE SOME FUN?
FIN... ARE YOU DEFLOWERING THAT MAID?
HEH HEH HEH
HEH HEH! YEAH! KINKY, NO? NOW ALL WE NEED ARE SOME FLOWERS...
UH... WHATEVER. HEY, DID THE PREDATOR USE A SWORD?
BECAUSE HE TOTALLY SHOULD HAVE DONE.
FIPP
THE FUCK?!
DID YOU SEE THAT?!
LOOK, FIN! I'M READY FOR THE OPERA! TEE-HEE!
HMM...
I MUST BE SEEING THINGS...

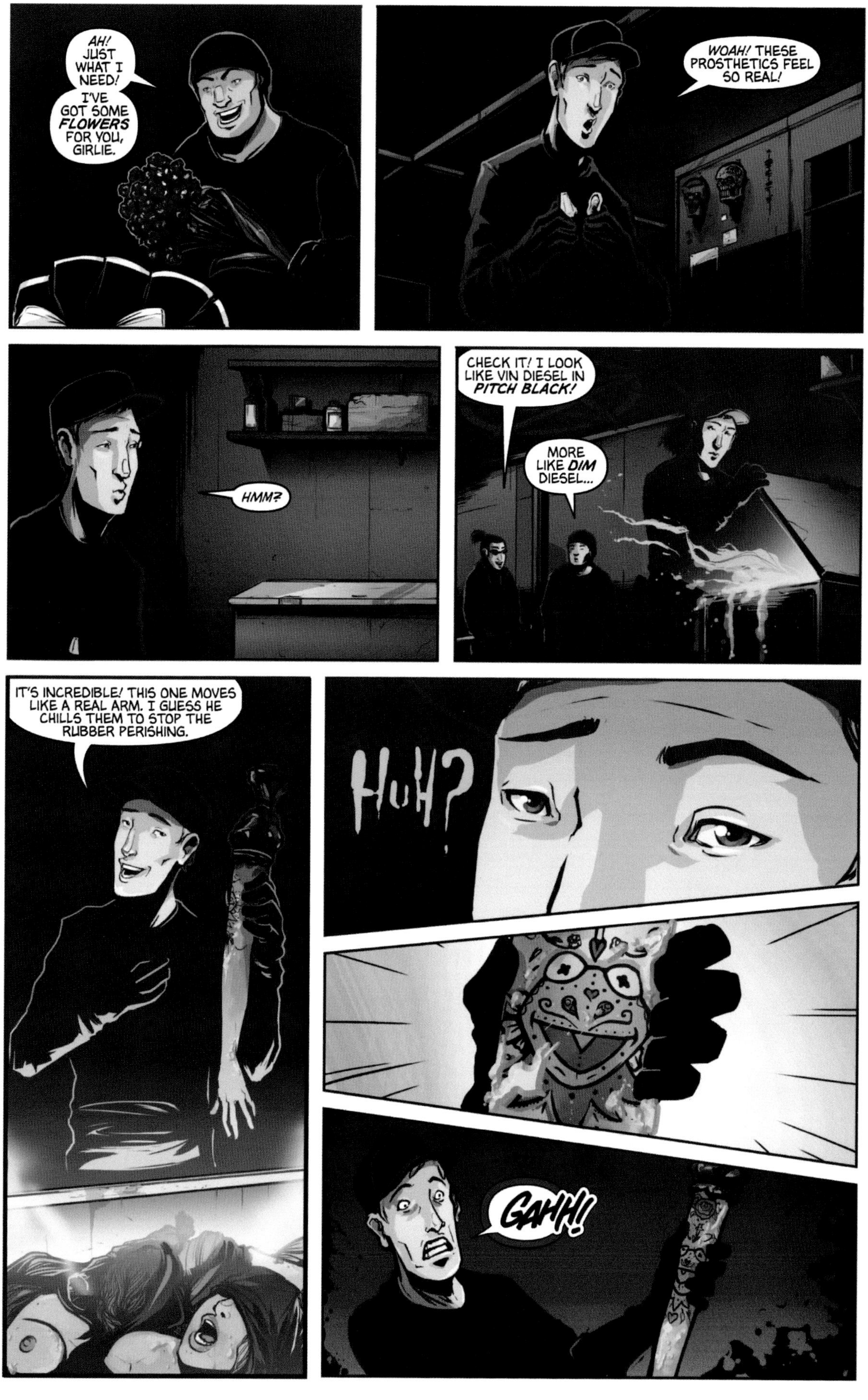
AH! JUST WHAT I NEED!
I'VE GOT SOME FLOWERS FOR YOU, GIRLIE.
WOAH! THESE PROSTHETICS FEEL SO REAL!
HMM?
CHECK IT! I LOOK LIKE VIN DIESEL IN PITCH BLACK!
MORE LIKE DIM DIESEL...
IT'S INCREDIBLE! THIS ONE MOVES LIKE A REAL ARM. I GUESS HE CHILLS THEM TO STOP THE RUBBER PERISHING.
HUH?
GAHH!

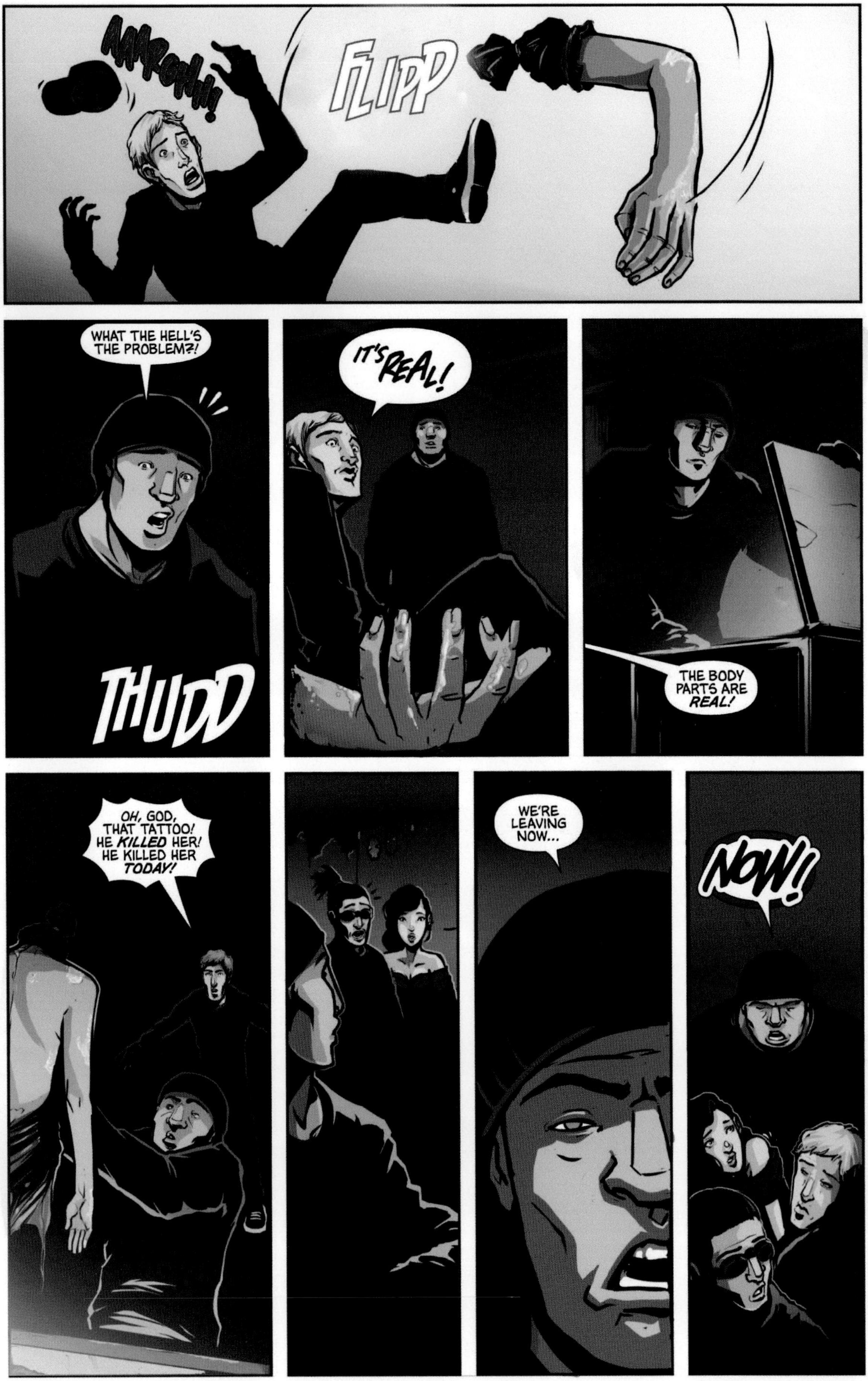
AAARGHHH!
FLIPP
WHAT THE HELL'S THE PROBLEM?!
THUDD
IT'S REAL!
THE BODY PARTS ARE REAL!
OH, GOD, THAT TATTOO! HE KILLED HER! HE KILLED HER TODAY!
WE'RE LEAVING NOW...
NOW!

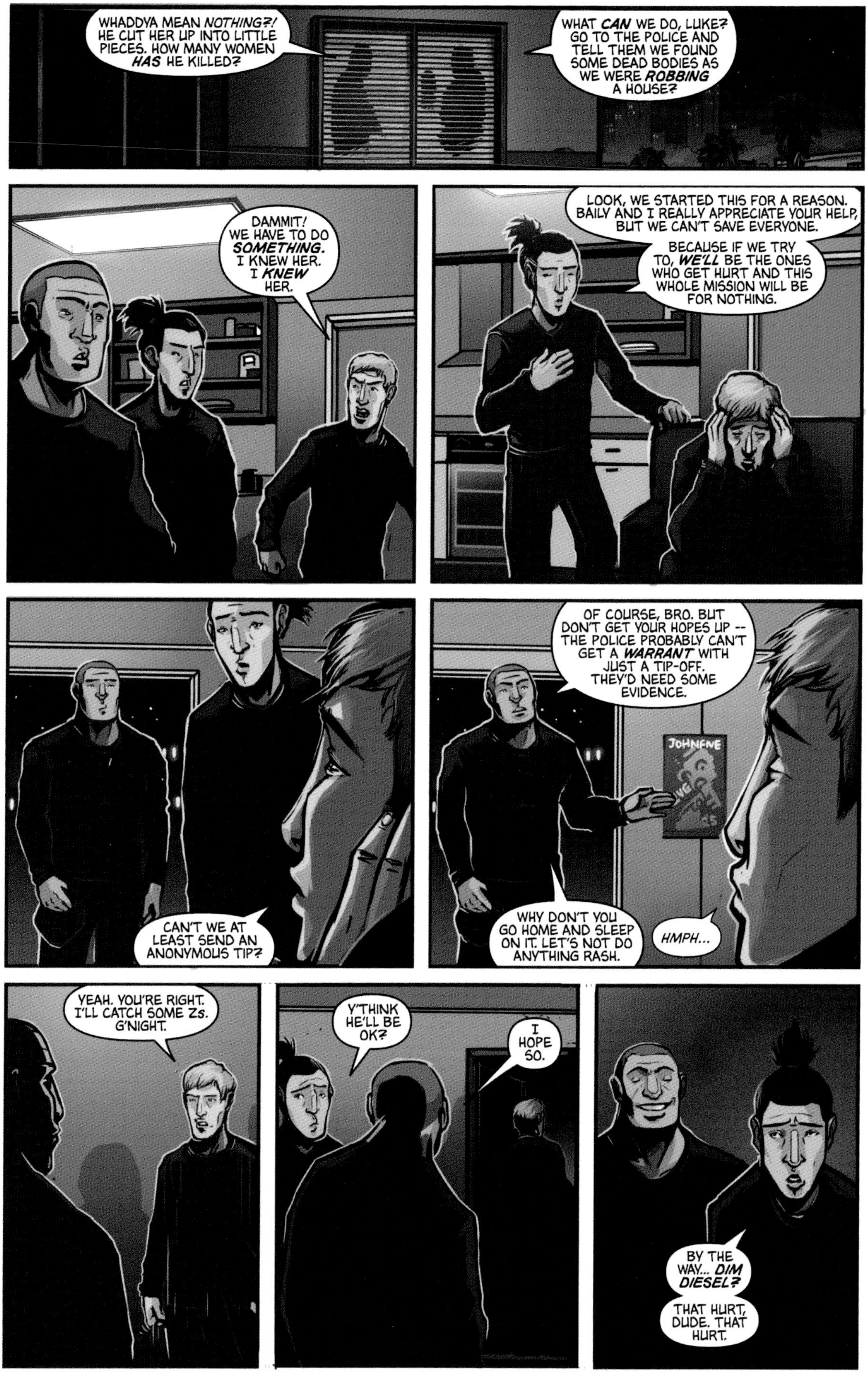
WHADDYA MEAN *NOTHING?!* HE CUT HER UP INTO LITTLE PIECES. HOW MANY WOMEN ***HAS*** HE KILLED?
WHAT ***CAN*** WE DO, LUKE? GO TO THE POLICE AND TELL THEM WE FOUND SOME DEAD BODIES AS WE WERE ***ROBBING*** A HOUSE?
DAMMIT! WE HAVE TO DO ***SOMETHING.*** I KNEW HER. I ***KNEW*** HER.
LOOK, WE STARTED THIS FOR A REASON. BAILY AND I REALLY APPRECIATE YOUR HELP, BUT WE CAN'T SAVE EVERYONE.
BECAUSE IF WE TRY TO, ***WE'LL*** BE THE ONES WHO GET HURT AND THIS WHOLE MISSION WILL BE FOR NOTHING.
CAN'T WE AT LEAST SEND AN ANONYMOUS TIP?
OF COURSE, BRO. BUT DON'T GET YOUR HOPES UP -- THE POLICE PROBABLY CAN'T GET A ***WARRANT*** WITH JUST A TIP-OFF. THEY'D NEED SOME EVIDENCE.
JOHNNE
WHY DON'T YOU GO HOME AND SLEEP ON IT. LET'S NOT DO ANYTHING RASH.
HMPH...
YEAH. YOU'RE RIGHT. I'LL CATCH SOME Zs. G'NIGHT.
Y'THINK HE'LL BE OK?
I HOPE SO.
BY THE WAY... ***DIM DIESEL?***
THAT HURT, DUDE. THAT HURT.

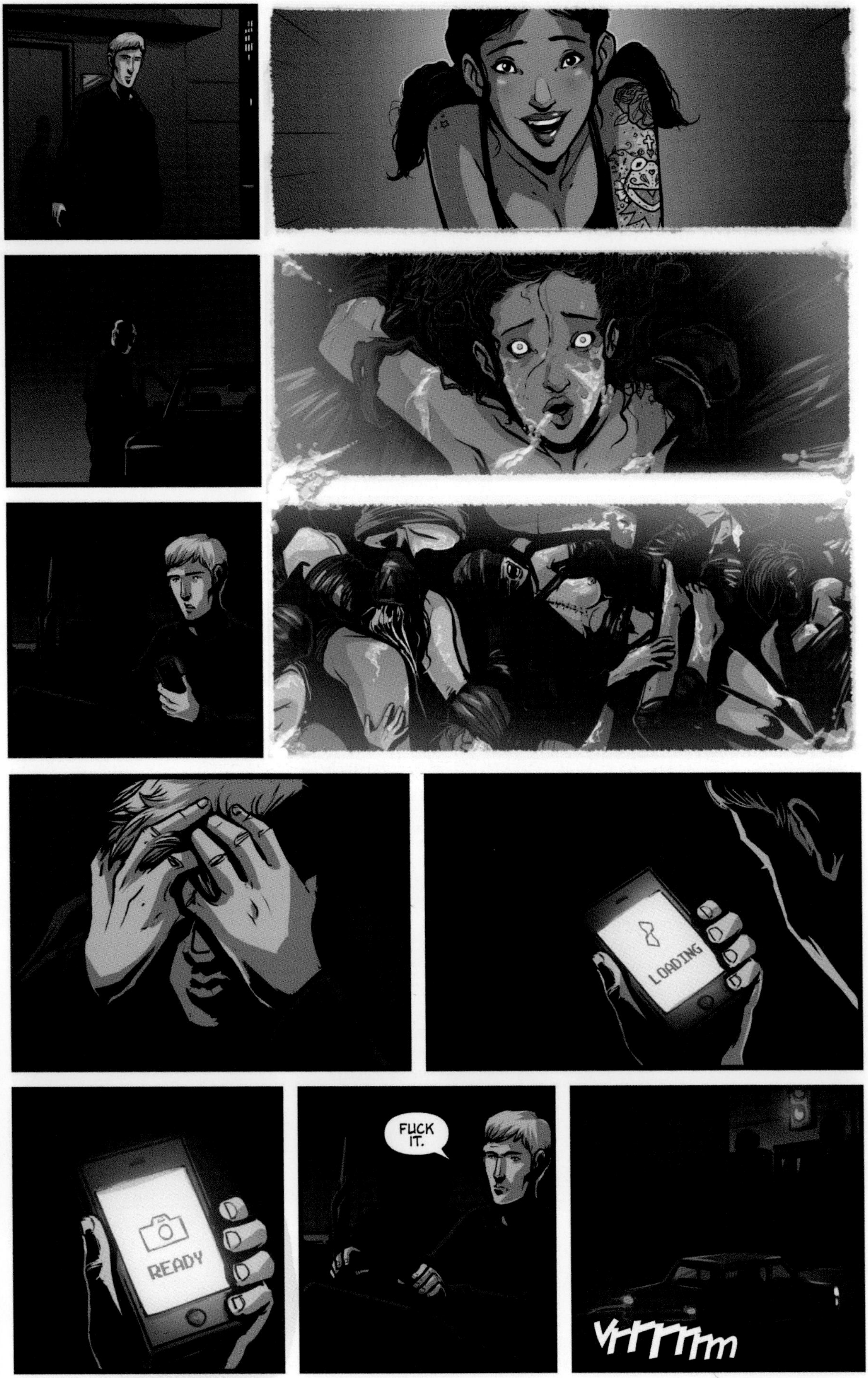
LOADING
READY
FUCK IT.
VRRRRMM

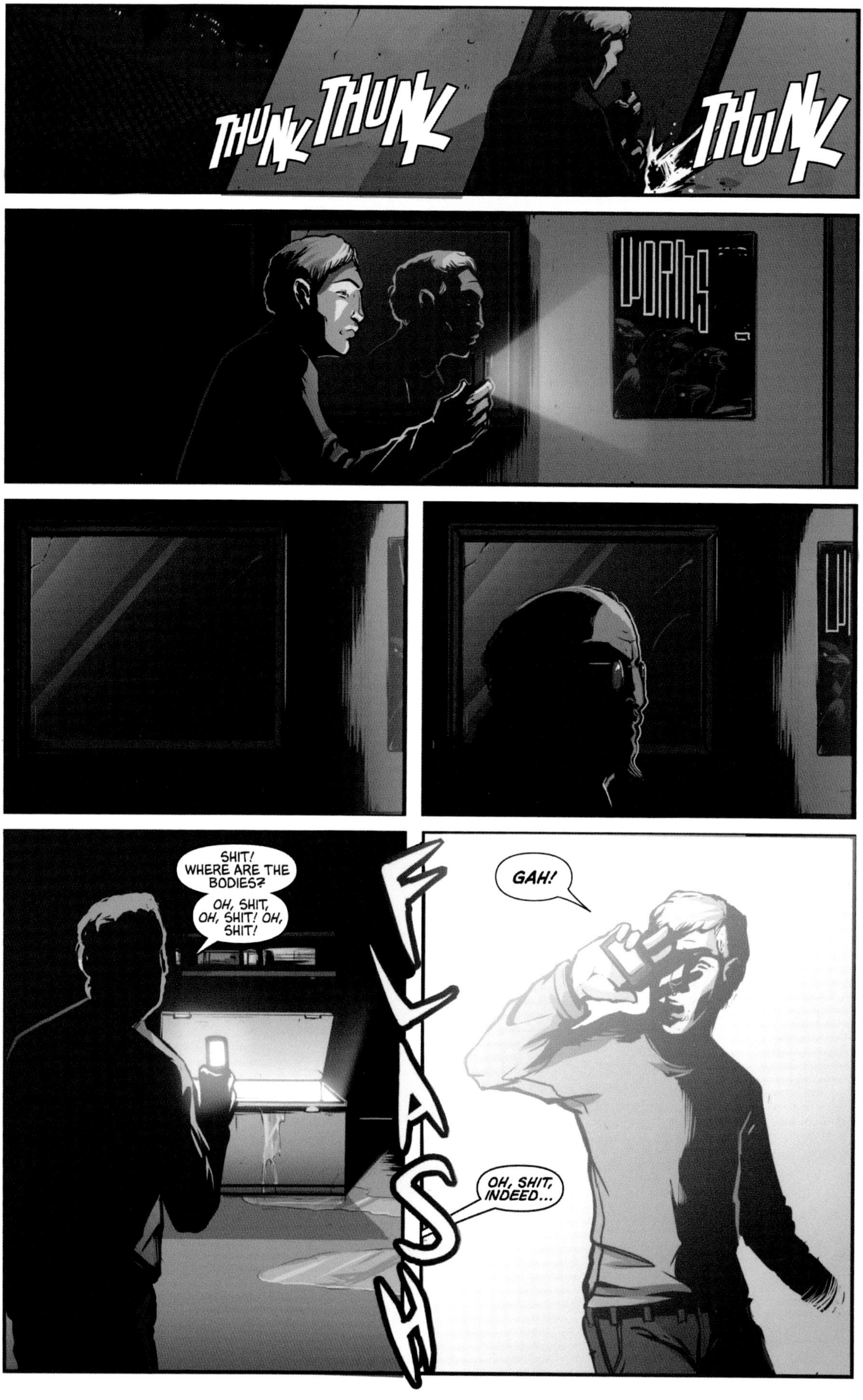
THUNK THUNK
THUNK
WORMS
SHIT! WHERE ARE THE BODIES? OH, SHIT, OH, SHIT! OH, SHIT!
FLASH
GAH!
OH, SHIT, INDEED...

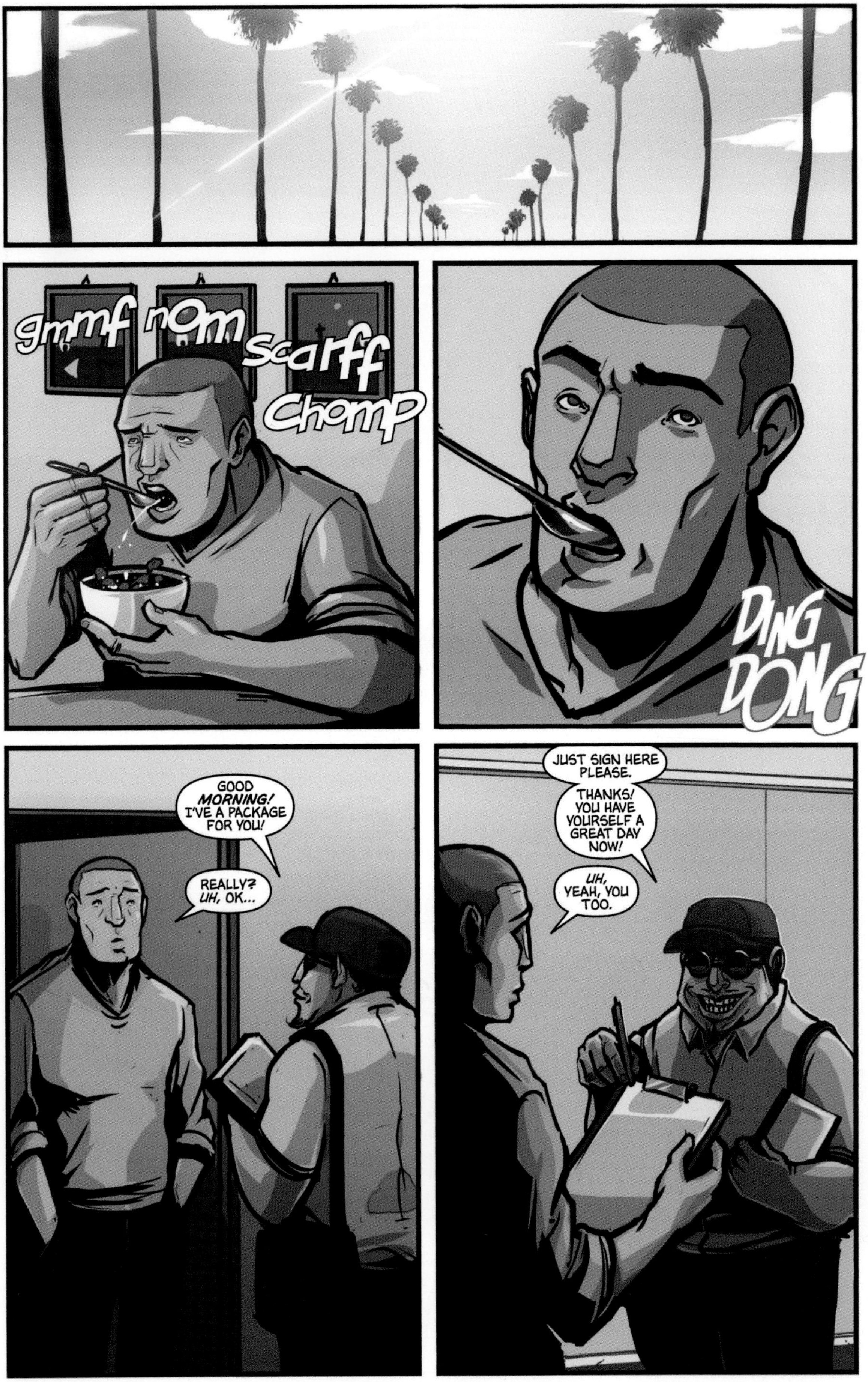
gmmf nom scarff
chomp
DING DONG
GOOD MORNING! I'VE A PACKAGE FOR YOU!
REALLY? UH, OK...
JUST SIGN HERE PLEASE.
THANKS! YOU HAVE YOURSELF A GREAT DAY NOW!
UH, YEAH, YOU TOO.

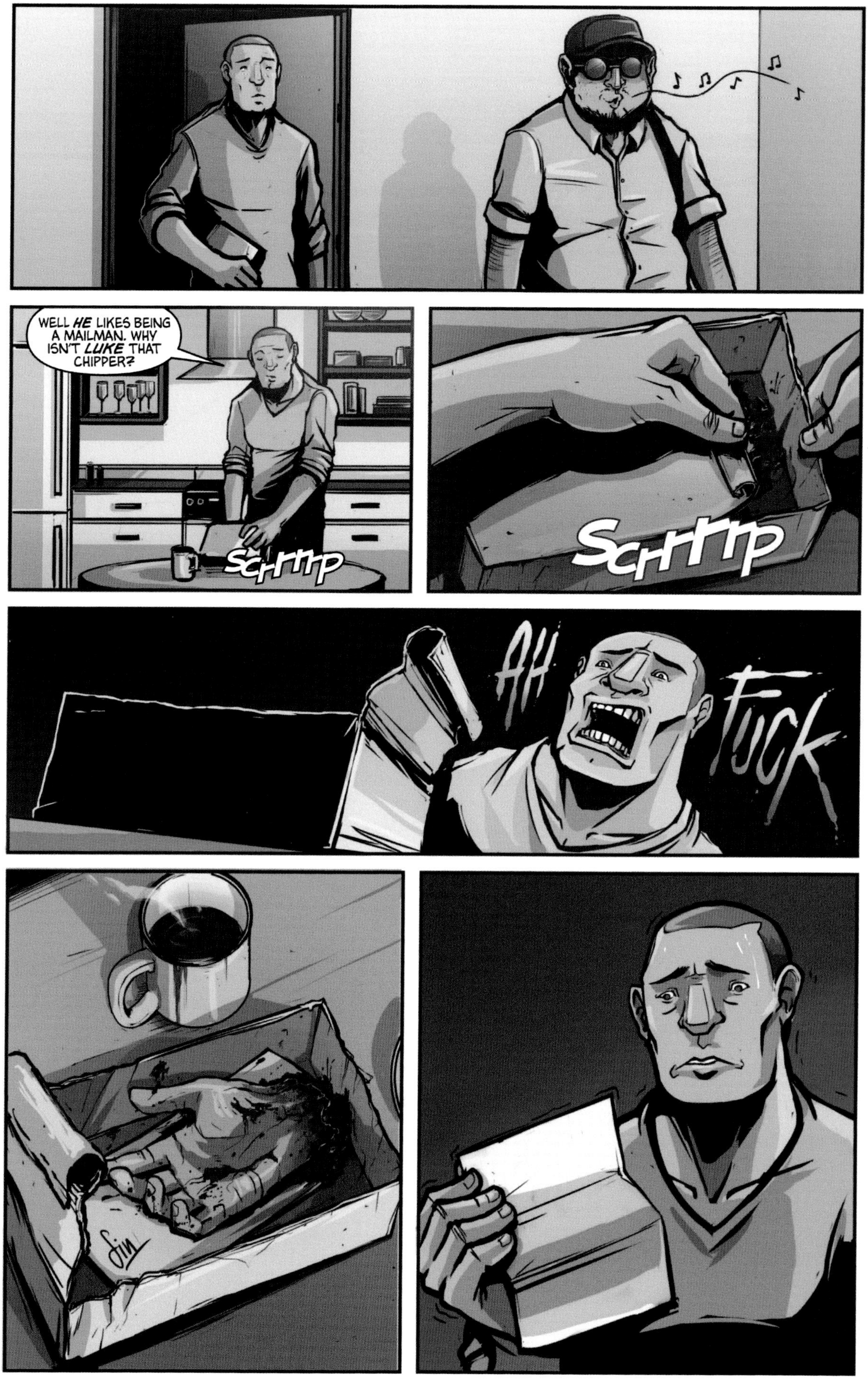
WELL HE LIKES BEING A MAILMAN. WHY ISN'T LUKE THAT CHIPPER?
SCRRRRP
SCRRRRP
AH
FUCK

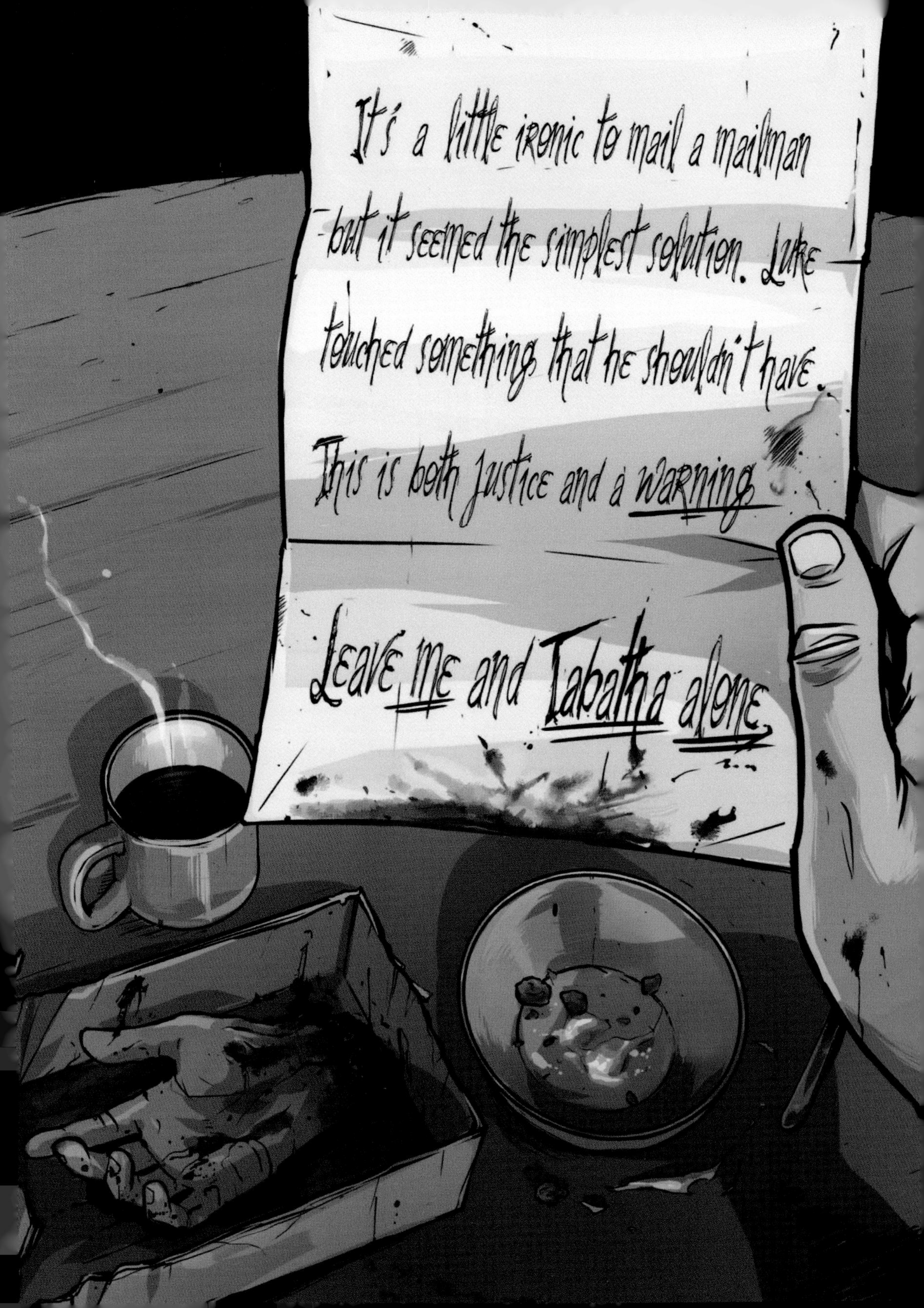
It's a little ironic to mail a mailman
but it seemed the simplest solution. Luke
touched something that he shouldn't have.
This is both justice and a warning.
Leave me and Tabatha alone.

CHAPTER TWO

"HER DEATH IS MEANINGLESS AND IT'S ON YOUR HANDS, NOT MINE, YOURS, NOT MINE."

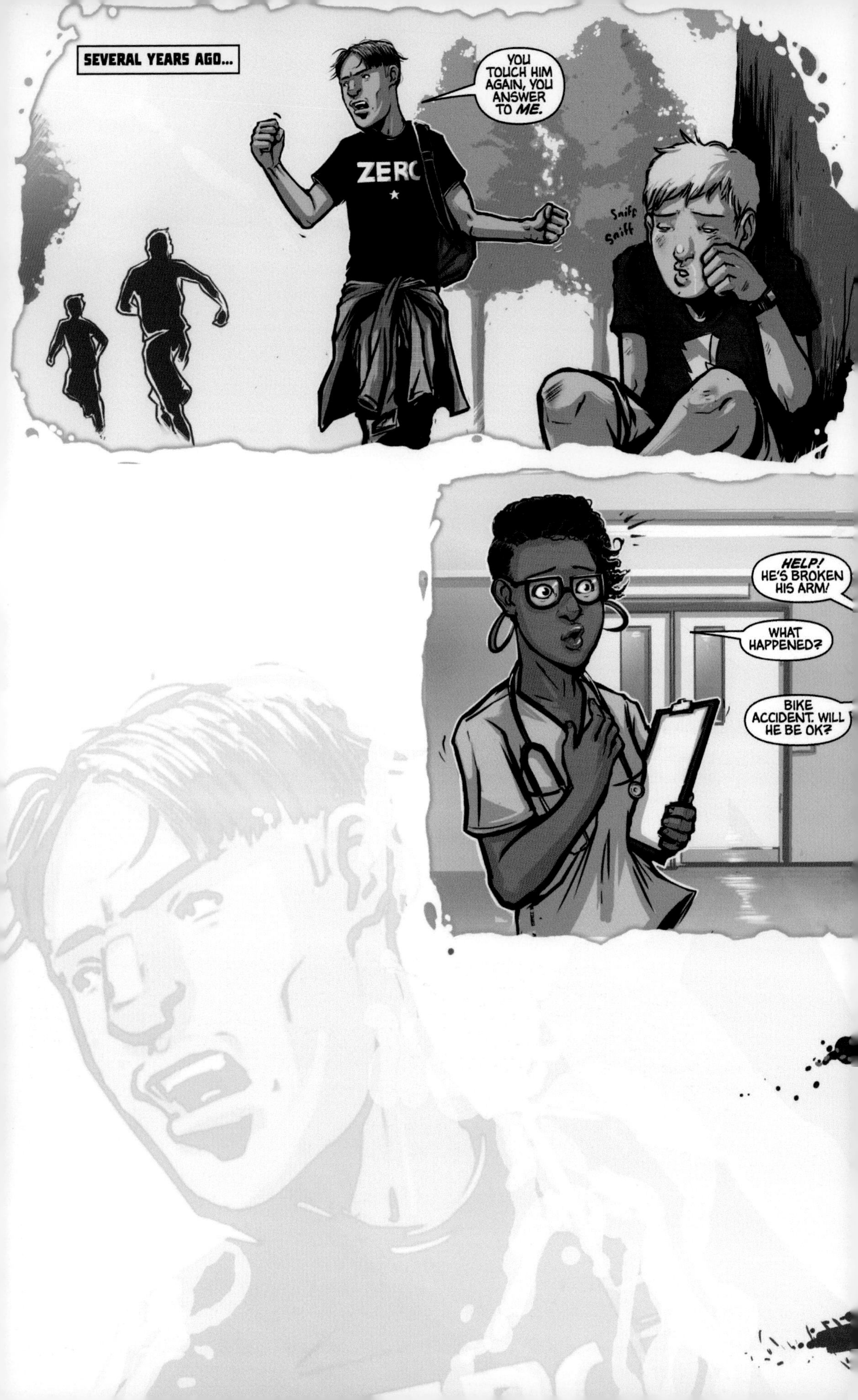
SEVERAL YEARS AGO...
YOU TOUCH HIM AGAIN, YOU ANSWER TO ME.
ZERO
Sniff
Sniff
HELP! HE'S BROKEN HIS ARM!
WHAT HAPPENED?
BIKE ACCIDENT. WILL HE BE OK?

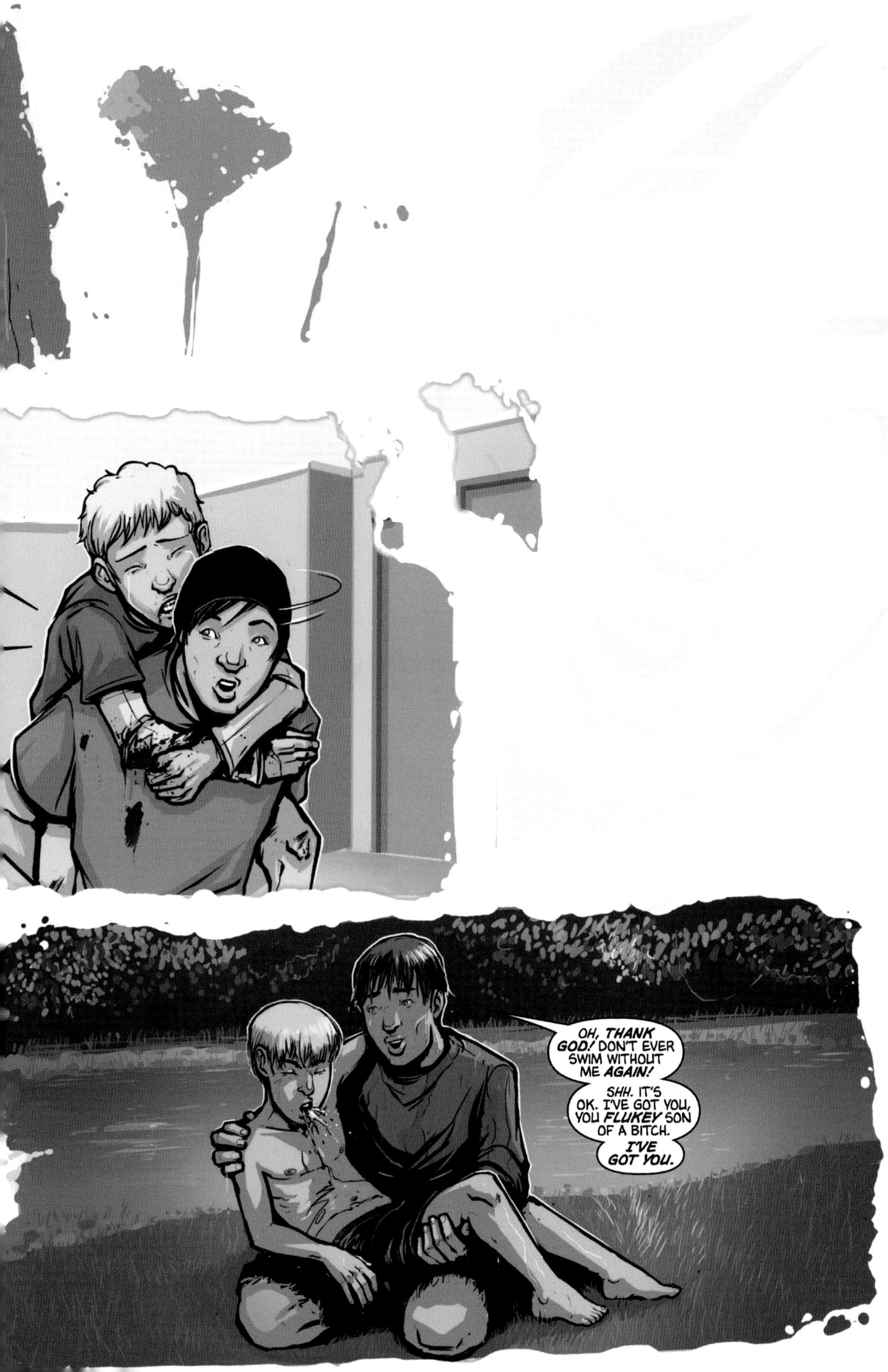
OH, THANK GOD! DON'T EVER SWIM WITHOUT ME AGAIN!
SHH. IT'S OK. I'VE GOT YOU, YOU FLUKEY SON OF A BITCH.
I'VE GOT YOU.

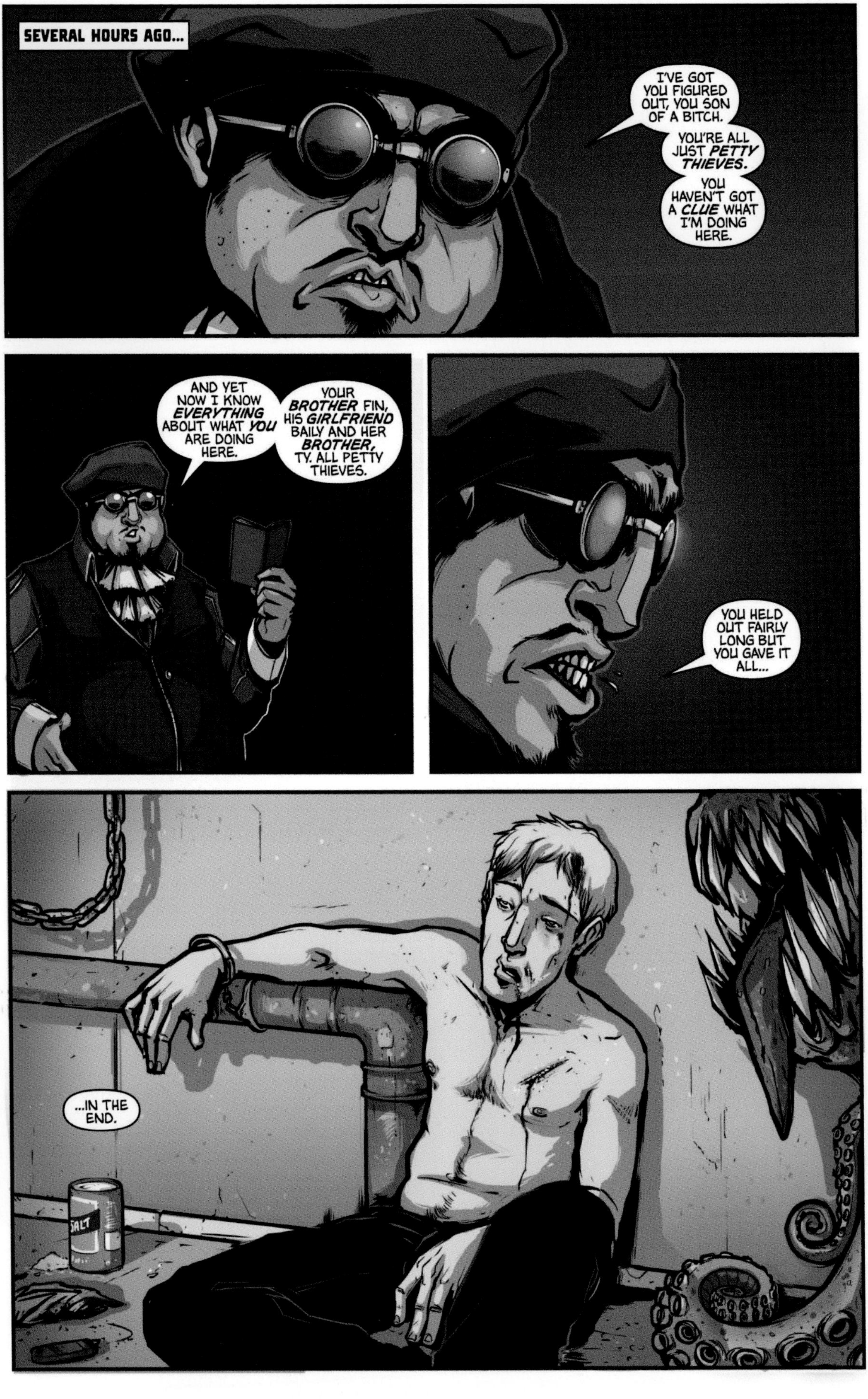
SEVERAL HOURS AGO...
I'VE GOT YOU FIGURED OUT, YOU SON OF A BITCH.
YOU'RE ALL JUST PETTY THIEVES.
YOU HAVEN'T GOT A CLUE WHAT I'M DOING HERE.
AND YET NOW I KNOW EVERYTHING ABOUT WHAT YOU ARE DOING HERE.
YOUR BROTHER FIN, HIS GIRLFRIEND BAILY AND HER BROTHER, TY. ALL PETTY THIEVES.
YOU HELD OUT FAIRLY LONG BUT YOU GAVE IT ALL...
...IN THE END.
SALT

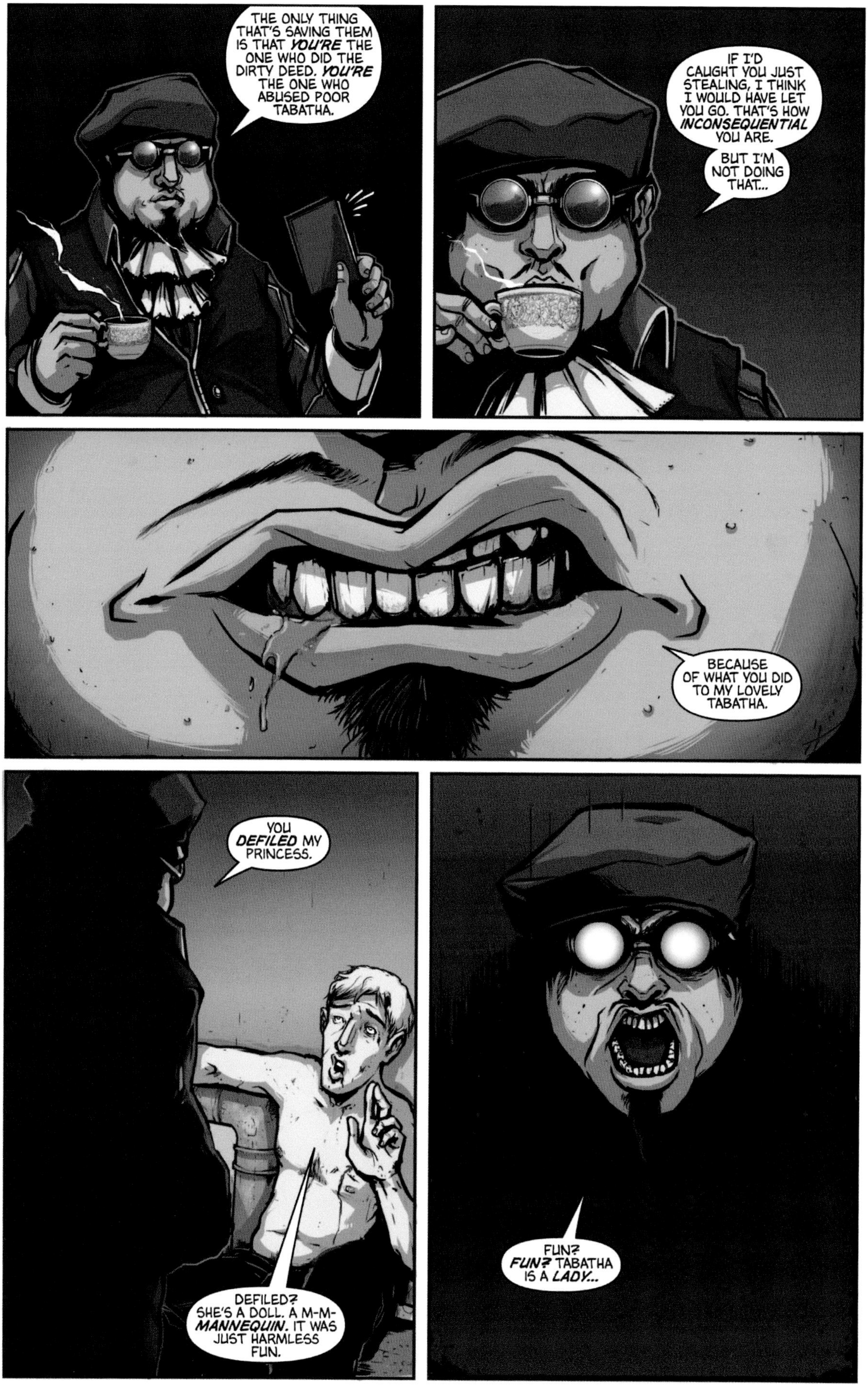
THE ONLY THING THAT'S SAVING THEM IS THAT *YOU'RE* THE ONE WHO DID THE DIRTY DEED. *YOU'RE* THE ONE WHO ABUSED POOR TABATHA.
IF I'D CAUGHT YOU JUST STEALING, I THINK I WOULD HAVE LET YOU GO. THAT'S HOW *INCONSEQUENTIAL* YOU ARE.
BUT I'M NOT DOING THAT...
BECAUSE OF WHAT YOU DID TO MY LOVELY TABATHA.
YOU *DEFILED* MY PRINCESS.
DEFILED? SHE'S A DOLL. A M-M-*MANNEQUIN*. IT WAS JUST HARMLESS FUN.
FUN? *FUN?* TABATHA IS A *LADY*...

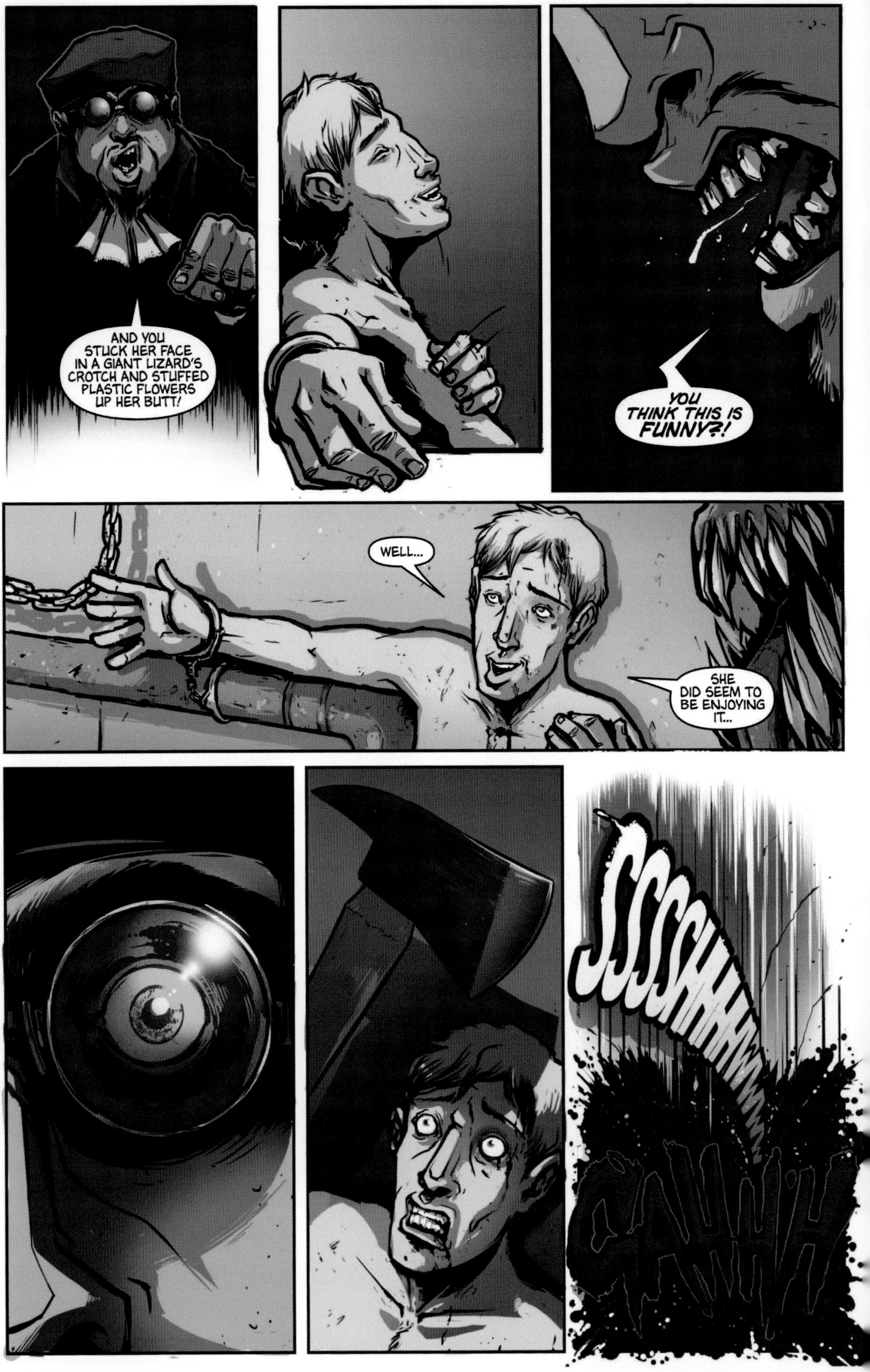

AND YOU STUCK HER FACE IN A GIANT LIZARD'S CROTCH AND STUFFED PLASTIC FLOWERS UP HER BUTT!
YOU THINK THIS IS FUNNY?!
WELL...
SHE DID SEEM TO BE ENJOYING IT...
SSSCHHHWWW

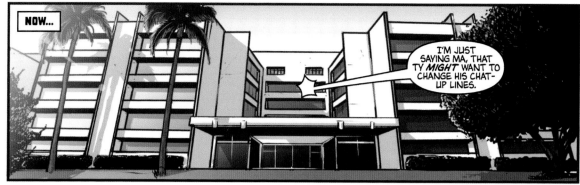

NOW...

I'M JUST SAYING MA, THAT TY *MIGHT* WANT TO CHANGE HIS CHAT-UP LINES.

BUT THEY'RE *FUNNY.*

I THINK THAT IN MATTERS OF ROMANCE, YOU SHOULD LISTEN TO BAILY.

HOLDING A RAG AND SAYING *"DOES THIS SMELL OF CHLOROFORM TO YOU"* MAY BE AMUSING TO *FRIENDS,* BUT IT'S GOING TO CREEP A GIRL OUT.

OK, OK, I'VE GOT A BETTER ONE. HOW ABOUT...

ARE YOU FREE TONIGHT...

...OR *WILL IT COST ME?*

YOU SEE! IF IT GETS A LAUGH I CAN'T *FAIL* TO GET A DATE.

HEH HEH HEH!

COFF... COFF

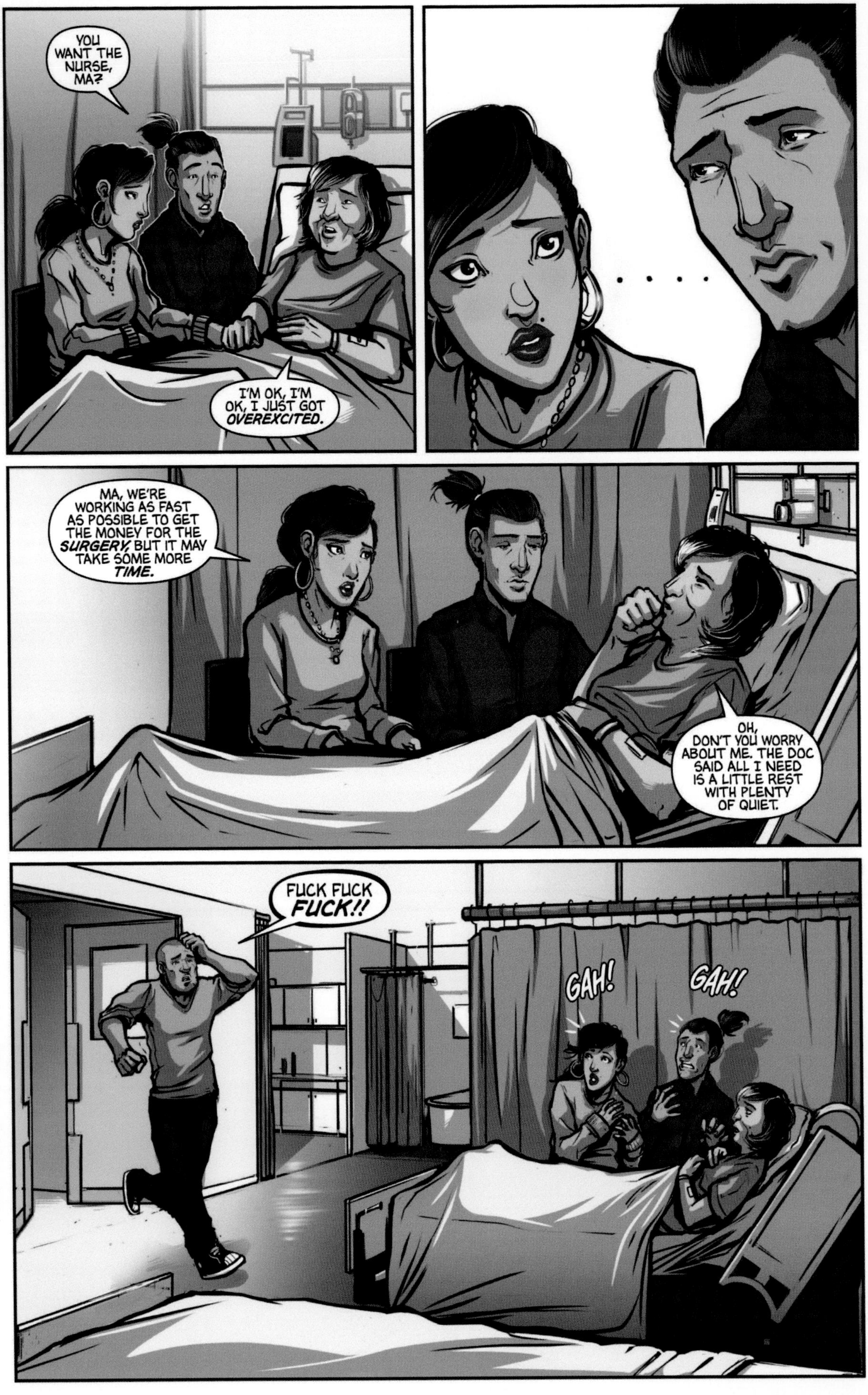
YOU WANT THE NURSE, MA?
I'M OK, I'M OK, I JUST GOT OVEREXCITED.
. . . .
MA, WE'RE WORKING AS FAST AS POSSIBLE TO GET THE MONEY FOR THE SURGERY, BUT IT MAY TAKE SOME MORE TIME.
OH, DON'T YOU WORRY ABOUT ME. THE DOC SAID ALL I NEED IS A LITTLE REST WITH PLENTY OF QUIET.
FUCK FUCK FUCK!!
GAH!
GAH!

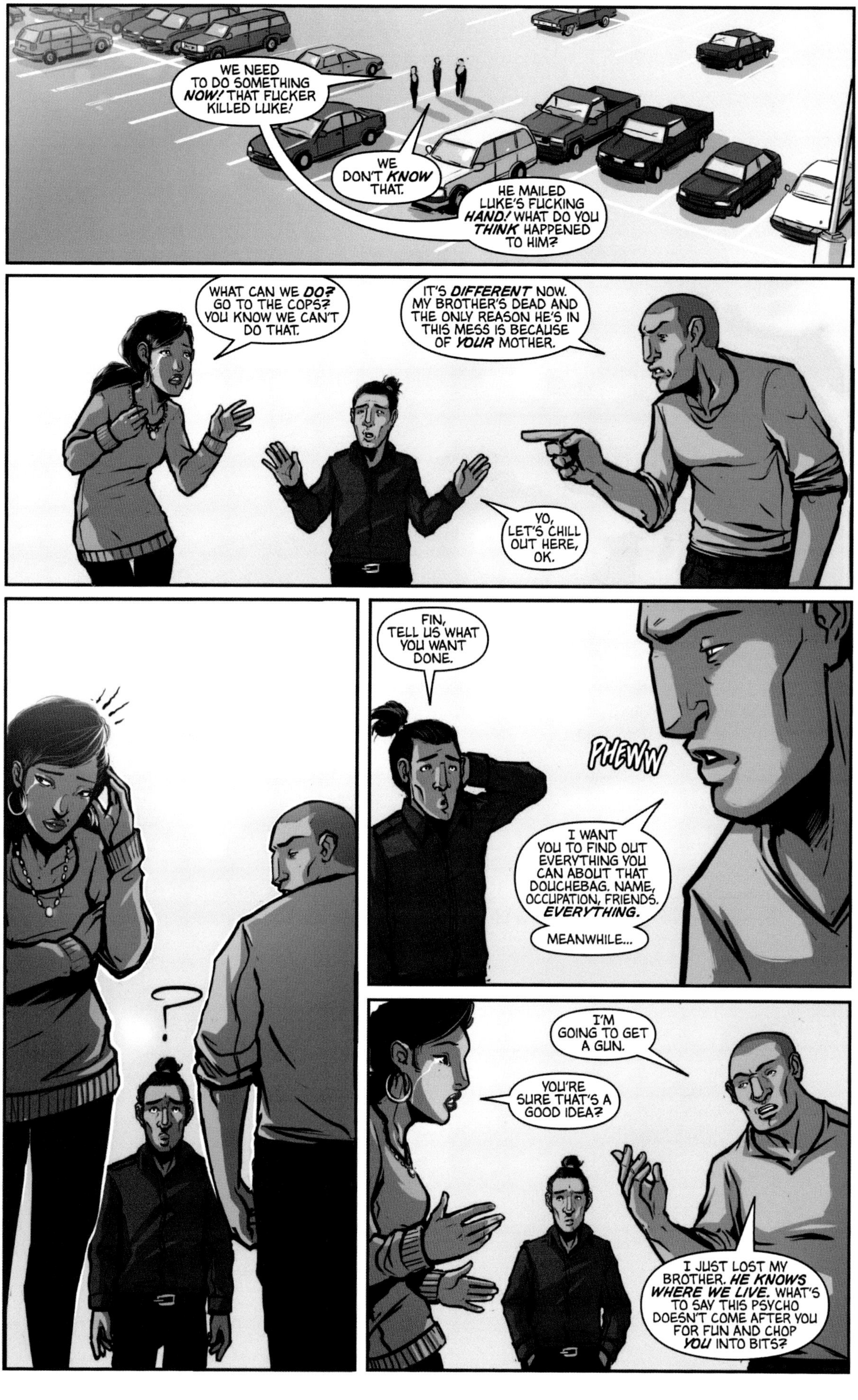
WE NEED TO DO SOMETHING NOW! THAT FUCKER KILLED LUKE!
WE DON'T KNOW THAT.
HE MAILED LUKE'S FUCKING HAND! WHAT DO YOU THINK HAPPENED TO HIM?
WHAT CAN WE DO? GO TO THE COPS? YOU KNOW WE CAN'T DO THAT.
IT'S DIFFERENT NOW. MY BROTHER'S DEAD AND THE ONLY REASON HE'S IN THIS MESS IS BECAUSE OF YOUR MOTHER.
YO, LET'S CHILL OUT HERE, OK.
?
FIN, TELL US WHAT YOU WANT DONE.
PHEWW
I WANT YOU TO FIND OUT EVERYTHING YOU CAN ABOUT THAT DOUCHEBAG. NAME, OCCUPATION, FRIENDS. EVERYTHING.
MEANWHILE...
I'M GOING TO GET A GUN.
YOU'RE SURE THAT'S A GOOD IDEA?
I JUST LOST MY BROTHER. HE KNOWS WHERE WE LIVE. WHAT'S TO SAY THIS PSYCHO DOESN'T COME AFTER YOU FOR FUN AND CHOP YOU INTO BITS?

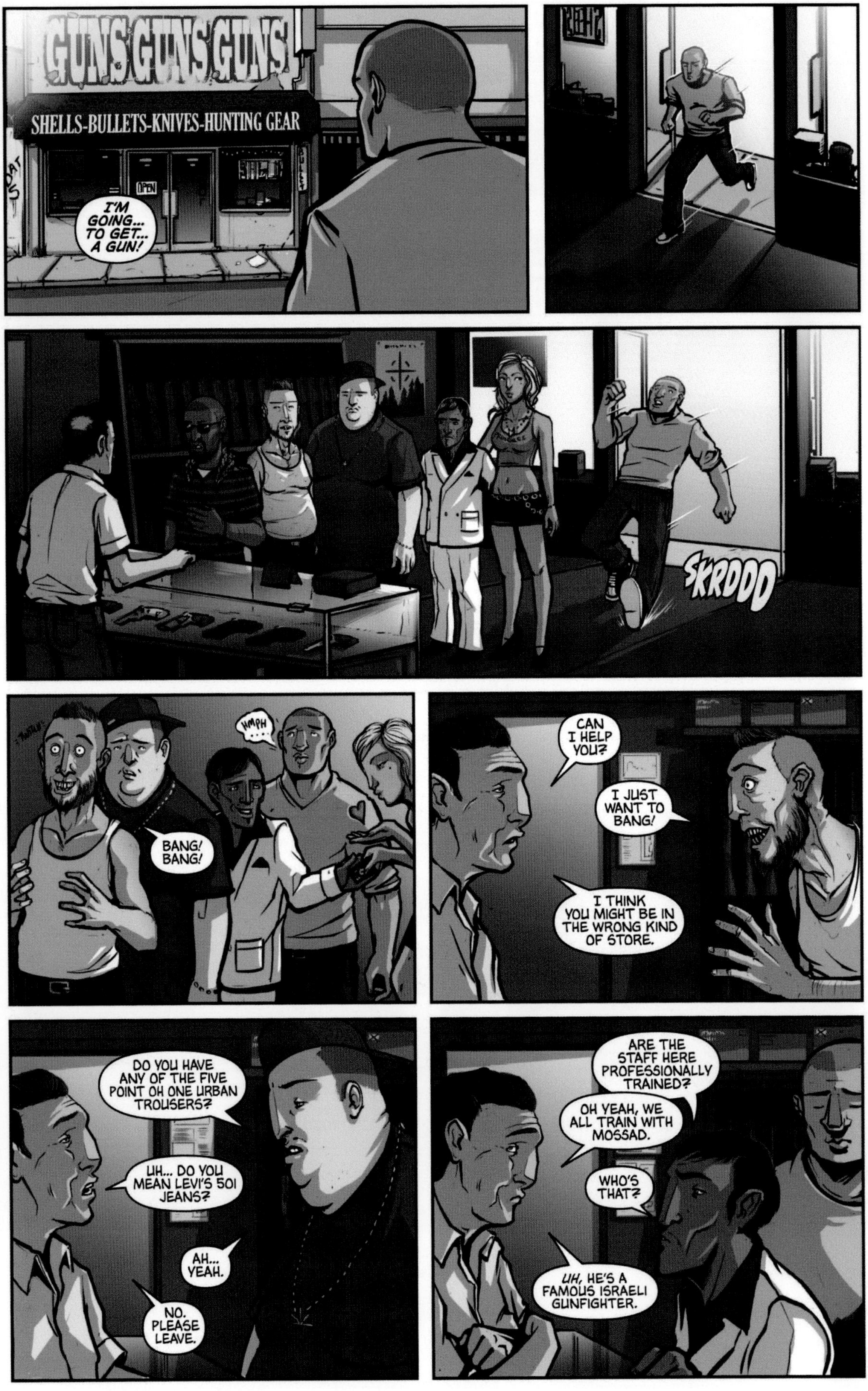
GUNS GUNS GUNS
SHELLS-BULLETS-KNIVES-HUNTING GEAR
OPEN
I'M GOING... TO GET... A GUN!
SKRDDD
HMPH...
BANG! BANG!
CAN I HELP YOU?
I JUST WANT TO BANG!
I THINK YOU MIGHT BE IN THE WRONG KIND OF STORE.
DO YOU HAVE ANY OF THE FIVE POINT OH ONE URBAN TROUSERS?
UH... DO YOU MEAN LEVI'S 501 JEANS?
AH... YEAH.
NO. PLEASE LEAVE.
ARE THE STAFF HERE PROFESSIONALLY TRAINED?
OH YEAH, WE ALL TRAIN WITH MOSSAD.
WHO'S THAT?
UH, HE'S A FAMOUS ISRAELI GUNFIGHTER.

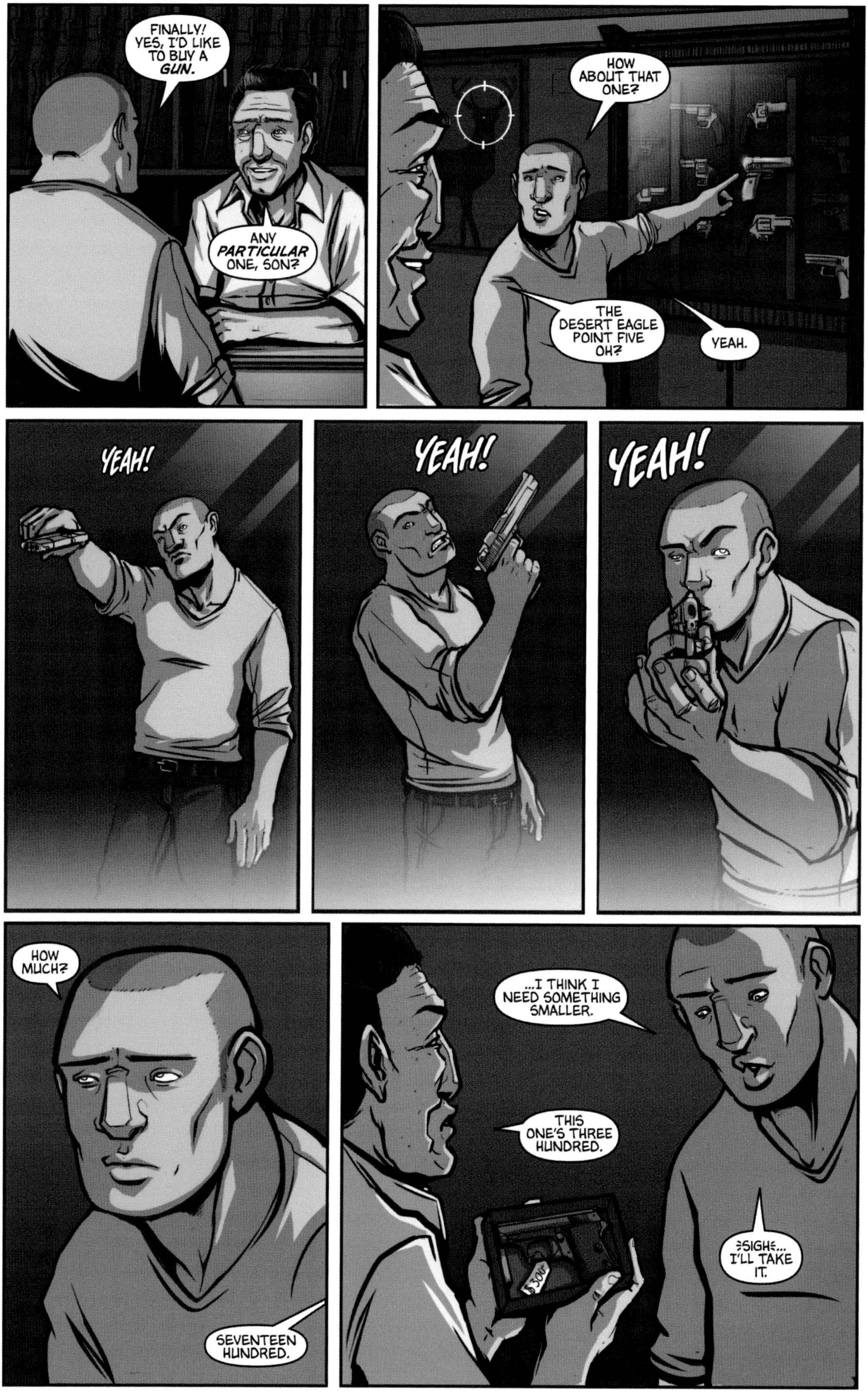

FINALLY! YES, I'D LIKE TO BUY A *GUN*.
ANY *PARTICULAR* ONE, SON?
HOW ABOUT THAT ONE?
THE DESERT EAGLE POINT FIVE OH?
YEAH.
YEAH!
YEAH!
YEAH!
HOW MUCH?
SEVENTEEN HUNDRED.
...I THINK I NEED SOMETHING SMALLER.
THIS ONE'S THREE HUNDRED.
$300
ƎSIGHƐ... I'LL TAKE IT.

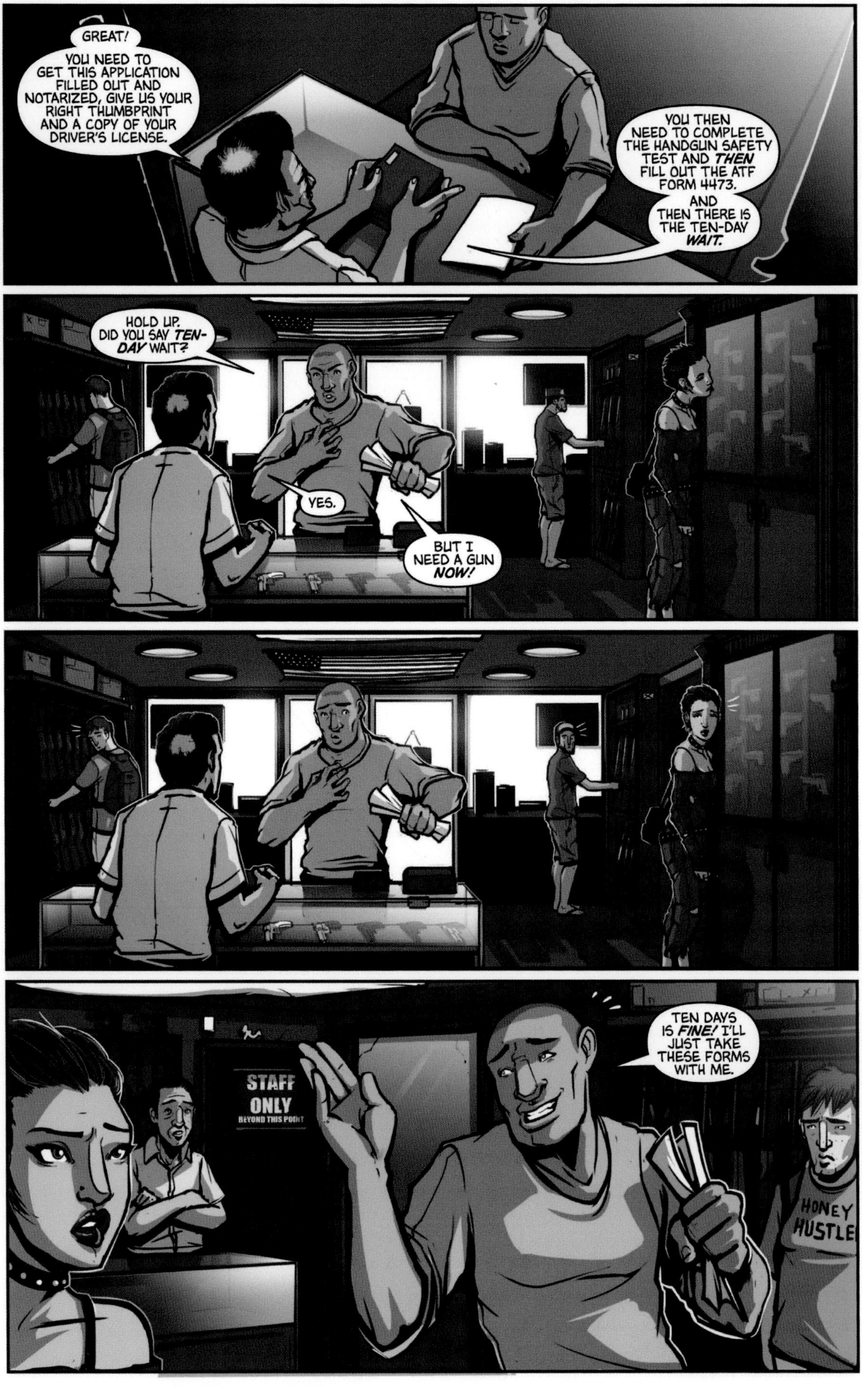
GREAT!
YOU NEED TO GET THIS APPLICATION FILLED OUT AND NOTARIZED, GIVE US YOUR RIGHT THUMBPRINT AND A COPY OF YOUR DRIVER'S LICENSE.
YOU THEN NEED TO COMPLETE THE HANDGUN SAFETY TEST AND *THEN* FILL OUT THE ATF FORM 4473.
AND THEN THERE IS THE TEN-DAY *WAIT.*
HOLD UP. DID YOU SAY *TEN-DAY* WAIT?
YES.
BUT I NEED A GUN *NOW!*
STAFF ONLY BEYOND THIS POINT
TEN DAYS IS *FINE!* I'LL JUST TAKE THESE FORMS WITH ME.
HONEY HUSTLE

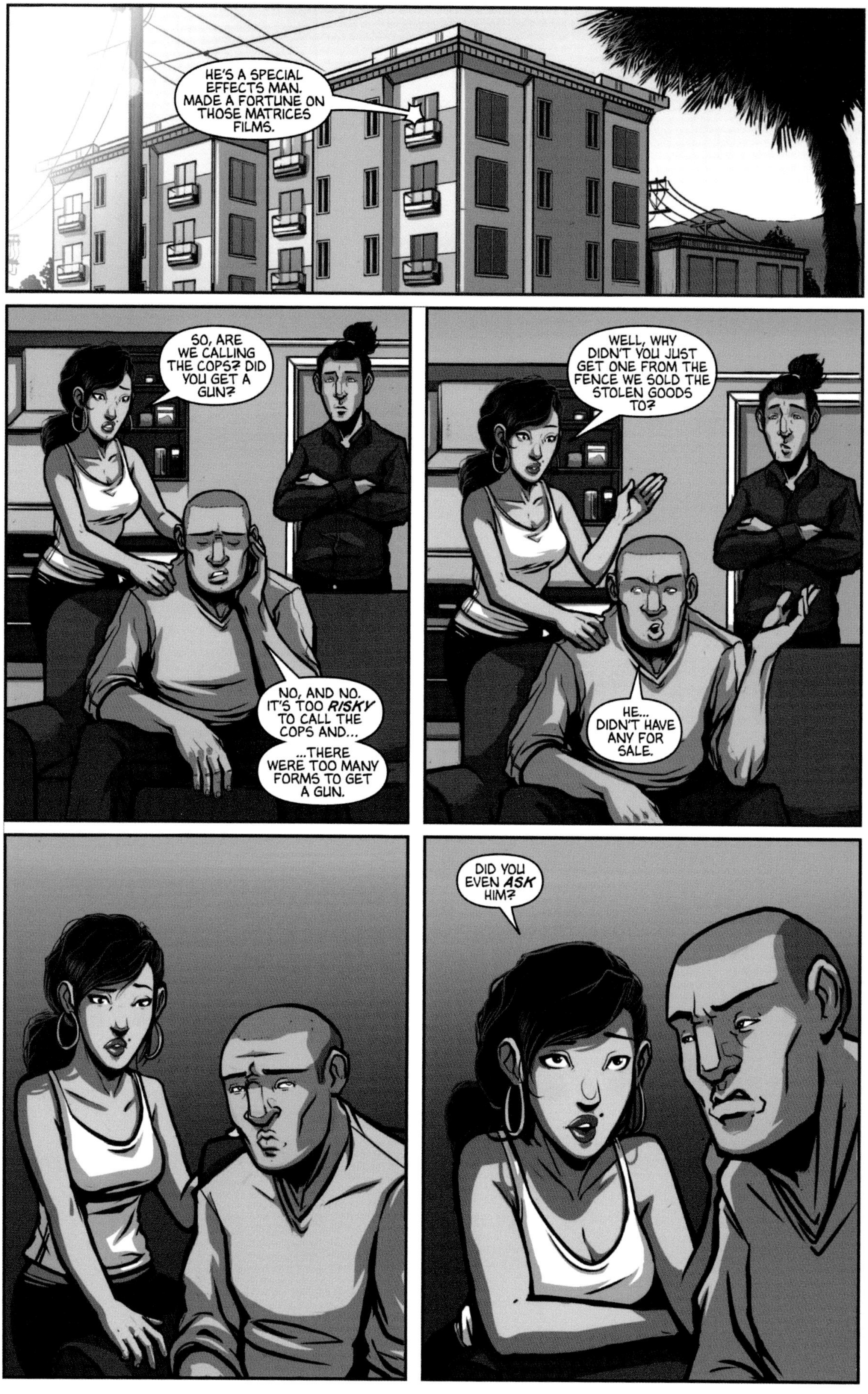
HE'S A SPECIAL EFFECTS MAN. MADE A FORTUNE ON THOSE MATRICES FILMS.
SO, ARE WE CALLING THE COPS? DID YOU GET A GUN?
NO, AND NO. IT'S TOO RISKY TO CALL THE COPS AND...
...THERE WERE TOO MANY FORMS TO GET A GUN.
WELL, WHY DIDN'T YOU JUST GET ONE FROM THE FENCE WE SOLD THE STOLEN GOODS TO?
HE... DIDN'T HAVE ANY FOR SALE.
DID YOU EVEN ASK HIM?

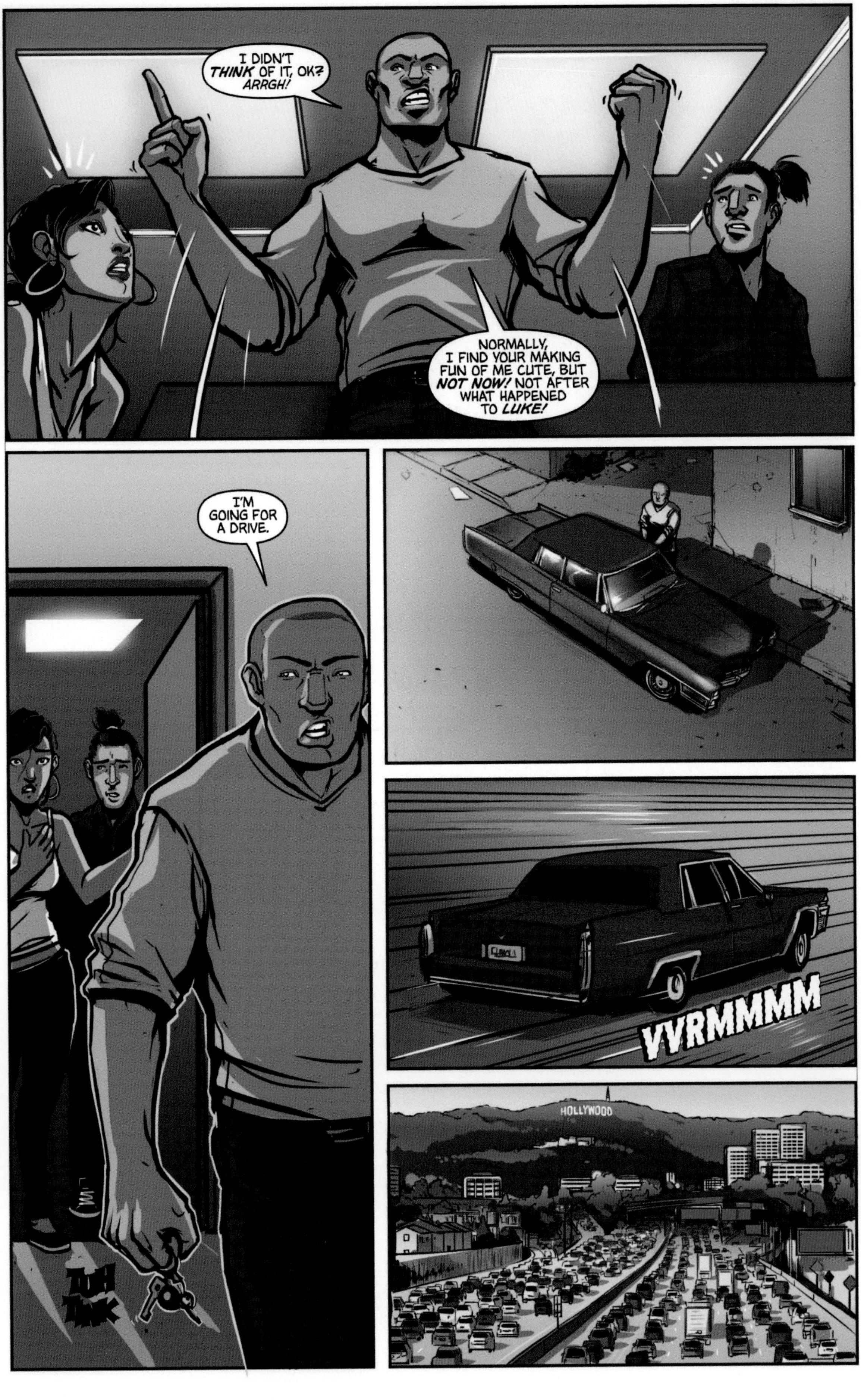
I DIDN'T THINK OF IT, OK? ARRGH!
NORMALLY, I FIND YOUR MAKING FUN OF ME CUTE, BUT NOT NOW! NOT AFTER WHAT HAPPENED TO LUKE!
I'M GOING FOR A DRIVE.
VVRMMMM
HOLLYWOOD

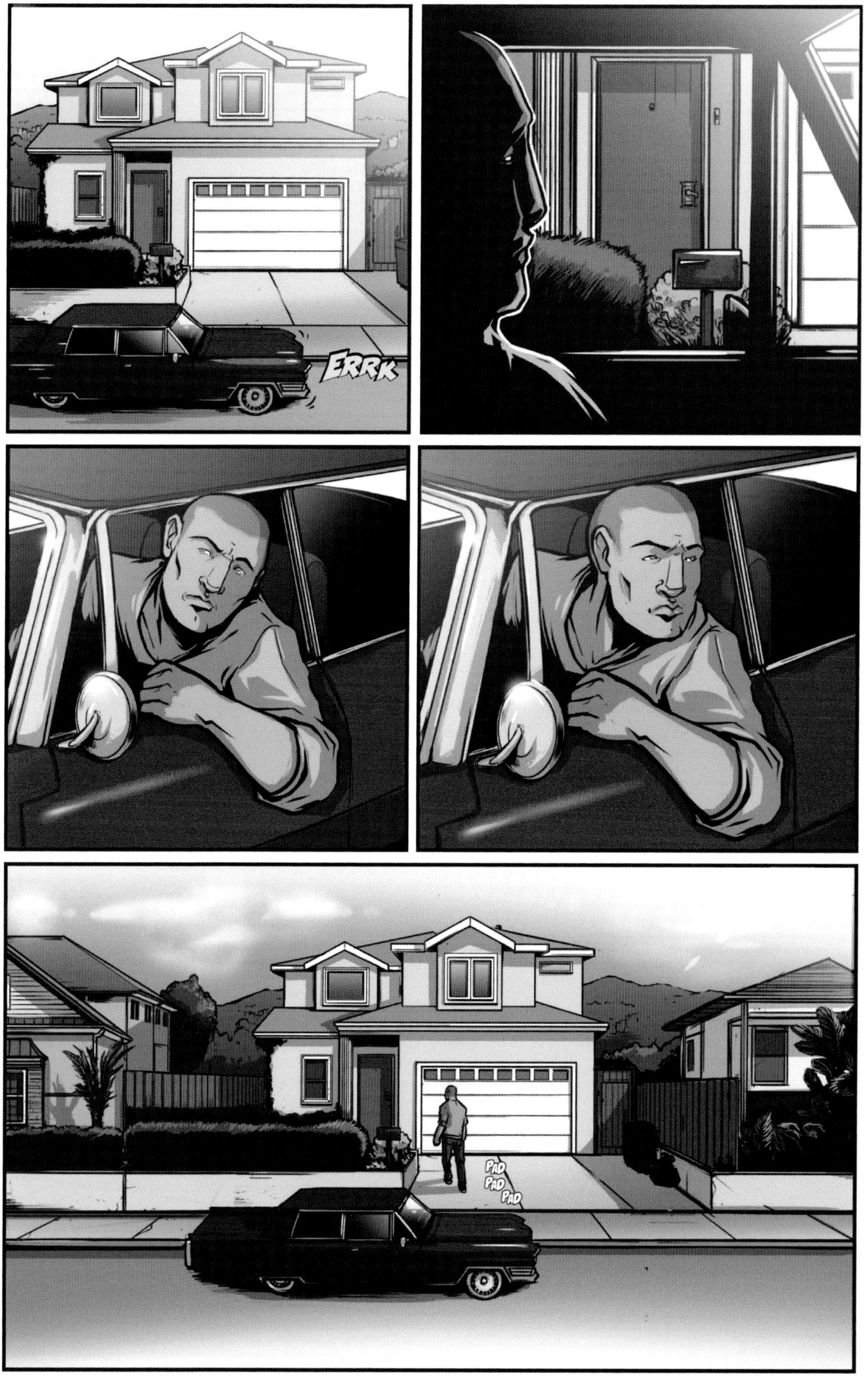
ERRK
PAD
PAD
PAD

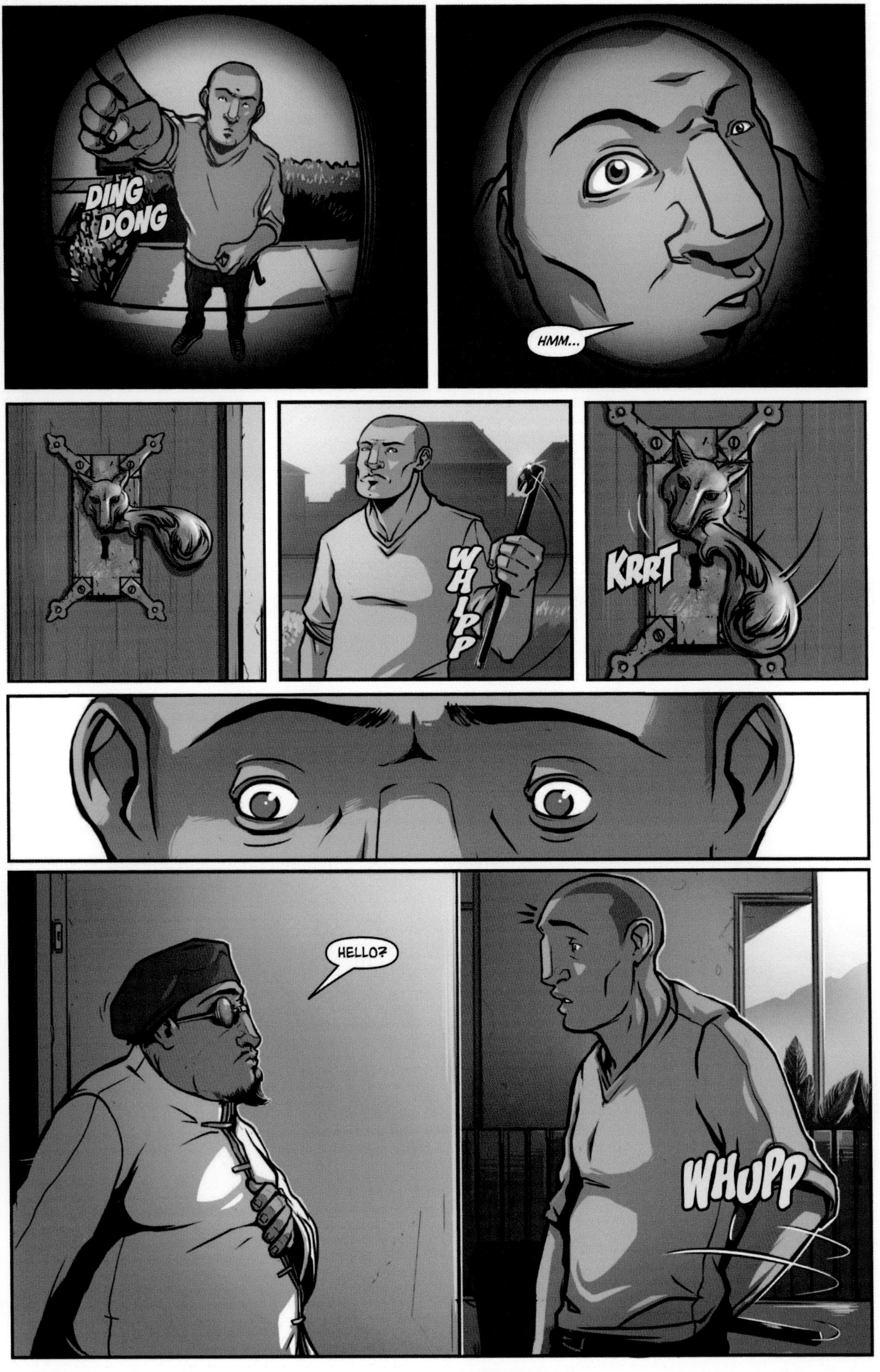
DING DONG
HMM...
WHIPP
KRRT
HELLO?
WHUPP

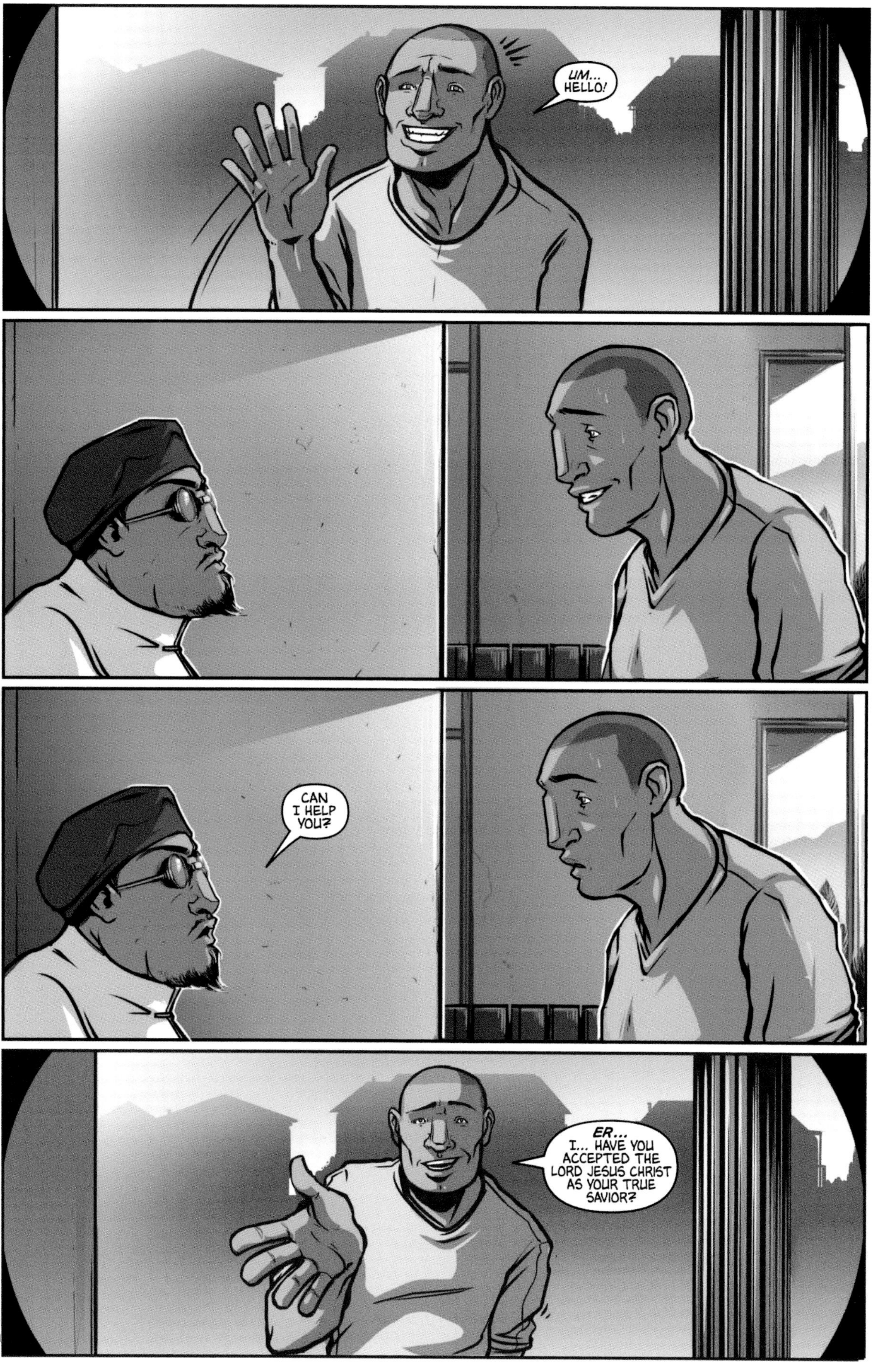
UM... HELLO!
CAN I HELP YOU?
ER... I... HAVE YOU ACCEPTED THE LORD JESUS CHRIST AS YOUR TRUE SAVIOR?

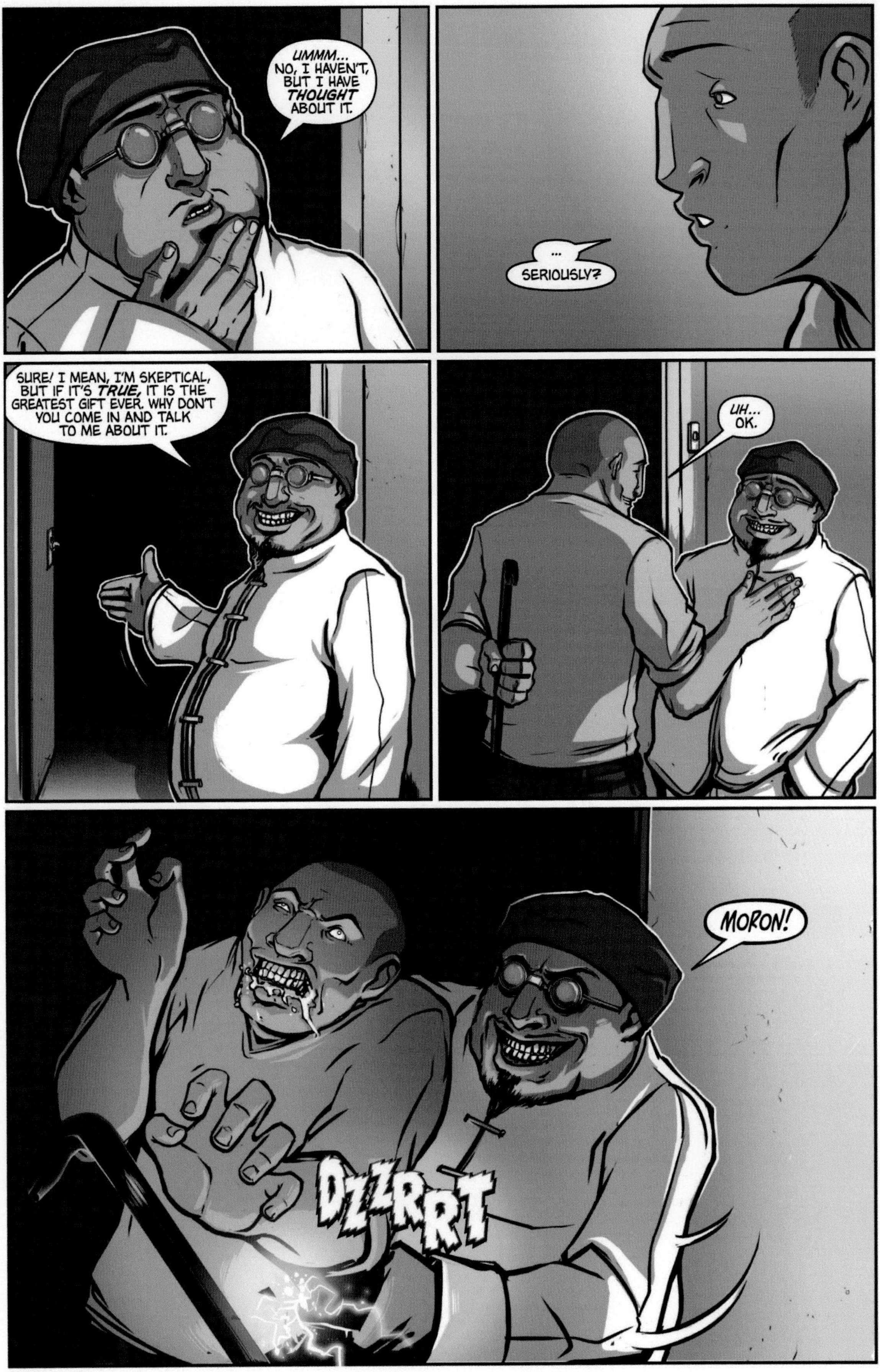
UMMM... NO, I HAVEN'T, BUT I HAVE *THOUGHT* ABOUT IT.
... SERIOUSLY?
SURE! I MEAN, I'M SKEPTICAL, BUT IF IT'S *TRUE*, IT IS THE GREATEST GIFT EVER. WHY DON'T YOU COME IN AND TALK TO ME ABOUT IT.
UH... OK.
MORON!
DZZRRRT

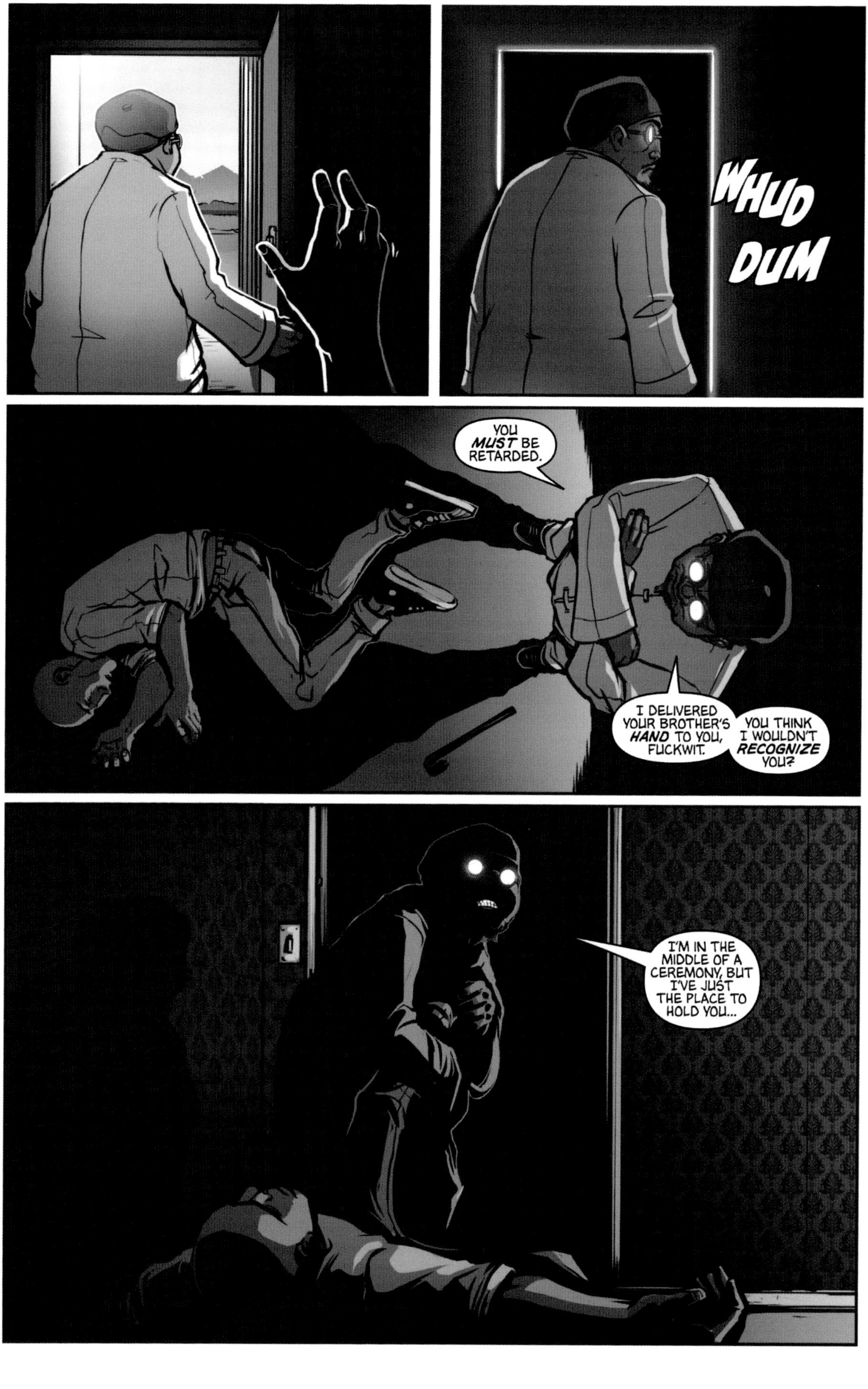
WHUD
DUM
YOU MUST BE RETARDED.
I DELIVERED YOUR BROTHER'S HAND TO YOU, FUCKWIT.
YOU THINK I WOULDN'T RECOGNIZE YOU?
I'M IN THE MIDDLE OF A CEREMONY, BUT I'VE JUST THE PLACE TO HOLD YOU...

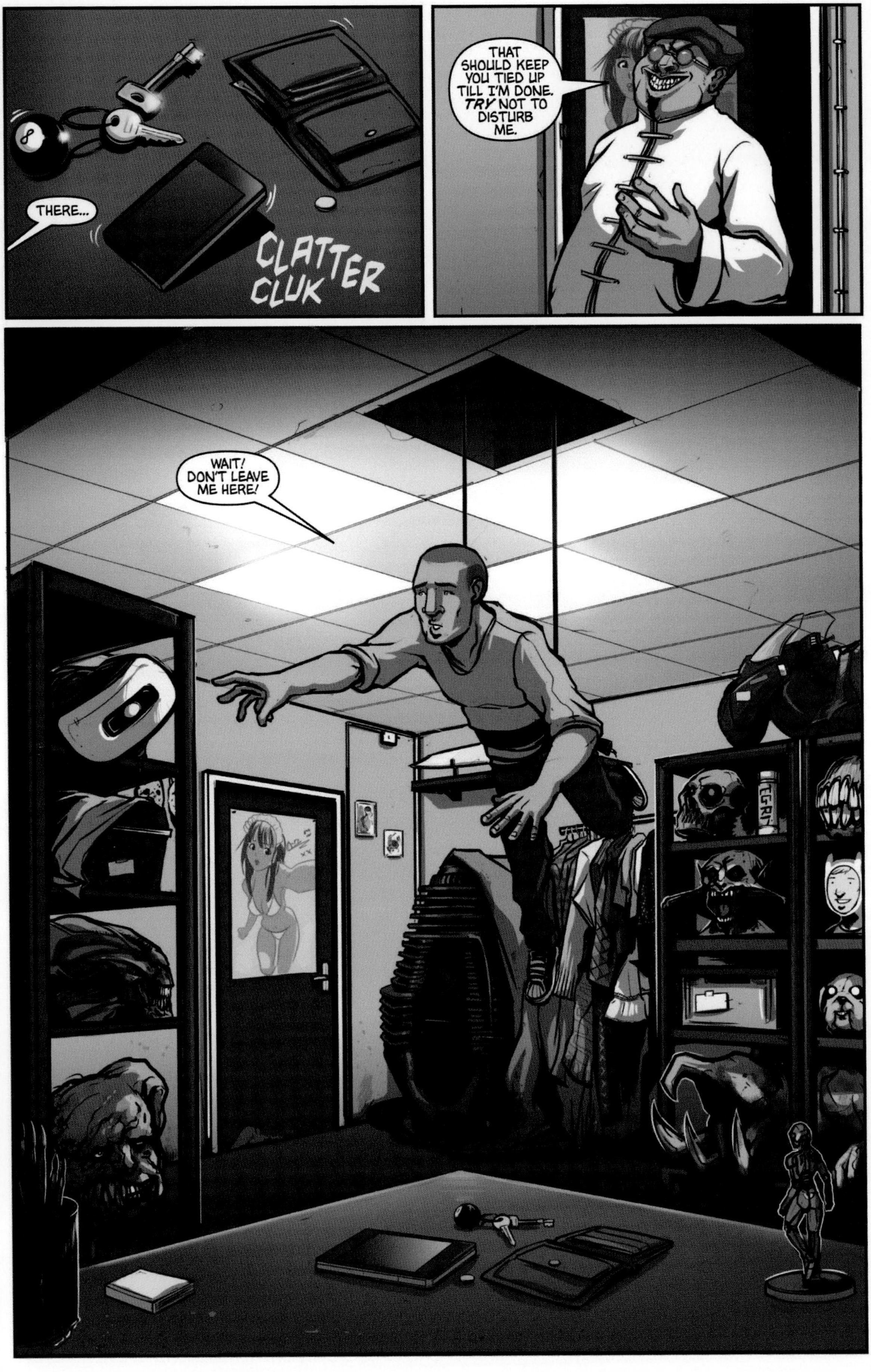
THERE...
CLATTER CLUK
THAT SHOULD KEEP YOU TIED UP TILL I'M DONE. *TRY* NOT TO DISTURB ME.
WAIT! DON'T LEAVE ME HERE!

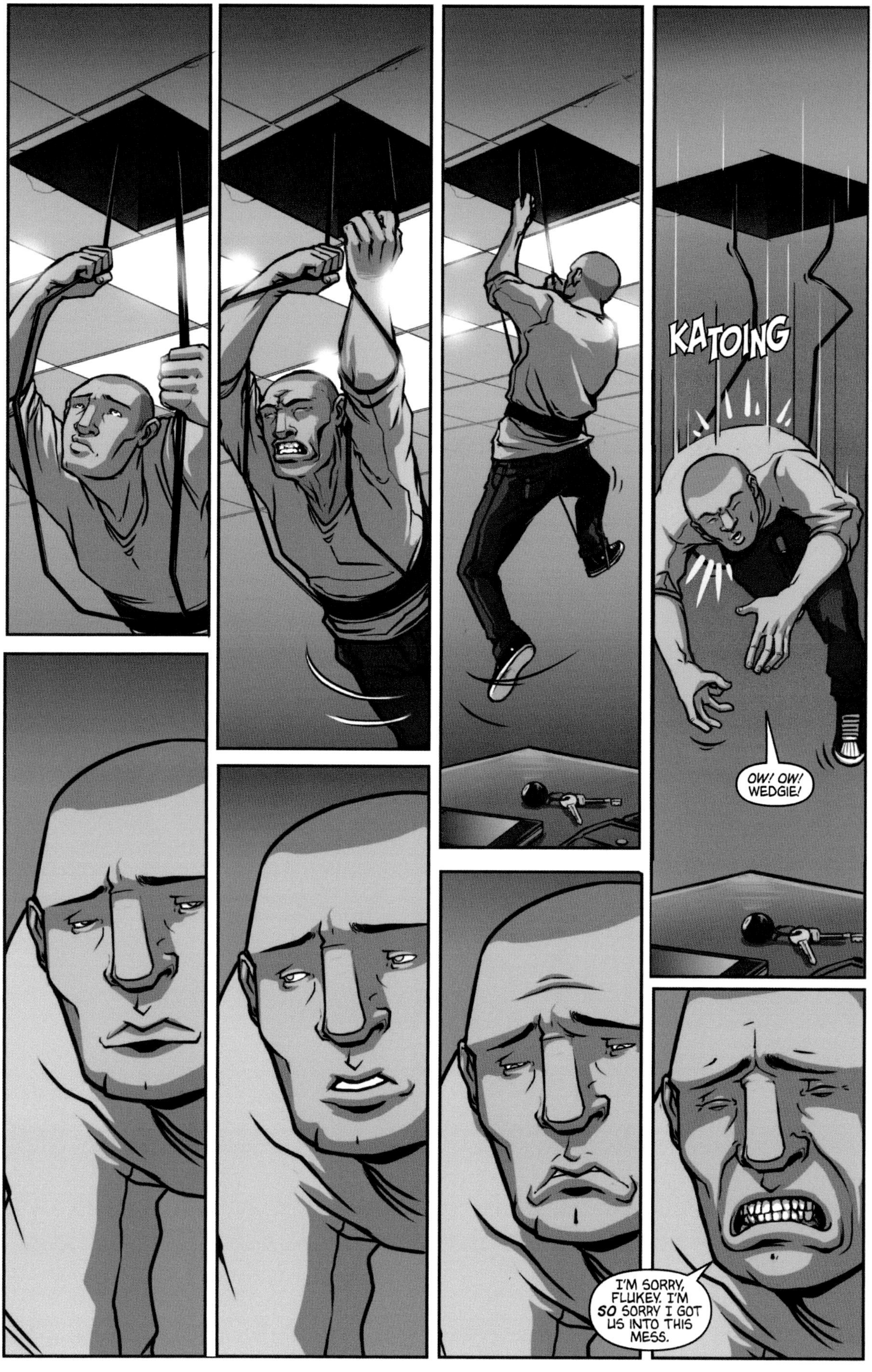
KATOING
OW! OW! WEDGIE!
I'M SORRY, FLUKEY. I'M SO SORRY I GOT US INTO THIS MESS.

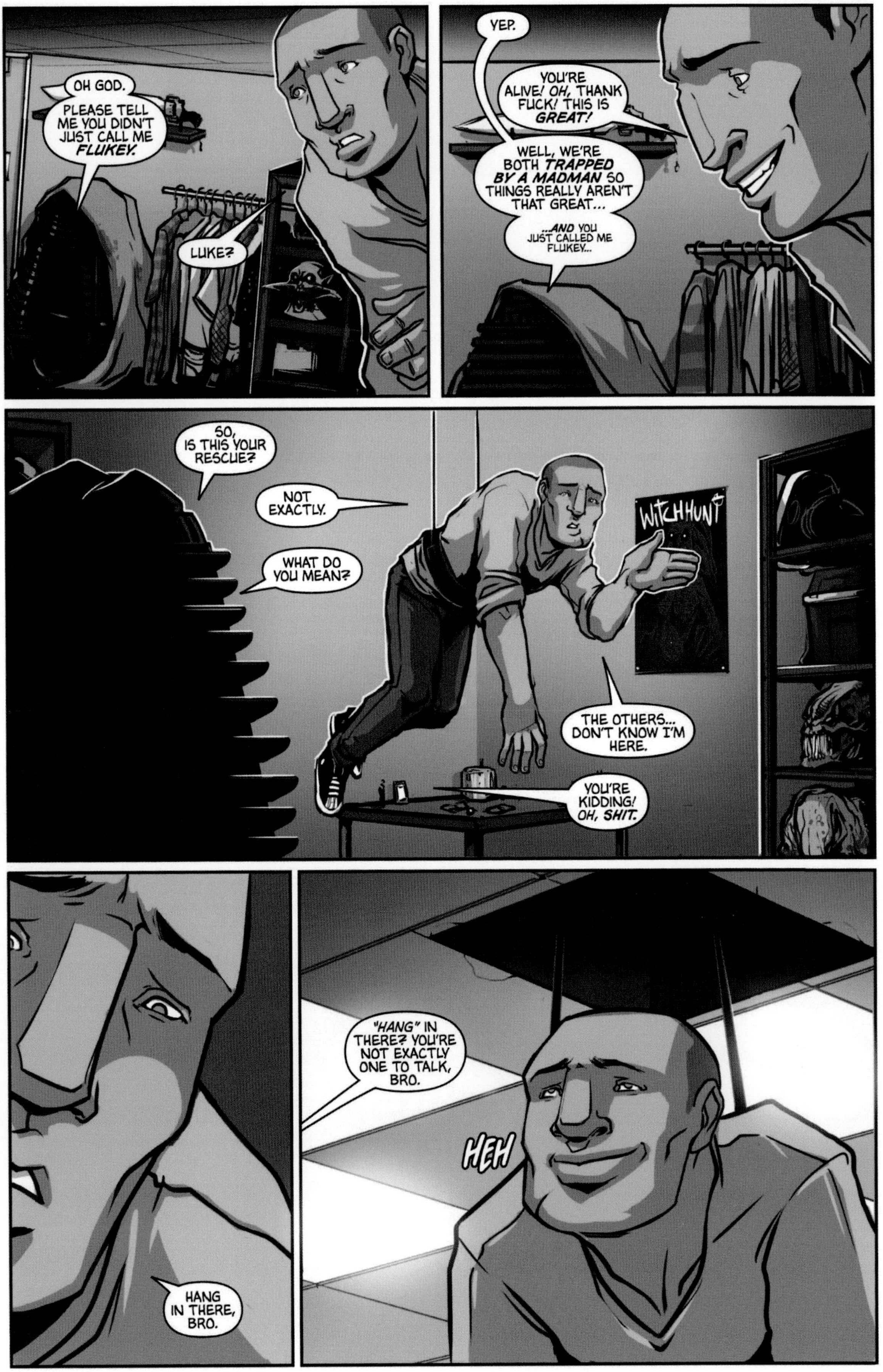
OH GOD.
PLEASE TELL ME YOU DIDN'T JUST CALL ME FLUKEY.
LUKE?
YEP.
YOU'RE ALIVE! OH, THANK FUCK! THIS IS GREAT!
WELL, WE'RE BOTH TRAPPED BY A MADMAN SO THINGS REALLY AREN'T THAT GREAT...
...AND YOU JUST CALLED ME FLUKEY...
SO, IS THIS YOUR RESCUE?
NOT EXACTLY.
WHAT DO YOU MEAN?
WITCHHUNT
THE OTHERS... DON'T KNOW I'M HERE.
YOU'RE KIDDING! OH, SHIT.
HANG IN THERE, BRO.
"HANG" IN THERE? YOU'RE NOT EXACTLY ONE TO TALK, BRO.
HEH

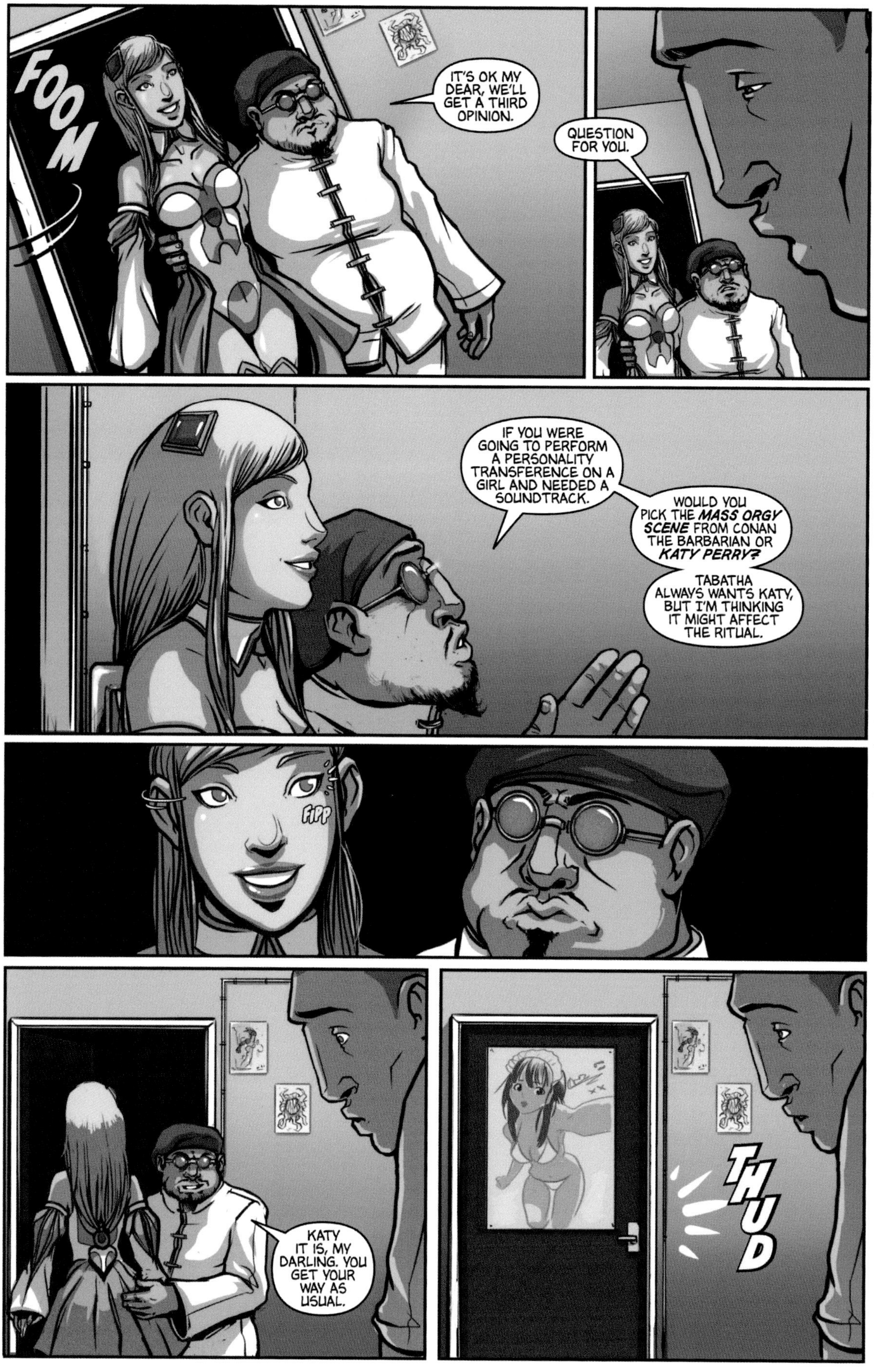
FOOM
IT'S OK MY DEAR, WE'LL GET A THIRD OPINION.
QUESTION FOR YOU.
IF YOU WERE GOING TO PERFORM A PERSONALITY TRANSFERENCE ON A GIRL AND NEEDED A SOUNDTRACK.
WOULD YOU PICK THE MASS ORGY SCENE FROM CONAN THE BARBARIAN OR KATY PERRY?
TABATHA ALWAYS WANTS KATY, BUT I'M THINKING IT MIGHT AFFECT THE RITUAL.
FIPP
KATY IT IS, MY DARLING. YOU GET YOUR WAY AS USUAL.
THUD

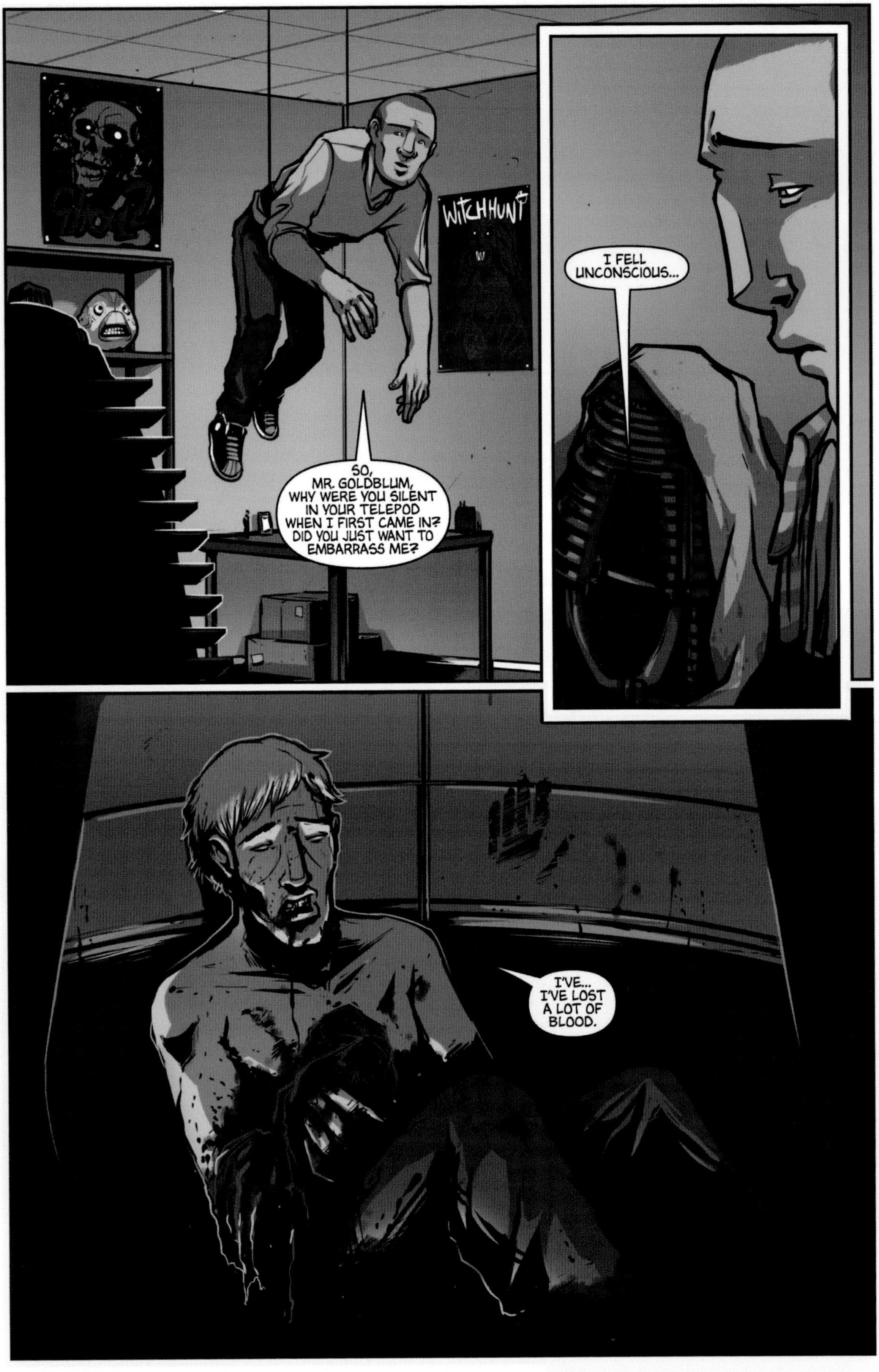
SO, MR. GOLDBLUM, WHY WERE YOU SILENT IN YOUR TELEPOD WHEN I FIRST CAME IN? DID YOU JUST WANT TO EMBARRASS ME?
WITCHHUNT
I FELL UNCONSCIOUS...
I'VE... I'VE LOST A LOT OF BLOOD.

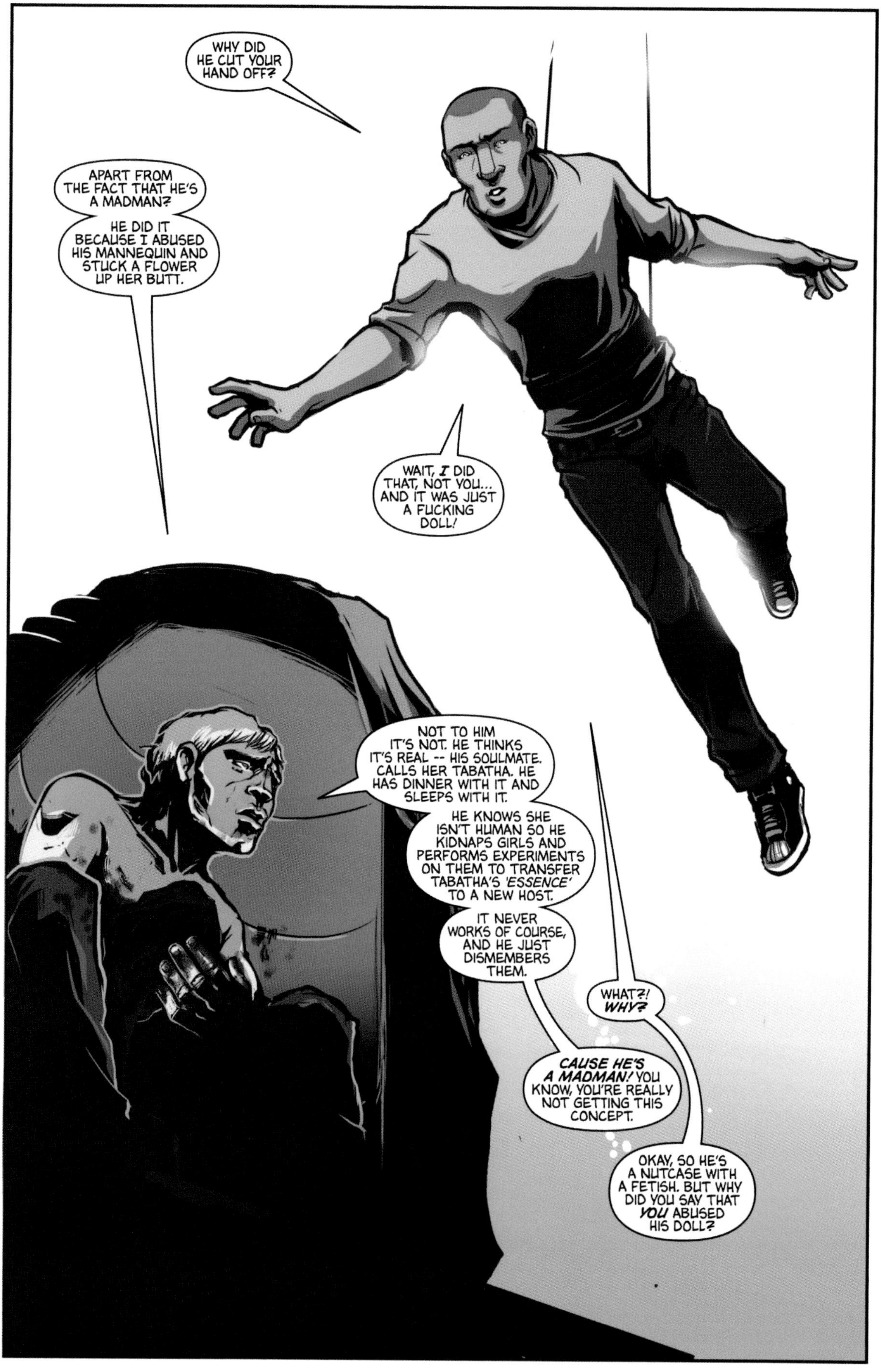
WHY DID HE CUT YOUR HAND OFF?
APART FROM THE FACT THAT HE'S A MADMAN?
HE DID IT BECAUSE I ABUSED HIS MANNEQUIN AND STUCK A FLOWER UP HER BUTT.
WAIT, *I* DID THAT, NOT YOU... AND IT WAS JUST A FUCKING DOLL!
NOT TO HIM IT'S NOT. HE THINKS IT'S REAL -- HIS SOULMATE. CALLS HER TABATHA. HE HAS DINNER WITH IT AND SLEEPS WITH IT.
HE KNOWS SHE ISN'T HUMAN SO HE KIDNAPS GIRLS AND PERFORMS EXPERIMENTS ON THEM TO TRANSFER TABATHA'S *'ESSENCE'* TO A NEW HOST.
IT NEVER WORKS OF COURSE, AND HE JUST DISMEMBERS THEM.
WHAT?! ***WHY?***
CAUSE HE'S A MADMAN! YOU KNOW, YOU'RE REALLY NOT GETTING THIS CONCEPT.
OKAY, SO HE'S A NUTCASE WITH A FETISH. BUT WHY DID YOU SAY THAT ***YOU*** ABUSED HIS DOLL?

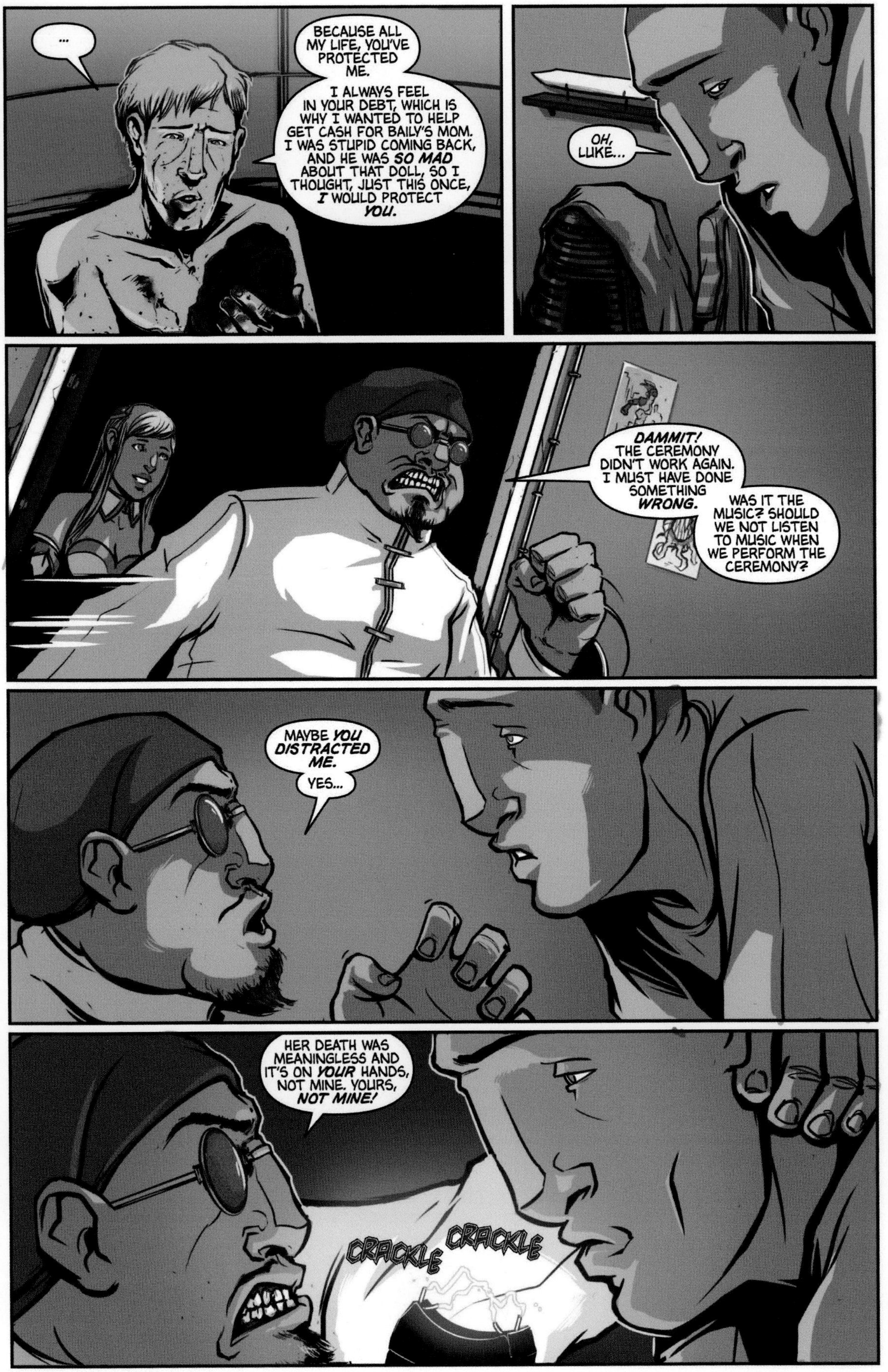
...
BECAUSE ALL MY LIFE, YOU'VE PROTECTED ME.
I ALWAYS FEEL IN YOUR DEBT, WHICH IS WHY I WANTED TO HELP GET CASH FOR BAILY'S MOM. I WAS STUPID COMING BACK, AND HE WAS SO MAD ABOUT THAT DOLL, SO I THOUGHT, JUST THIS ONCE, I WOULD PROTECT YOU.
OH, LUKE...
DAMMIT! THE CEREMONY DIDN'T WORK AGAIN. I MUST HAVE DONE SOMETHING WRONG.
WAS IT THE MUSIC? SHOULD WE NOT LISTEN TO MUSIC WHEN WE PERFORM THE CEREMONY?
MAYBE YOU DISTRACTED ME.
YES...
HER DEATH WAS MEANINGLESS AND IT'S ON YOUR HANDS, NOT MINE. YOURS, NOT MINE!
CRACKLE
CRACKLE

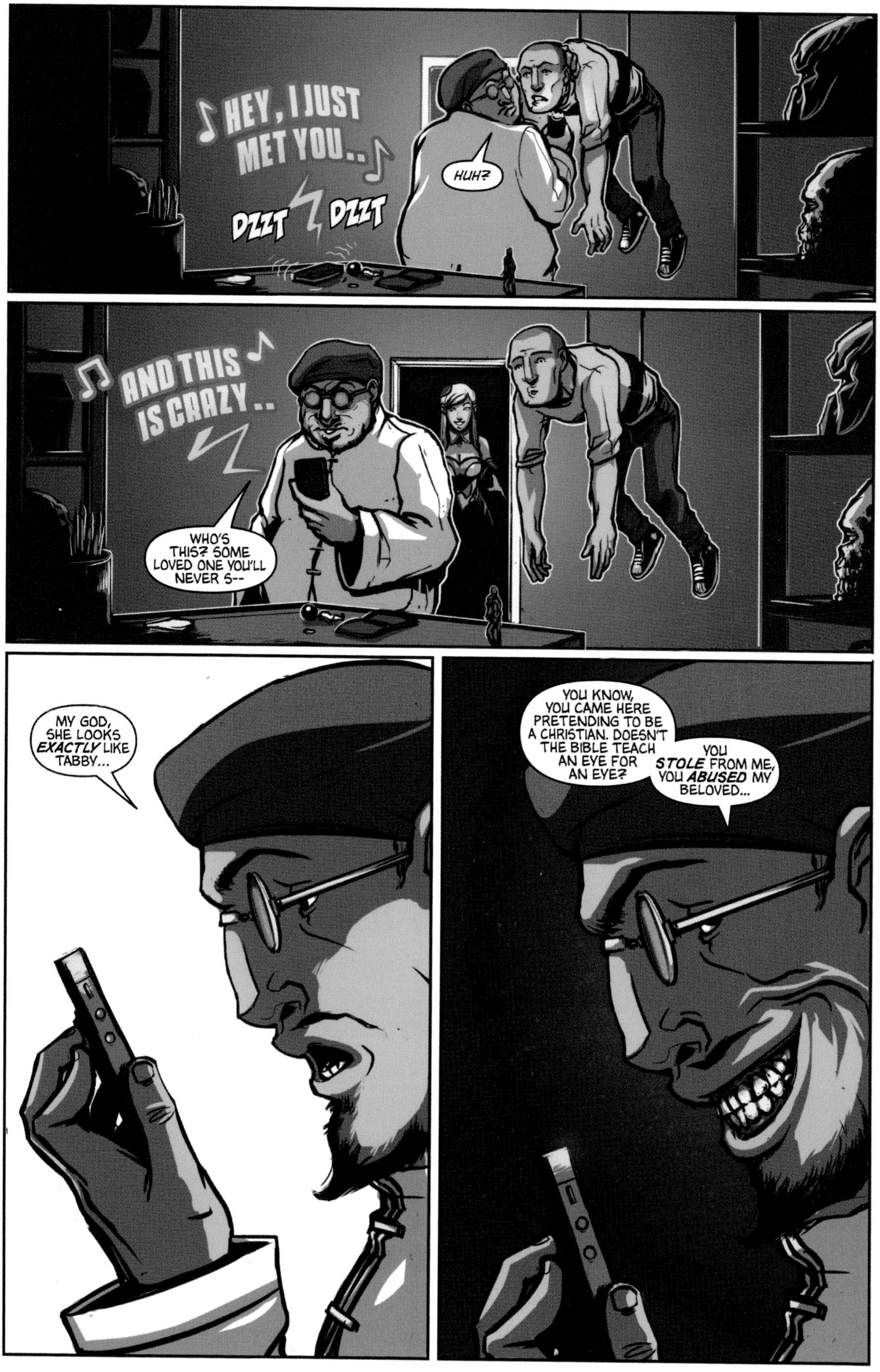
♪ HEY, I JUST MET YOU..♪
DZZT DZZT
HUH?
♫ AND THIS IS CRAZY..♪
WHO'S THIS? SOME LOVED ONE YOU'LL NEVER S--
MY GOD, SHE LOOKS EXACTLY LIKE TABBY...
YOU KNOW, YOU CAME HERE PRETENDING TO BE A CHRISTIAN. DOESN'T THE BIBLE TEACH AN EYE FOR AN EYE?
YOU STOLE FROM ME, YOU ABUSED MY BELOVED...

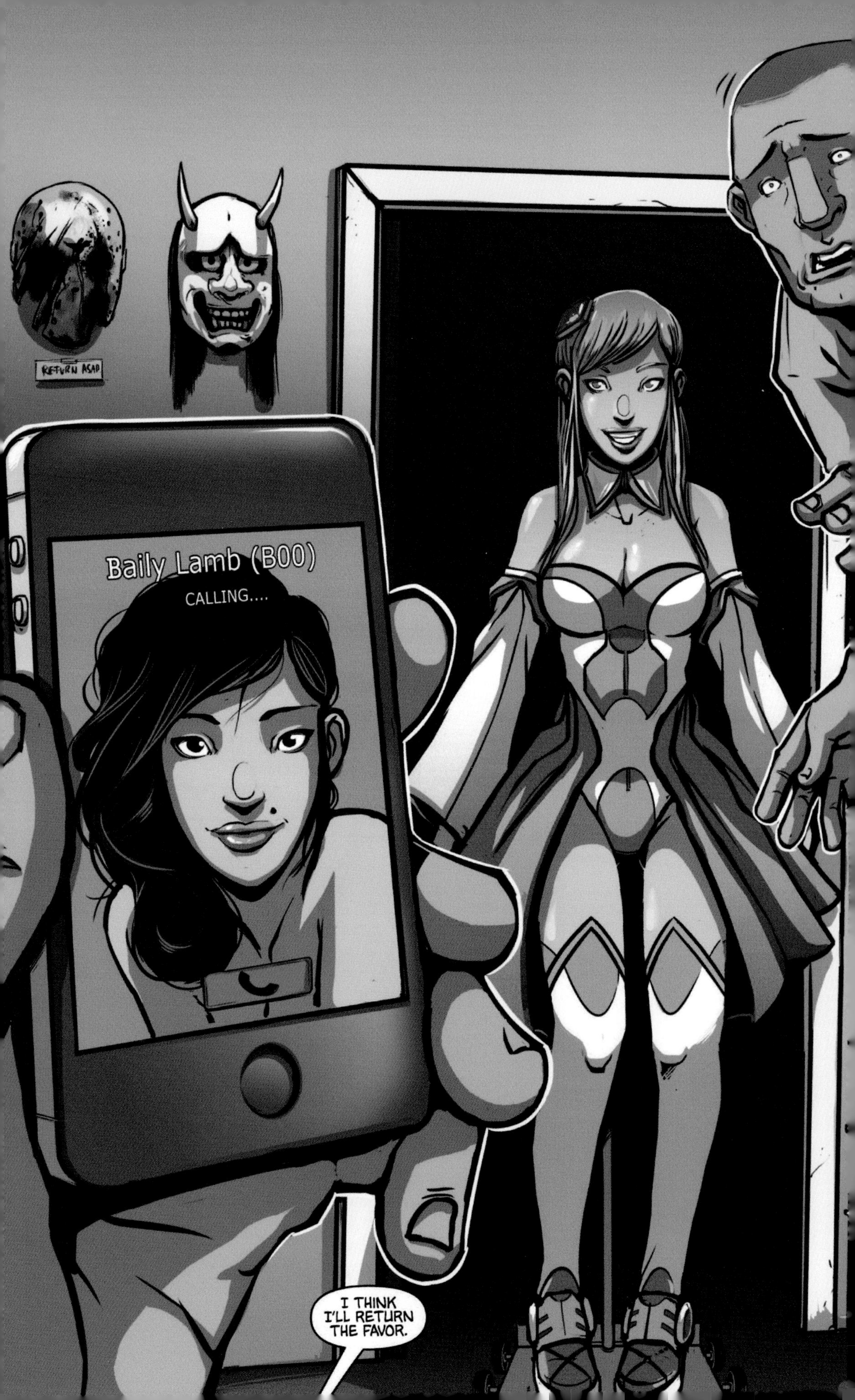
RETURN ASAP
Baily Lamb (B00)
CALLING....
I THINK I'LL RETURN THE FAVOR.

CHAPTER THREE

"I GUESS IT'S TIME TO START THE PROCEDURE."

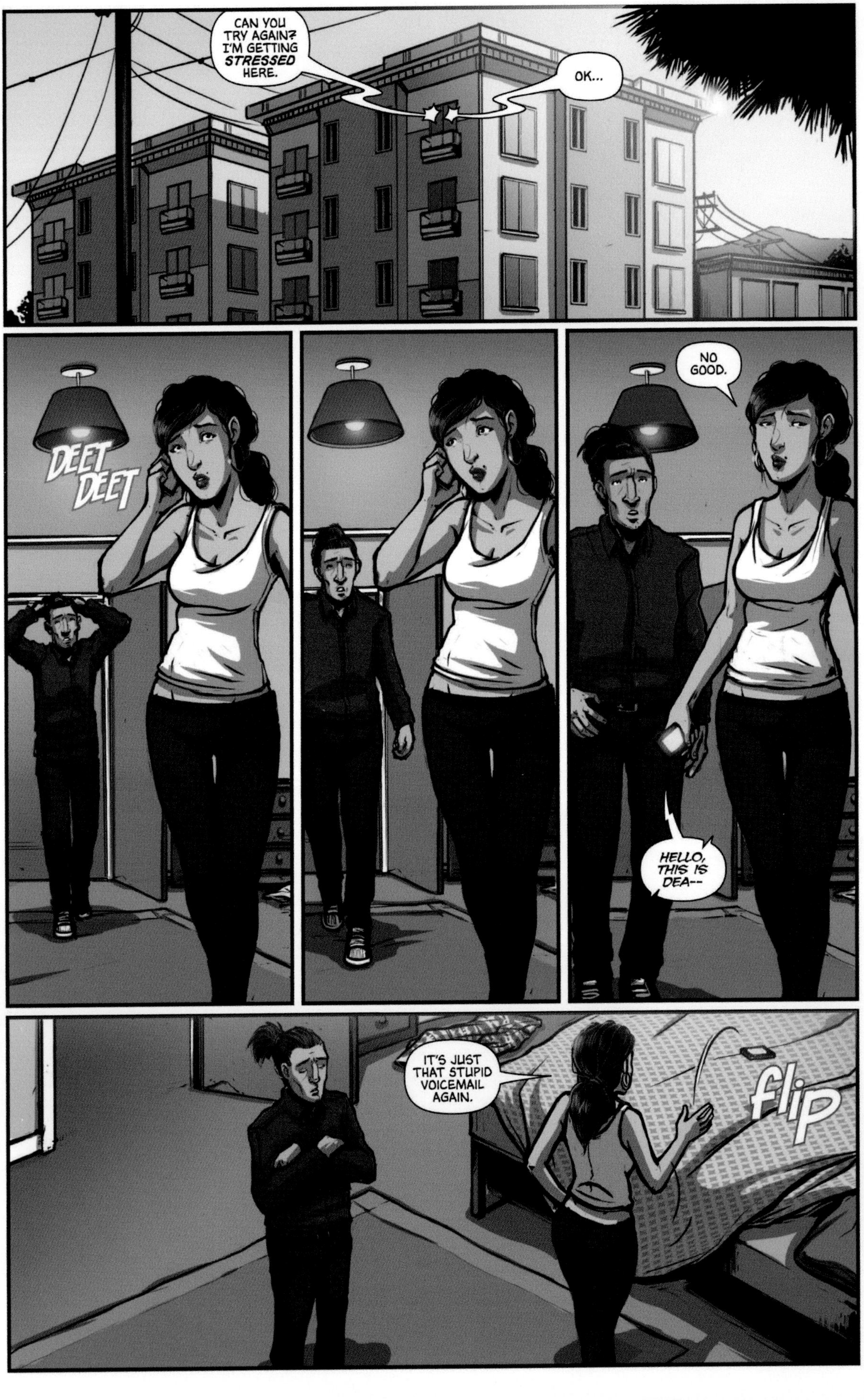
CAN YOU TRY AGAIN? I'M GETTING STRESSED HERE.
OK...
DEET DEET
NO GOOD.
HELLO, THIS IS DEA--
IT'S JUST THAT STUPID VOICEMAIL AGAIN.
flip

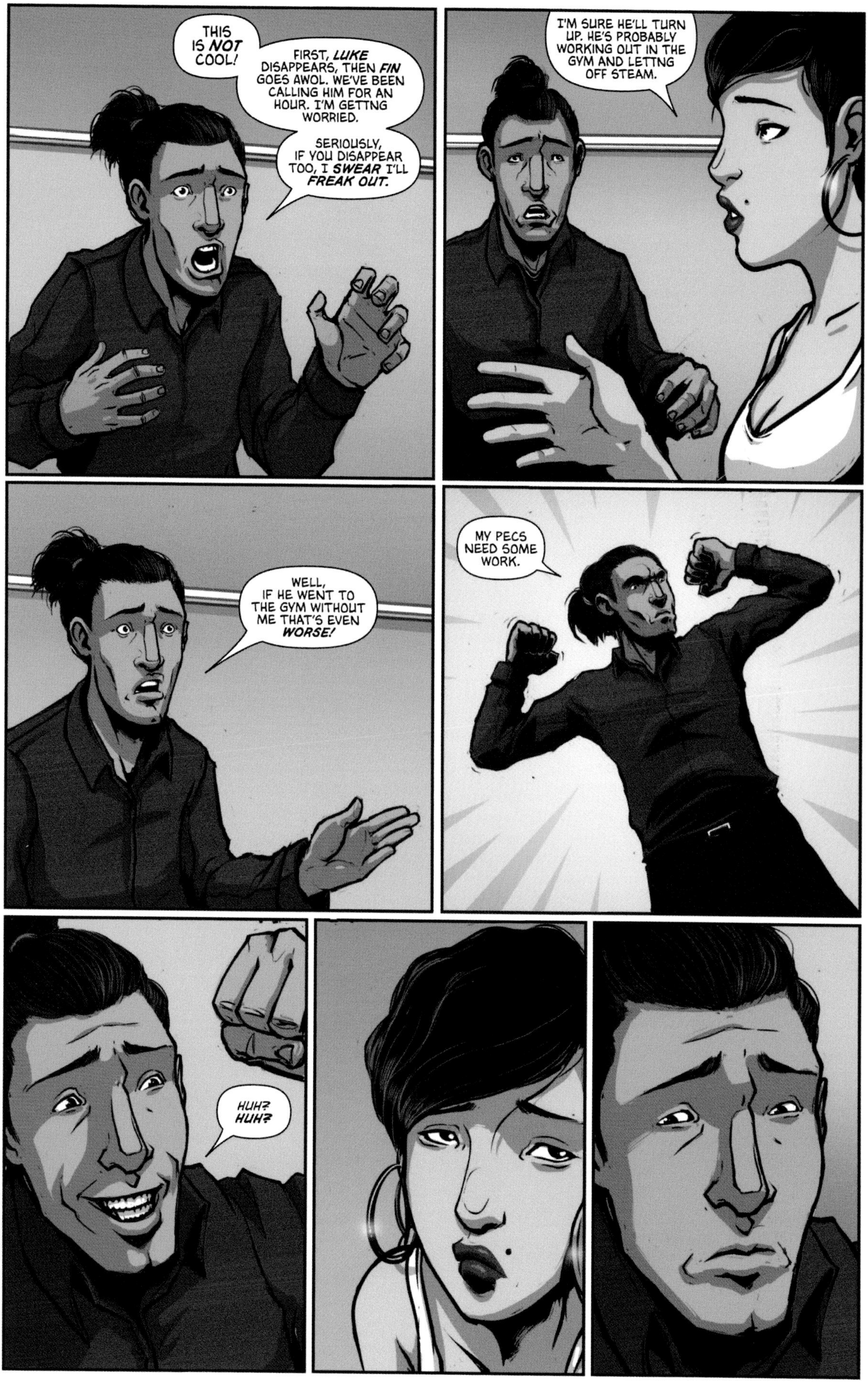
THIS IS NOT COOL!
FIRST, LUKE DISAPPEARS, THEN FIN GOES AWOL. WE'VE BEEN CALLING HIM FOR AN HOUR. I'M GETTNG WORRIED.
SERIOUSLY, IF YOU DISAPPEAR TOO, I SWEAR I'LL FREAK OUT.
I'M SURE HE'LL TURN UP. HE'S PROBABLY WORKING OUT IN THE GYM AND LETTNG OFF STEAM.
WELL, IF HE WENT TO THE GYM WITHOUT ME THAT'S EVEN WORSE!
MY PECS NEED SOME WORK.
HUH? HUH?

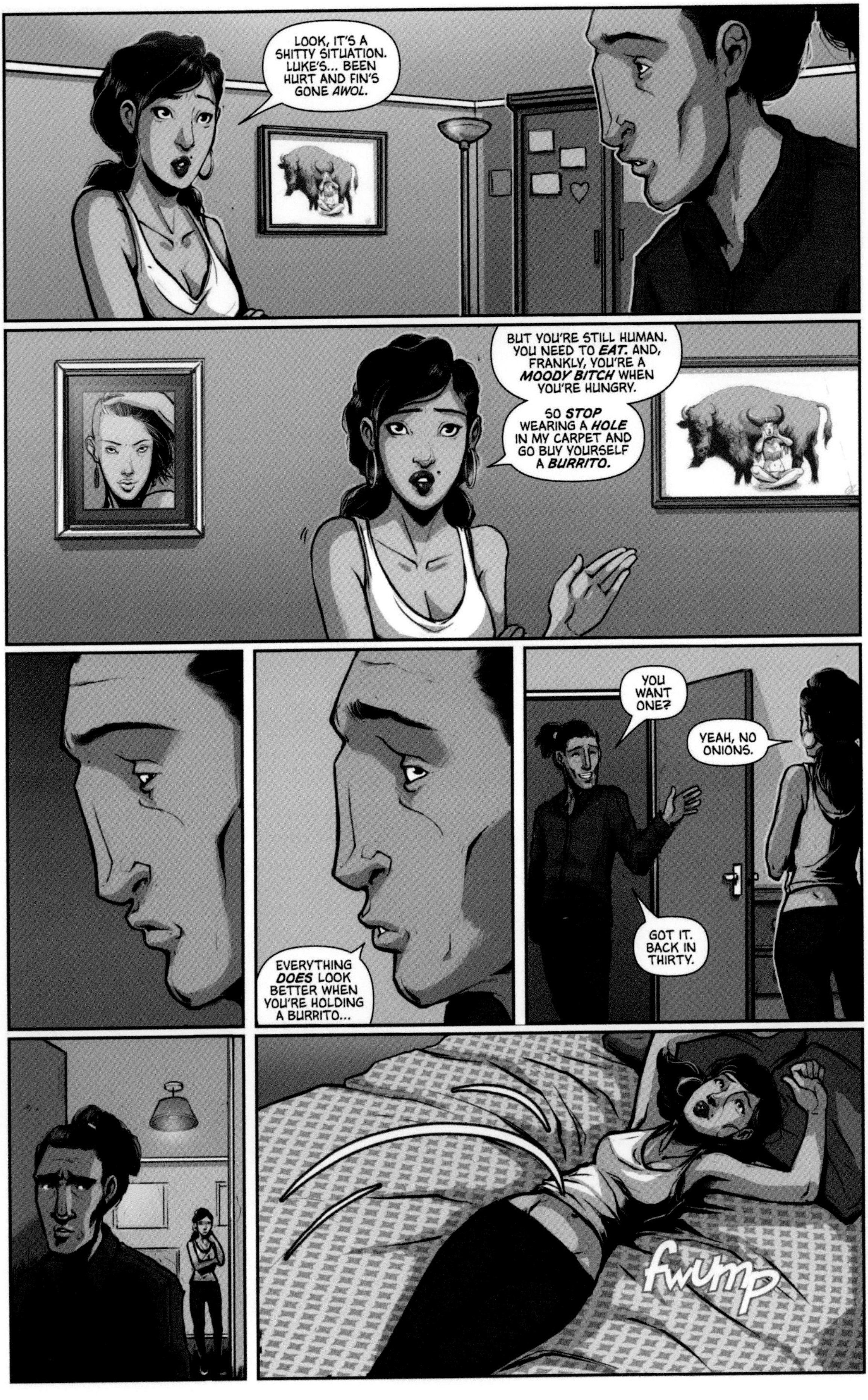
LOOK, IT'S A SHITTY SITUATION. LUKE'S... BEEN HURT AND FIN'S GONE *AWOL*.
BUT YOU'RE STILL HUMAN. YOU NEED TO *EAT*. AND, FRANKLY, YOU'RE A ***MOODY BITCH*** WHEN YOU'RE HUNGRY.
SO ***STOP*** WEARING A ***HOLE*** IN MY CARPET AND GO BUY YOURSELF A ***BURRITO***.
EVERYTHING ***DOES*** LOOK BETTER WHEN YOU'RE HOLDING A BURRITO...
YOU WANT ONE?
YEAH, NO ONIONS.
GOT IT. BACK IN THIRTY.
fwump

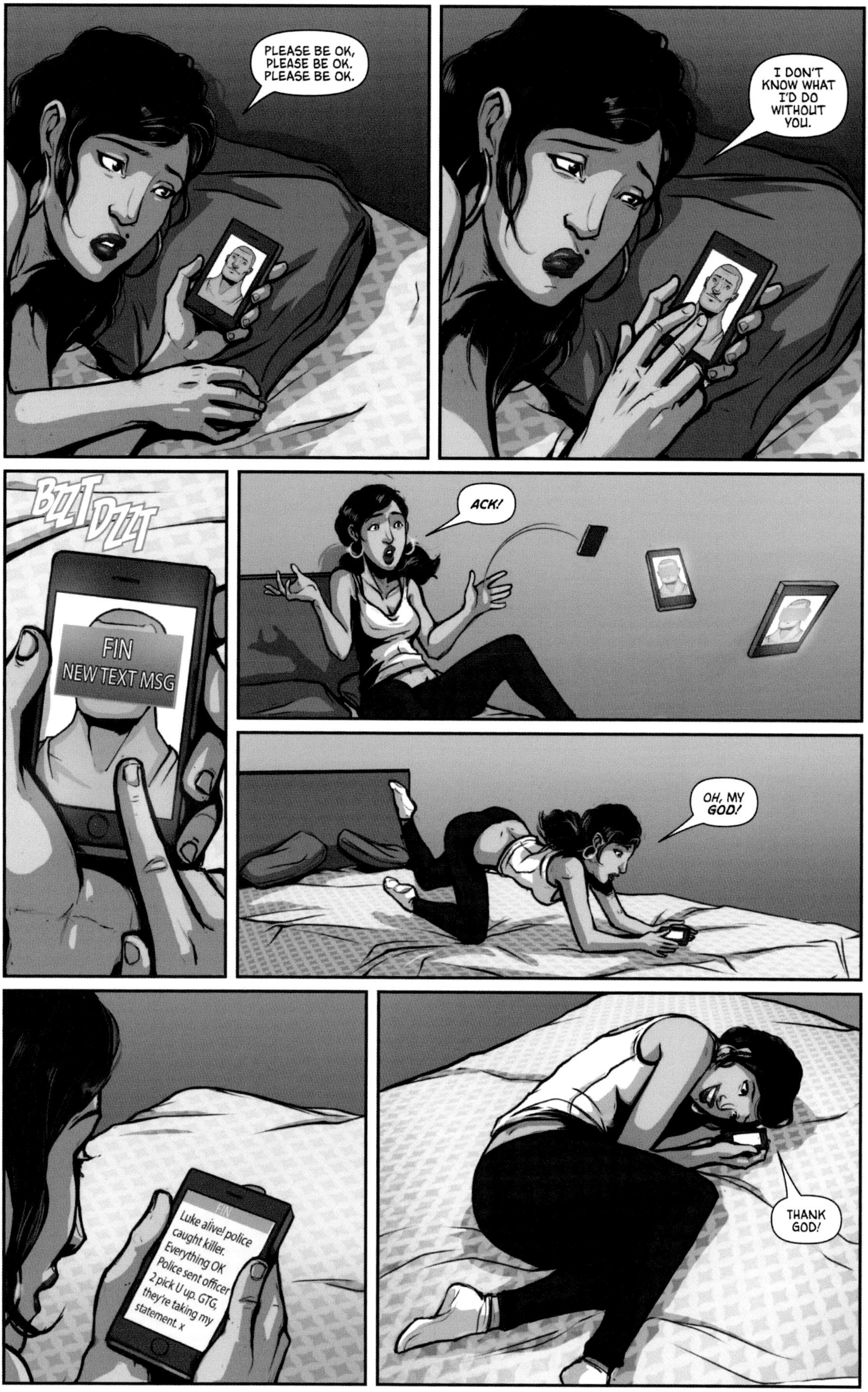
PLEASE BE OK, PLEASE BE OK. PLEASE BE OK.
I DON'T KNOW WHAT I'D DO WITHOUT YOU.
BZZT DZZT
FIN
NEW TEXT MSG
ACK!
OH, MY GOD!
FIN
Luke alive! police caught killer. Everything OK Police sent officer 2 pick U up. GTG, they're taking my statement. x
THANK GOD!

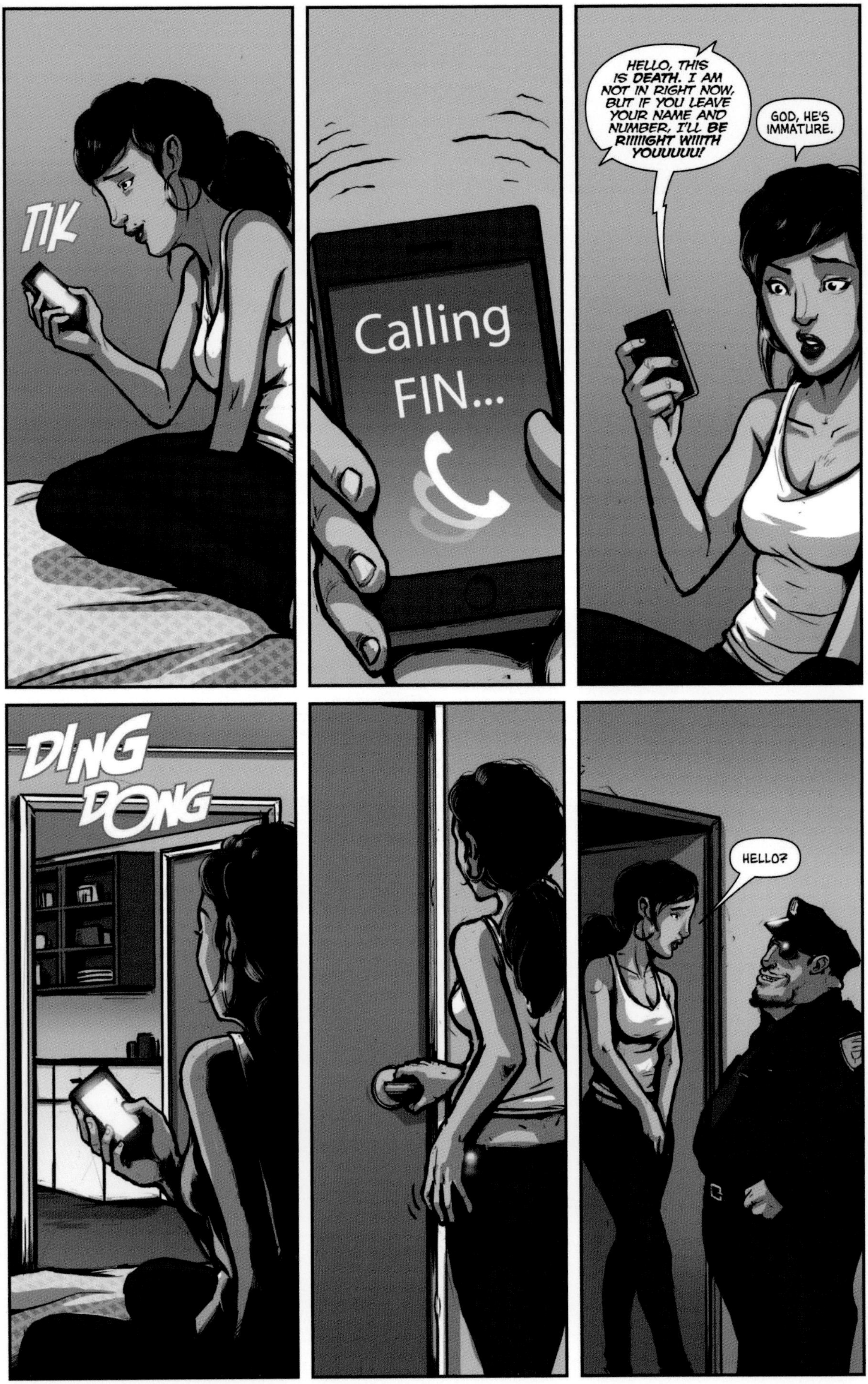
TIK
Calling FIN...
HELLO, THIS IS DEATH. I AM NOT IN RIGHT NOW, BUT IF YOU LEAVE YOUR NAME AND NUMBER, I'LL BE RIIIIGHT WIIITH YOUUUUU!
GOD, HE'S IMMATURE.
DING DONG
HELLO?

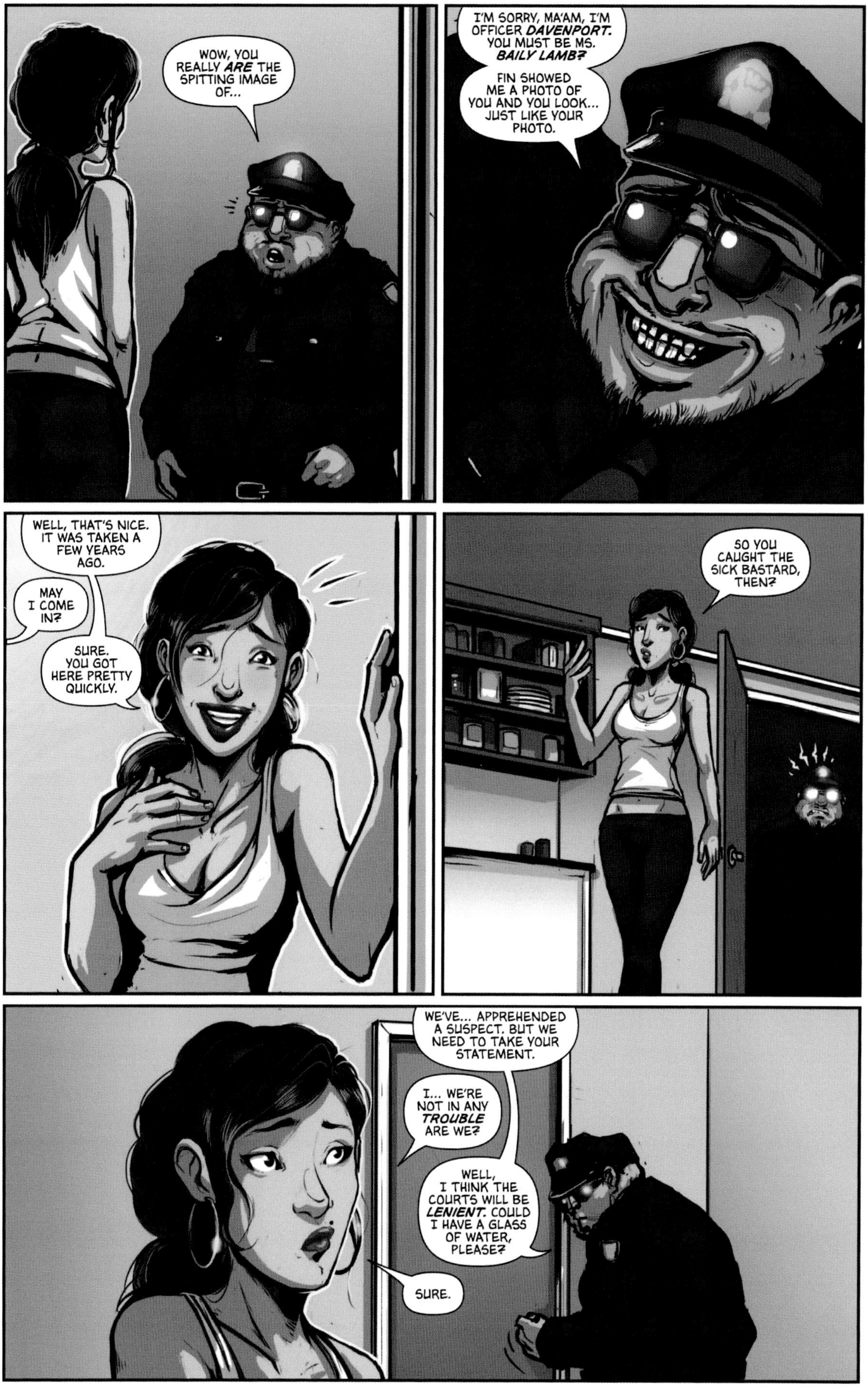
WOW, YOU REALLY ARE THE SPITTING IMAGE OF...
I'M SORRY, MA'AM, I'M OFFICER DAVENPORT. YOU MUST BE MS. BAILY LAMB?
FIN SHOWED ME A PHOTO OF YOU AND YOU LOOK... JUST LIKE YOUR PHOTO.
WELL, THAT'S NICE. IT WAS TAKEN A FEW YEARS AGO.
MAY I COME IN?
SURE. YOU GOT HERE PRETTY QUICKLY.
SO YOU CAUGHT THE SICK BASTARD, THEN?
WE'VE... APPREHENDED A SUSPECT. BUT WE NEED TO TAKE YOUR STATEMENT.
I... WE'RE NOT IN ANY TROUBLE ARE WE?
WELL, I THINK THE COURTS WILL BE LENIENT. COULD I HAVE A GLASS OF WATER, PLEASE?
SURE.

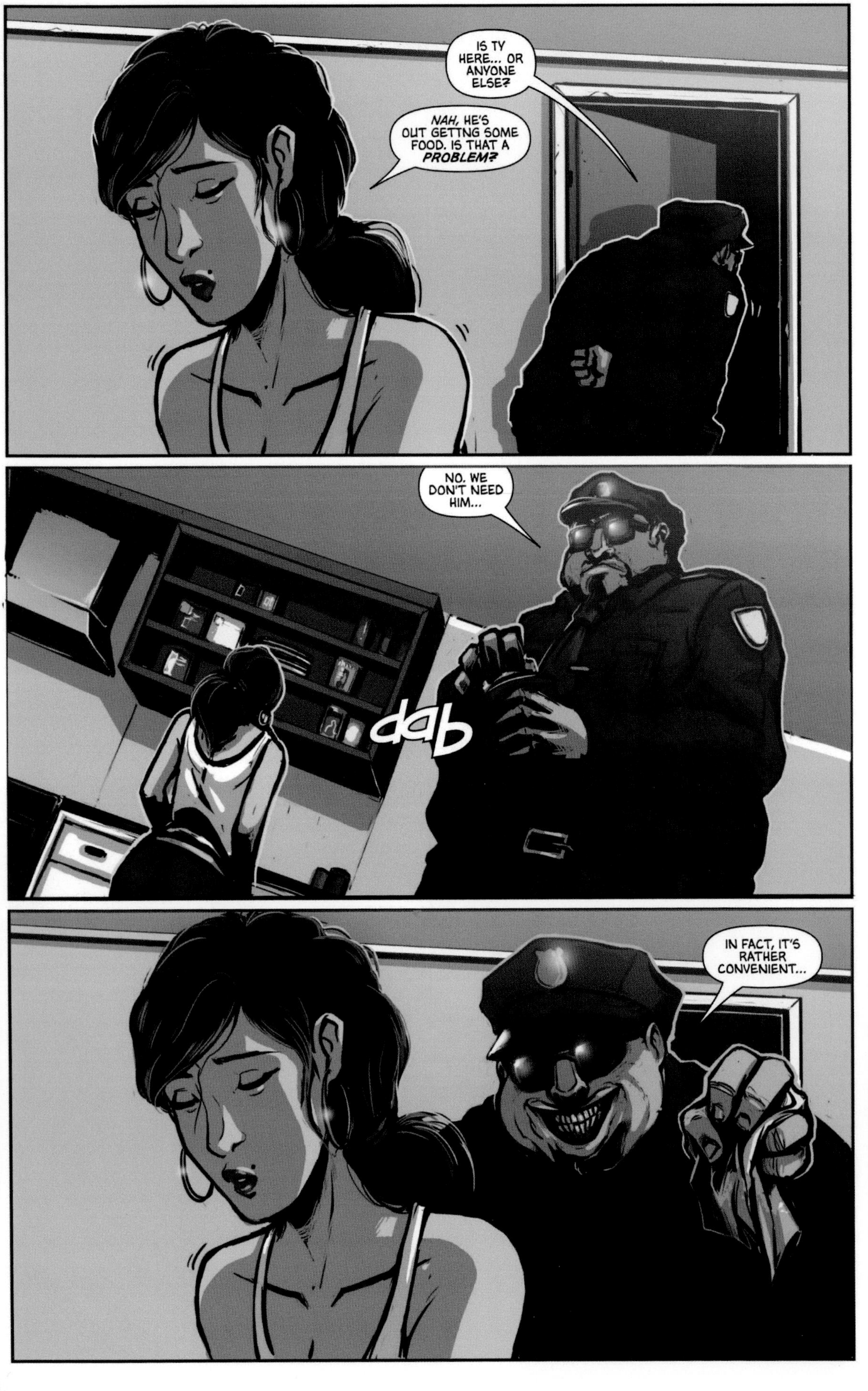
IS TY HERE... OR ANYONE ELSE?
NAH, HE'S OUT GETTNG SOME FOOD. IS THAT A PROBLEM?
NO. WE DON'T NEED HIM...
dab
IN FACT, IT'S RATHER CONVENIENT...

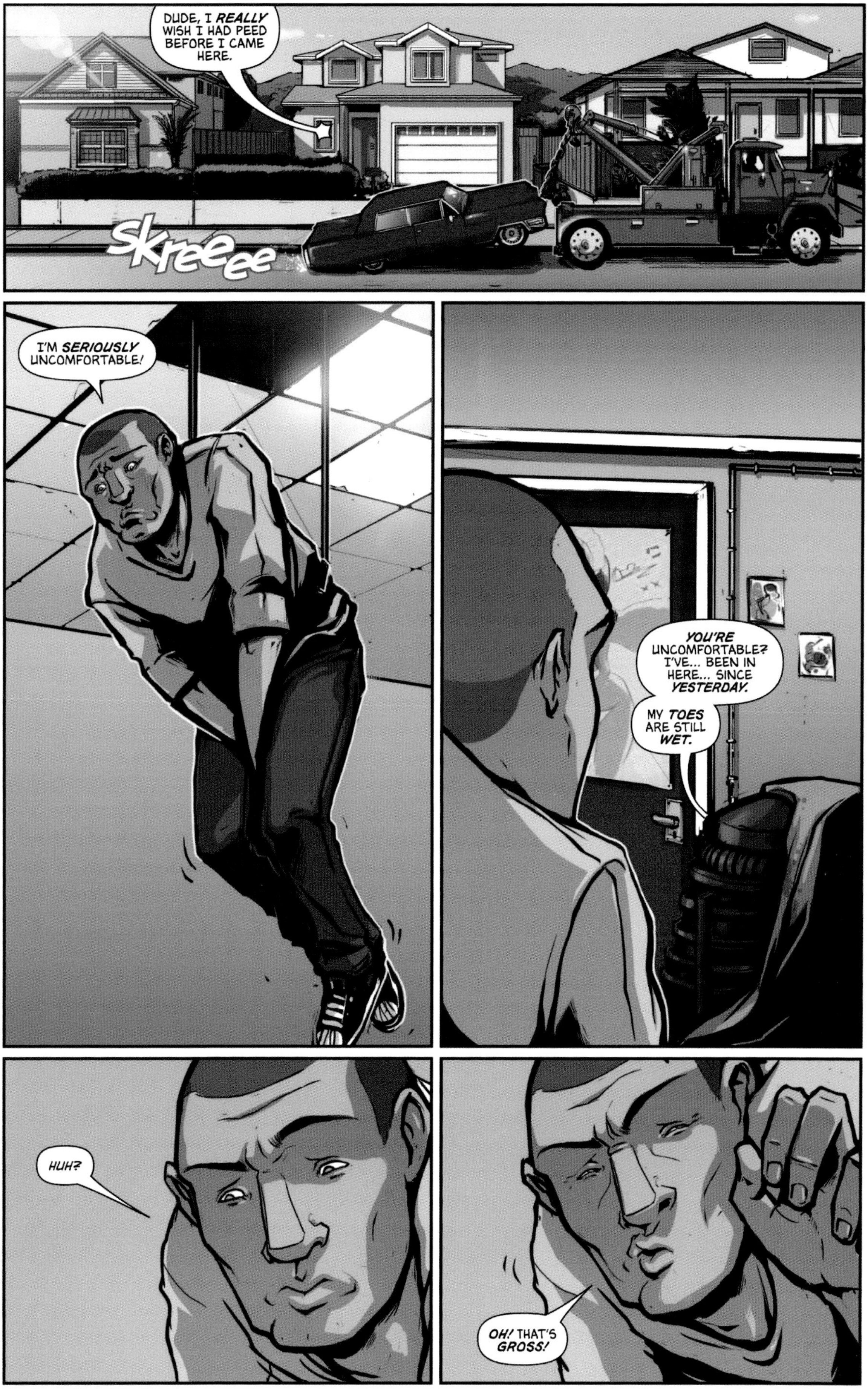
DUDE, I REALLY WISH I HAD PEED BEFORE I CAME HERE.
SKREEEEE
I'M SERIOUSLY UNCOMFORTABLE!
YOU'RE UNCOMFORTABLE? I'VE... BEEN IN HERE... SINCE YESTERDAY.
MY TOES ARE STILL WET.
HUH?
OH! THAT'S GROSS!

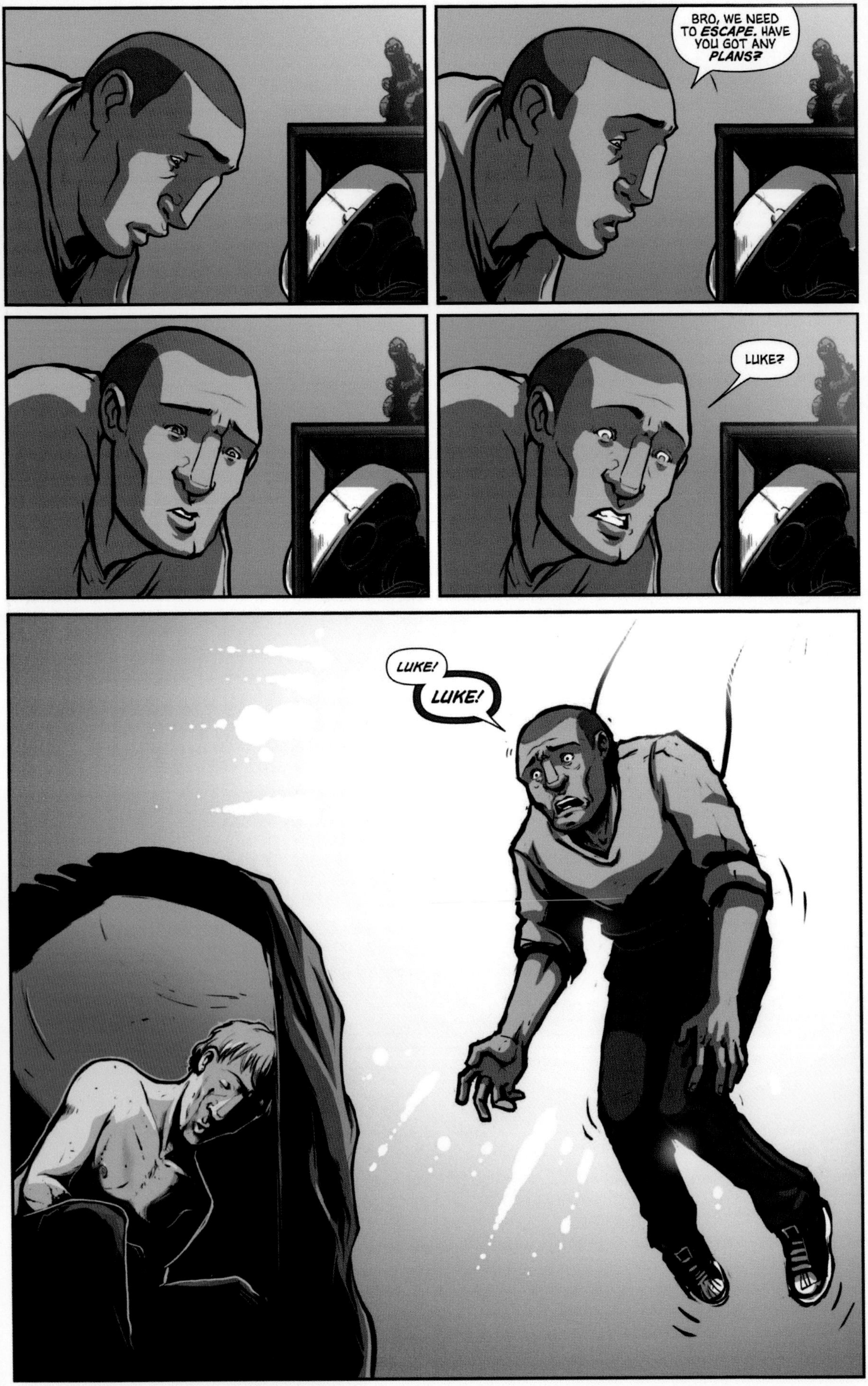
BRO, WE NEED TO ESCAPE. HAVE YOU GOT ANY PLANS?
LUKE?
LUKE!
LUKE!

I'M OK. I'M OK. YOU ALRIGHT?

AM *I* OK?! WHAT HAPPENED TO *YOU?*

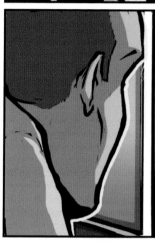

I... I'M *TIRED.* JUST LET ME SLEEP... THEN WE CAN TALK.

... WELL.

"AT LEAST THINGS CAN'T GET WORSE."

TABATHA, SWEETIE, I'VE GOT A *SURPRISE* FOR YOU...

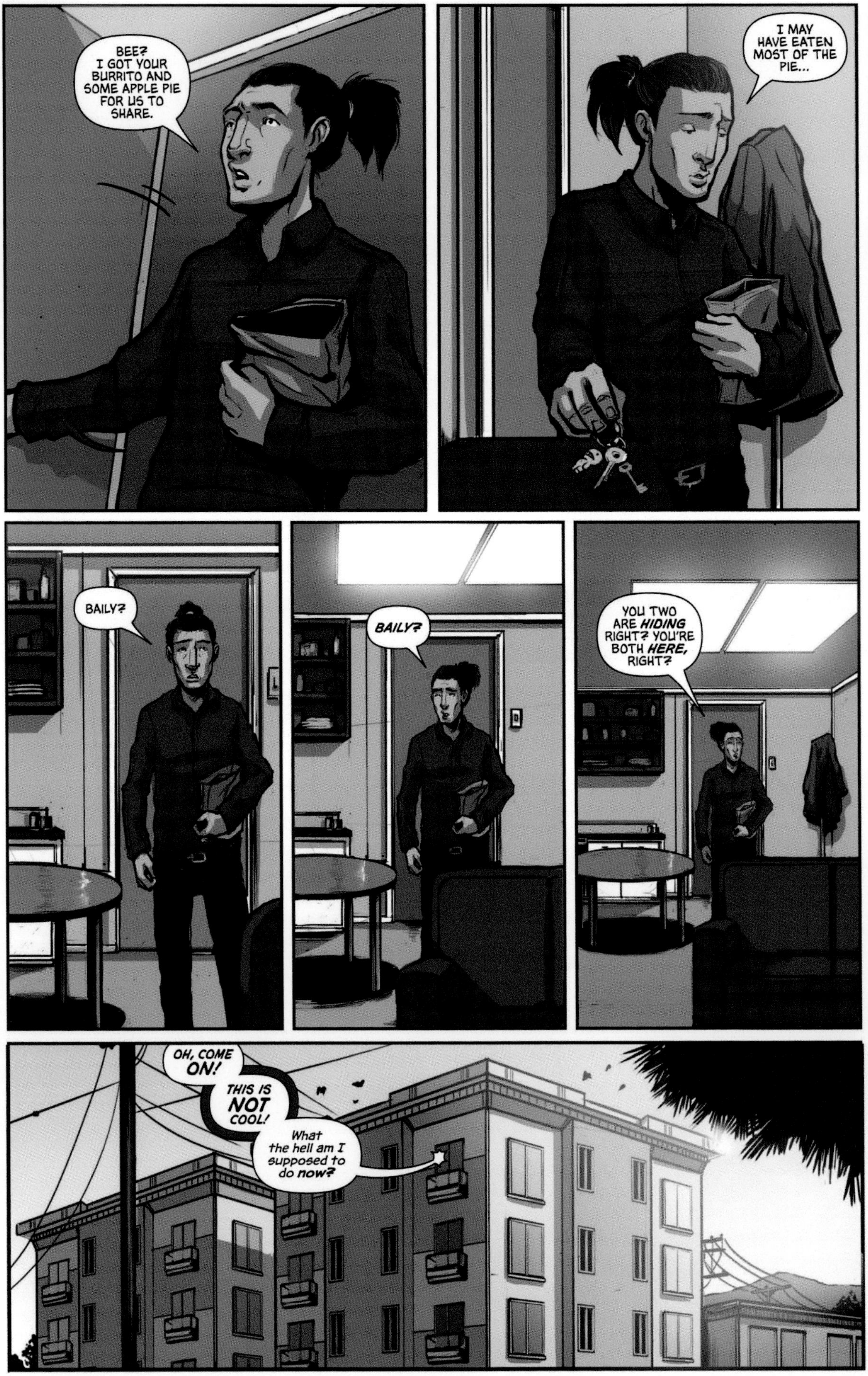
BEE? I GOT YOUR BURRITO AND SOME APPLE PIE FOR US TO SHARE.
I MAY HAVE EATEN MOST OF THE PIE...
BAILY?
BAILY?
YOU TWO ARE HIDING RIGHT? YOU'RE BOTH HERE, RIGHT?
OH, COME ON!
THIS IS NOT COOL!
What the hell am I supposed to do now?

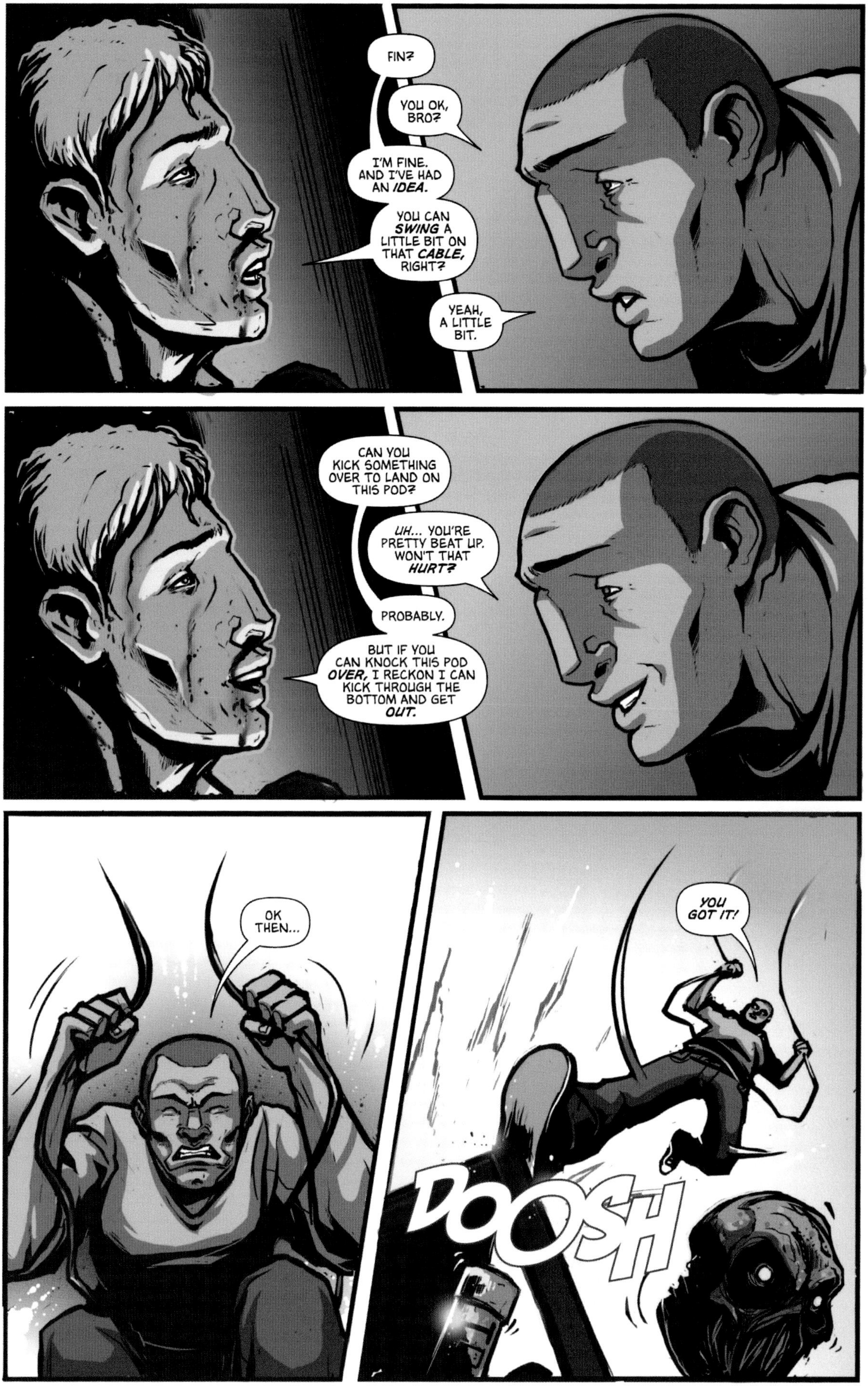
FIN?
YOU OK, BRO?
I'M FINE. AND I'VE HAD AN *IDEA.*
YOU CAN ***SWING*** A LITTLE BIT ON THAT ***CABLE,*** RIGHT?
YEAH, A LITTLE BIT.
CAN YOU KICK SOMETHING OVER TO LAND ON THIS POD?
UH... YOU'RE PRETTY BEAT UP. WON'T THAT ***HURT?***
PROBABLY.
BUT IF YOU CAN KNOCK THIS POD ***OVER,*** I RECKON I CAN KICK THROUGH THE BOTTOM AND GET ***OUT.***
OK THEN...
YOU GOT IT!
DOOSH

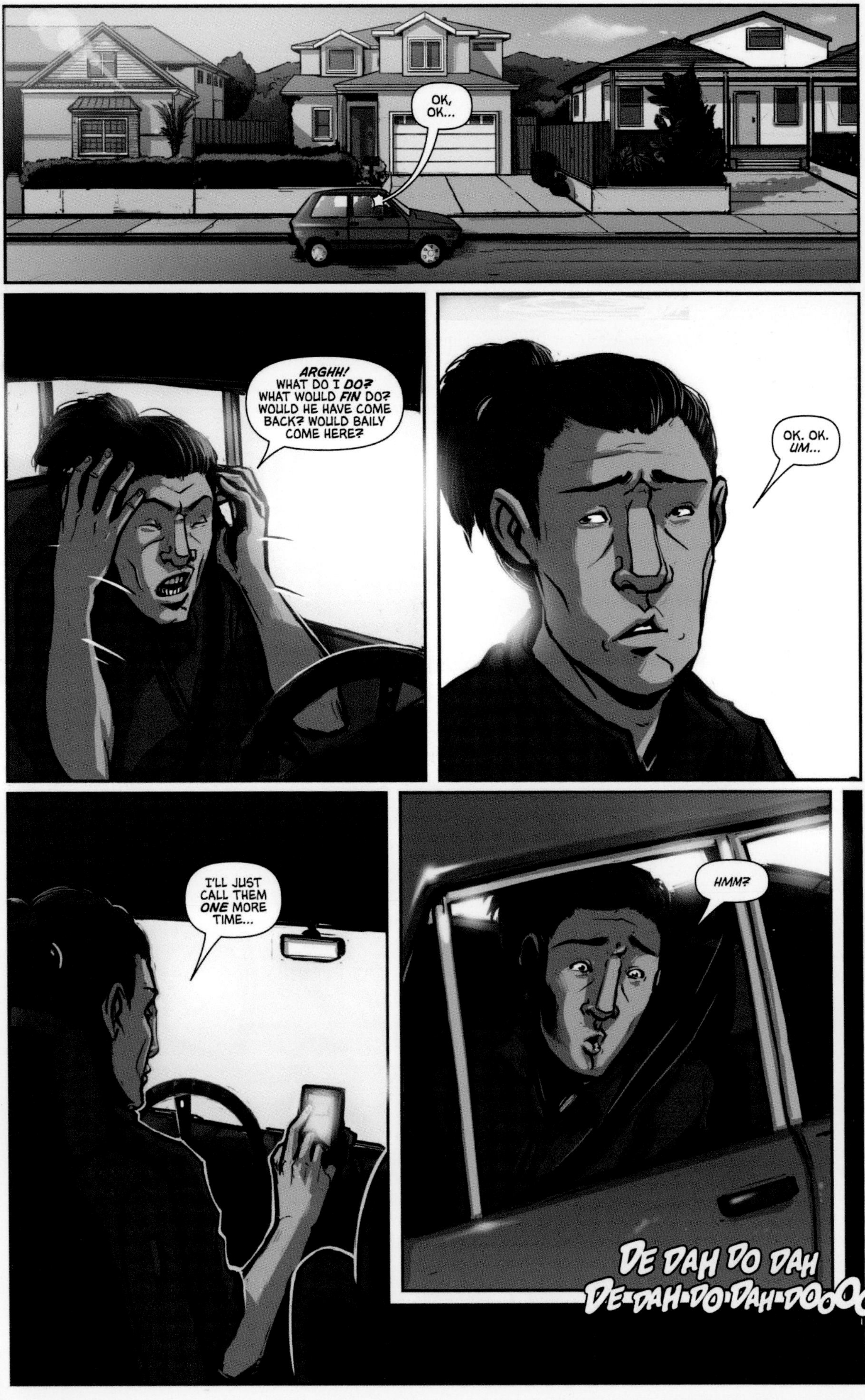
OK,
OK...
ARGHH!
WHAT DO I DO?
WHAT WOULD FIN DO?
WOULD HE HAVE COME
BACK? WOULD BAILY
COME HERE?
OK. OK.
UM...
I'LL JUST
CALL THEM
ONE MORE
TIME...
HMM?
DE DAH DO DAH
DE-DAH-DO-DAH-DOOOO

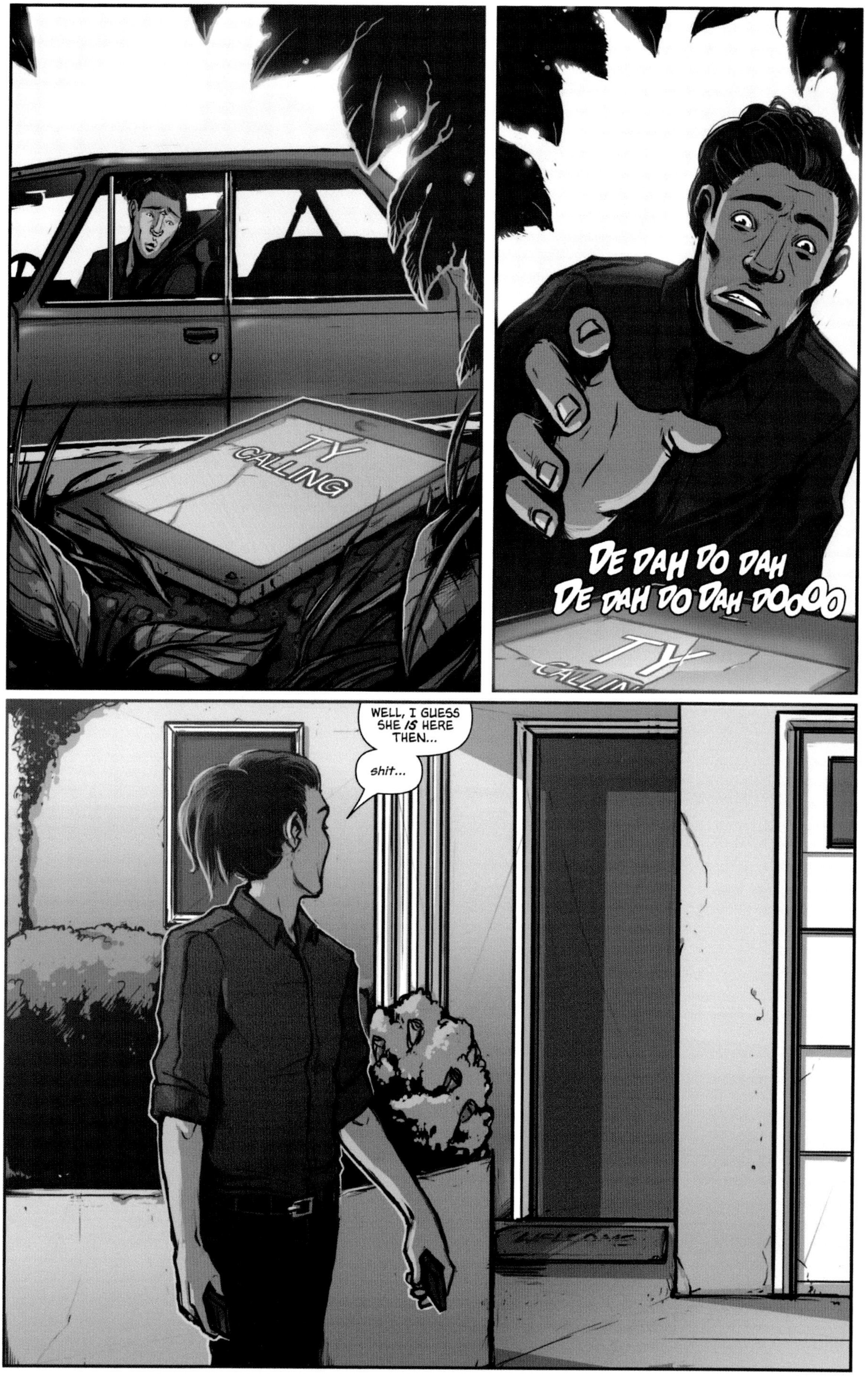
TY
CALLING
DE DAH DO DAH
DE DAH DO DAH DOOOOO
TY
WELL, I GUESS SHE *IS* HERE THEN...
shit...

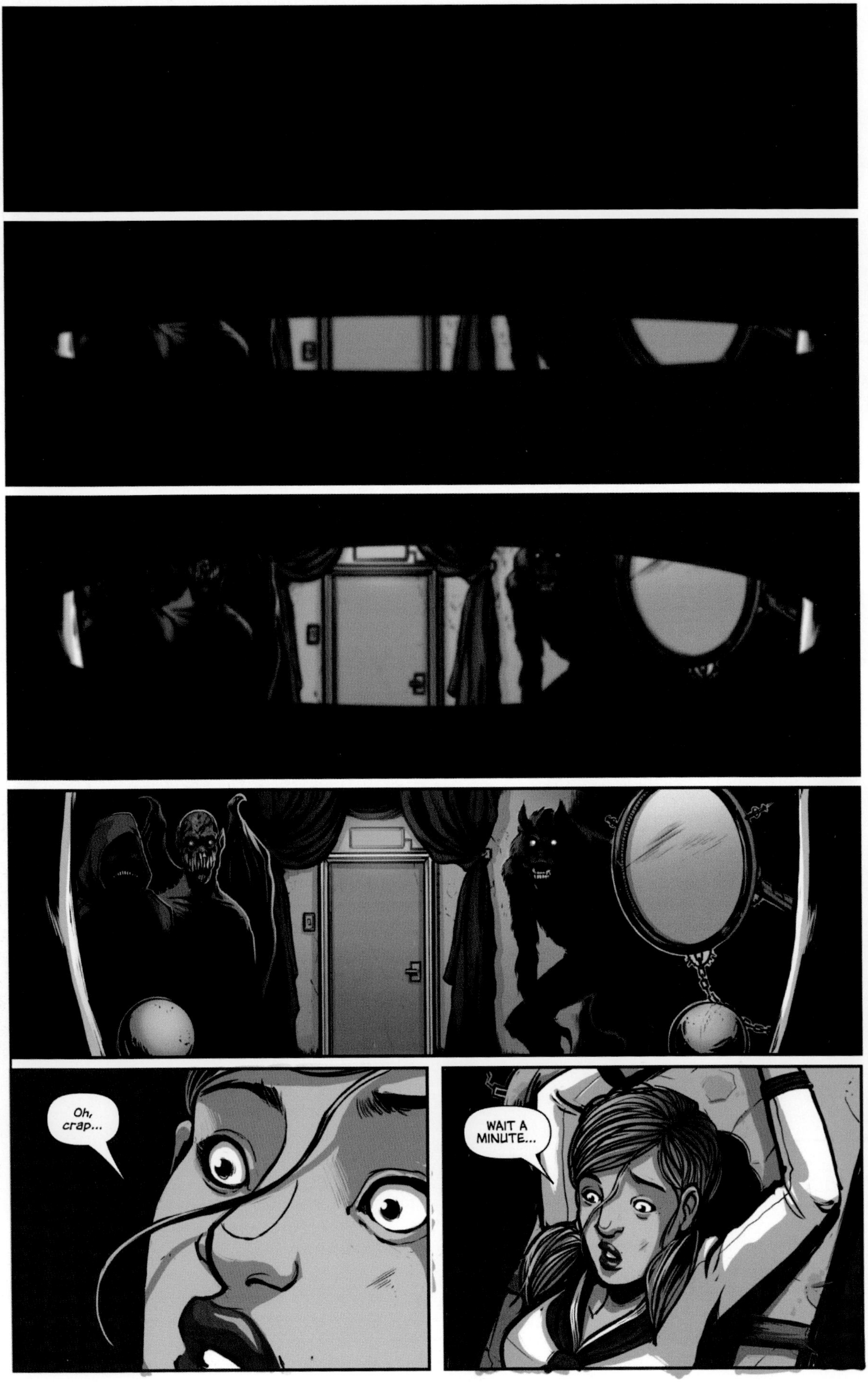
Oh, crap...
WAIT A MINUTE...

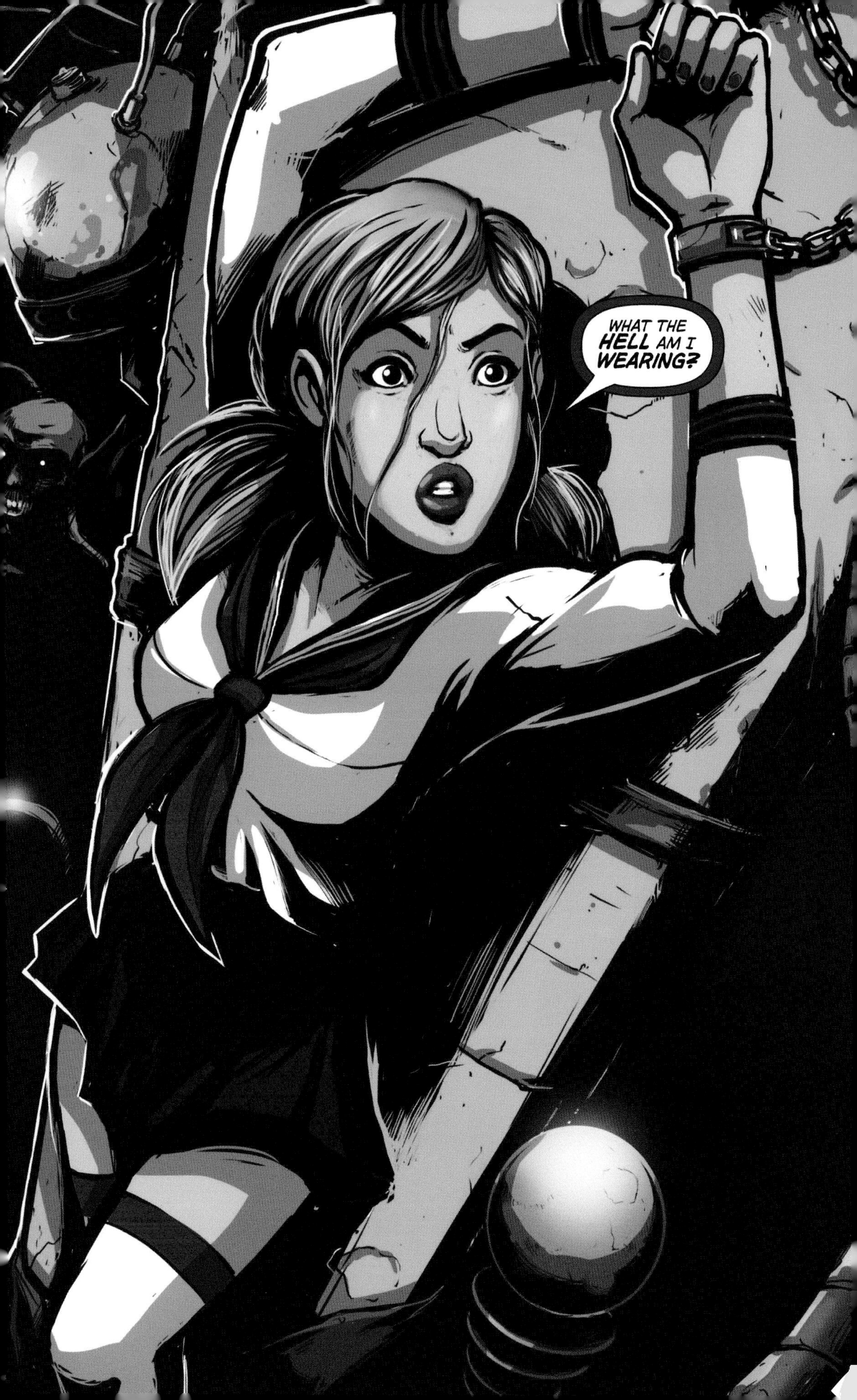
WHAT THE HELL AM I WEARING?

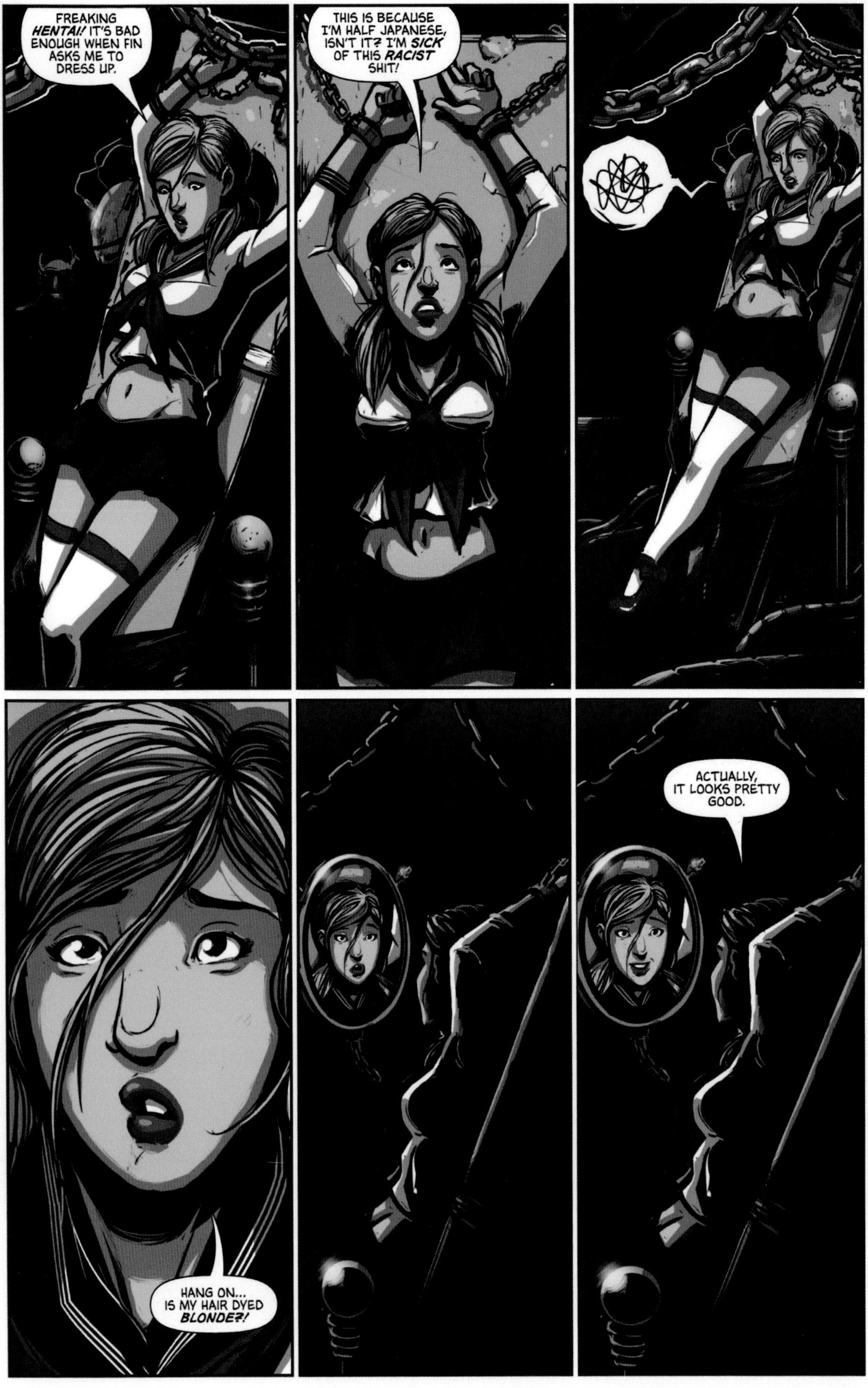
FREAKING HENTAI!! IT'S BAD ENOUGH WHEN FIN ASKS ME TO DRESS UP.
THIS IS BECAUSE I'M HALF JAPANESE, ISN'T IT? I'M SICK OF THIS RACIST SHIT!
HANG ON... IS MY HAIR DYED BLONDE?!
ACTUALLY, IT LOOKS PRETTY GOOD.

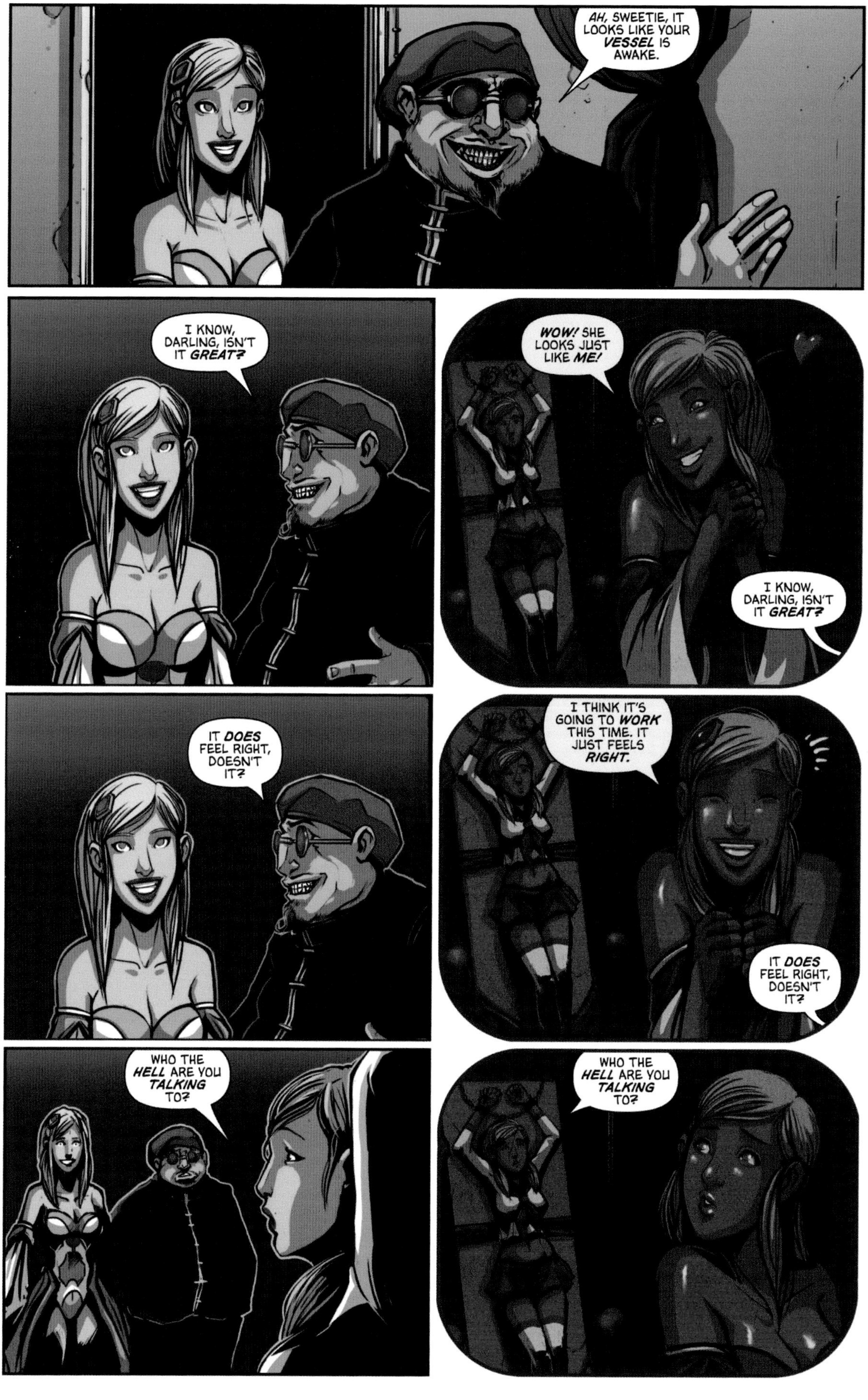
AH, SWEETIE, IT LOOKS LIKE YOUR VESSEL IS AWAKE.
I KNOW, DARLING, ISN'T IT GREAT?
WOW! SHE LOOKS JUST LIKE ME!
I KNOW, DARLING, ISN'T IT GREAT?
IT DOES FEEL RIGHT, DOESN'T IT?
I THINK IT'S GOING TO WORK THIS TIME. IT JUST FEELS RIGHT.
IT DOES FEEL RIGHT, DOESN'T IT?
WHO THE HELL ARE YOU TALKING TO?
WHO THE HELL ARE YOU TALKING TO?

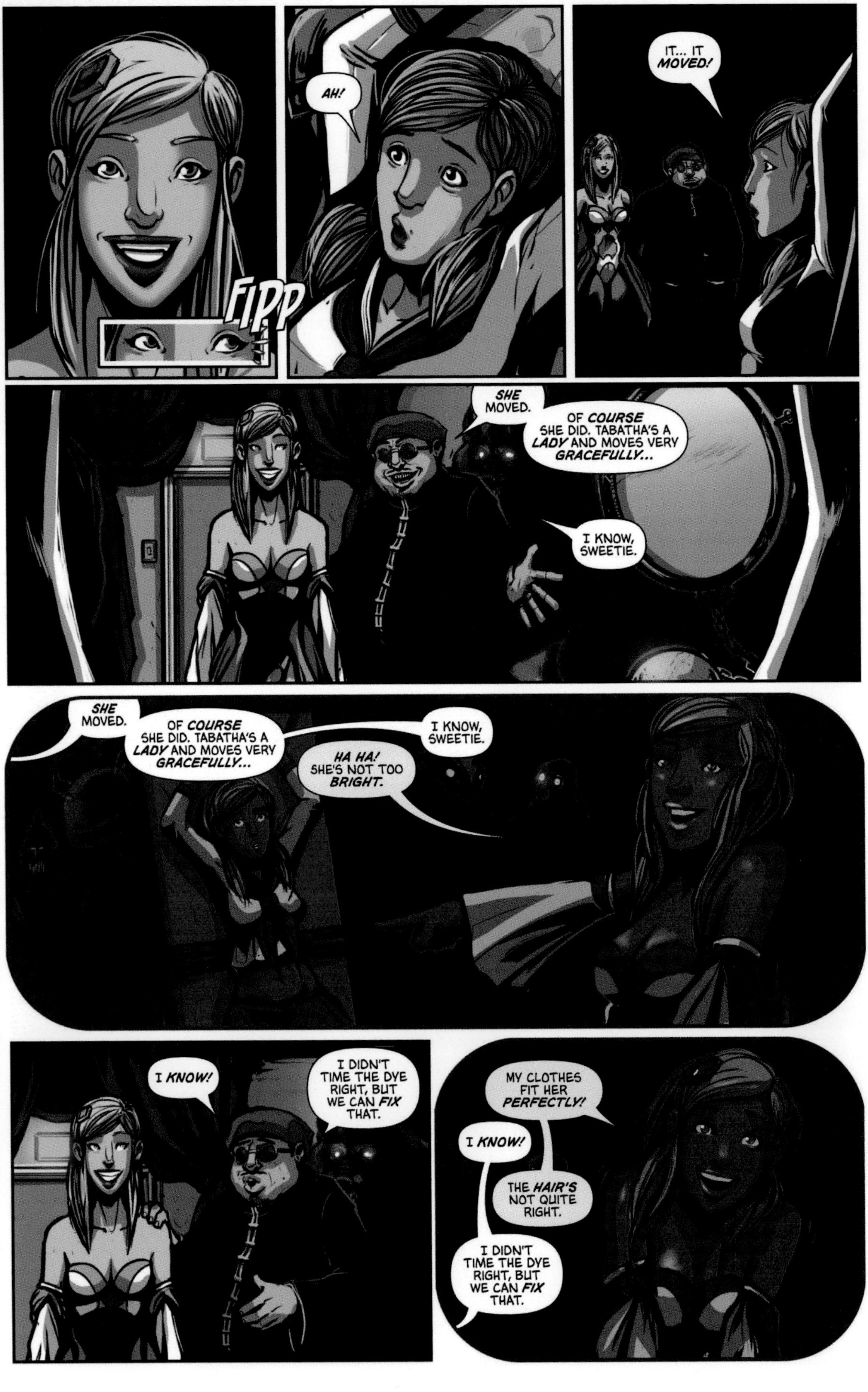
FIPP
AH!
IT... IT MOVED!
SHE MOVED.
OF COURSE SHE DID. TABATHA'S A LADY AND MOVES VERY GRACEFULLY...
I KNOW, SWEETIE.
SHE MOVED.
OF COURSE SHE DID. TABATHA'S A LADY AND MOVES VERY GRACEFULLY...
I KNOW, SWEETIE.
HA HA! SHE'S NOT TOO BRIGHT.
I KNOW!
I DIDN'T TIME THE DYE RIGHT, BUT WE CAN FIX THAT.
MY CLOTHES FIT HER PERFECTLY!
I KNOW!
THE HAIR'S NOT QUITE RIGHT.
I DIDN'T TIME THE DYE RIGHT, BUT WE CAN FIX THAT.

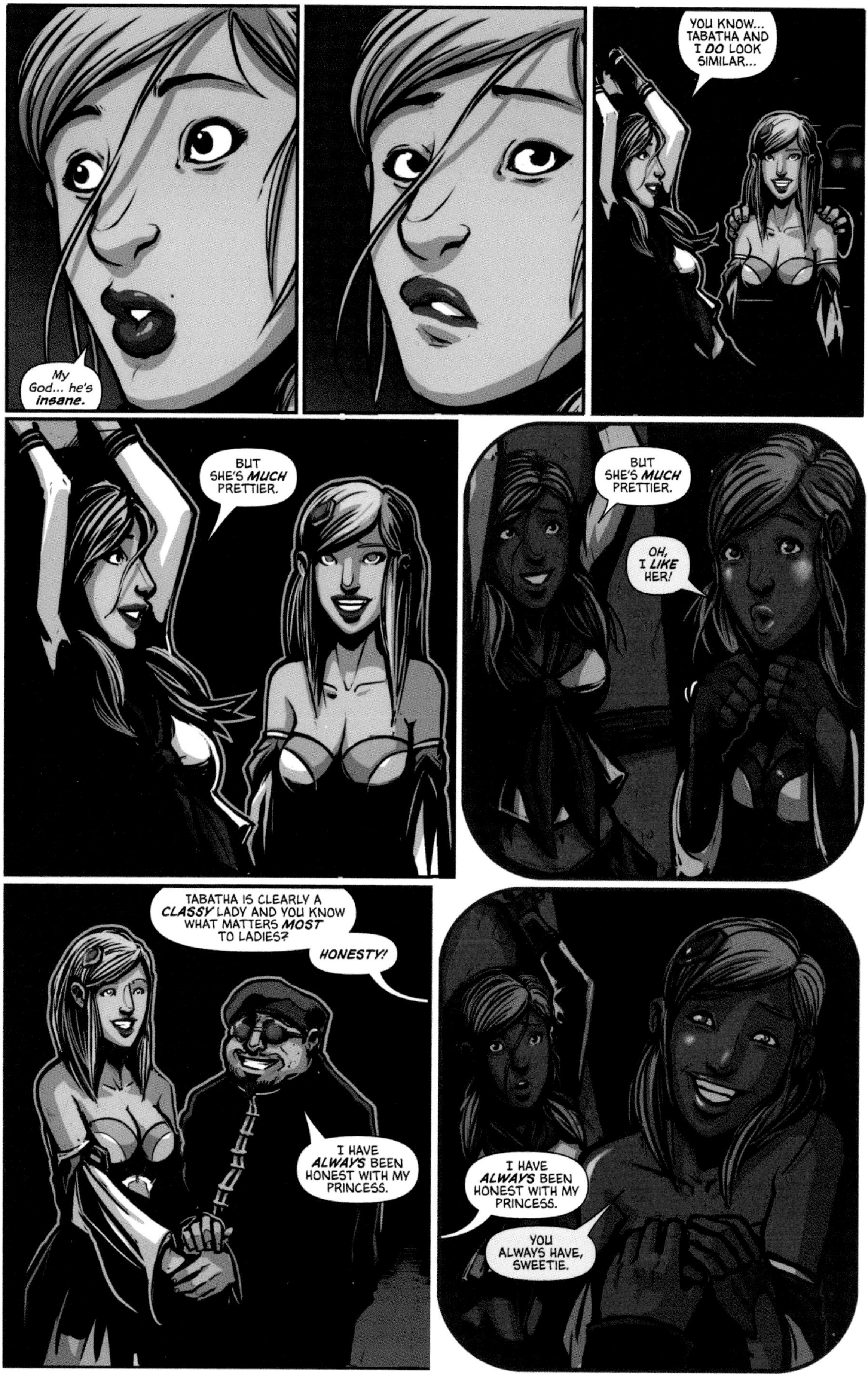
My God... he's *insane.*
YOU KNOW... TABATHA AND I *DO* LOOK SIMILAR...
BUT SHE'S *MUCH* PRETTIER.
BUT SHE'S *MUCH* PRETTIER.
OH, I *LIKE* HER!
TABATHA IS CLEARLY A *CLASSY* LADY AND YOU KNOW WHAT MATTERS *MOST* TO LADIES?
HONESTY!
I HAVE *ALWAYS* BEEN HONEST WITH MY PRINCESS.
I HAVE *ALWAYS* BEEN HONEST WITH MY PRINCESS.
YOU ALWAYS HAVE, SWEETIE.

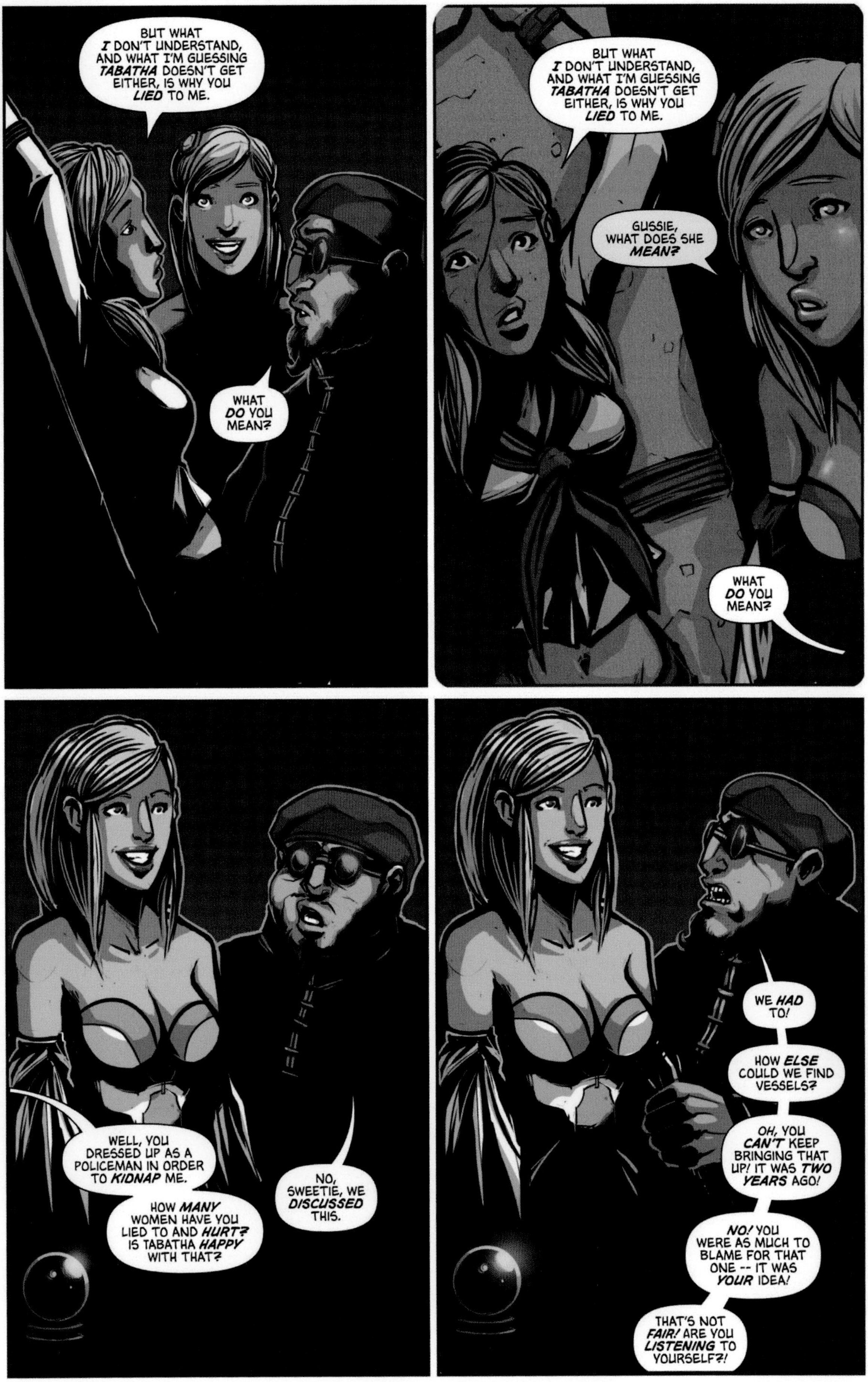
BUT WHAT I DON'T UNDERSTAND, AND WHAT I'M GUESSING TABATHA DOESN'T GET EITHER, IS WHY YOU LIED TO ME.
WHAT DO YOU MEAN?
BUT WHAT I DON'T UNDERSTAND, AND WHAT I'M GUESSING TABATHA DOESN'T GET EITHER, IS WHY YOU LIED TO ME.
GUSSIE, WHAT DOES SHE MEAN?
WHAT DO YOU MEAN?
WELL, YOU DRESSED UP AS A POLICEMAN IN ORDER TO KIDNAP ME.
HOW MANY WOMEN HAVE YOU LIED TO AND HURT? IS TABATHA HAPPY WITH THAT?
NO, SWEETIE, WE DISCUSSED THIS.
WE HAD TO!
HOW ELSE COULD WE FIND VESSELS?
OH, YOU CAN'T KEEP BRINGING THAT UP! IT WAS TWO YEARS AGO!
NO! YOU WERE AS MUCH TO BLAME FOR THAT ONE -- IT WAS YOUR IDEA!
THAT'S NOT FAIR! ARE YOU LISTENING TO YOURSELF?!

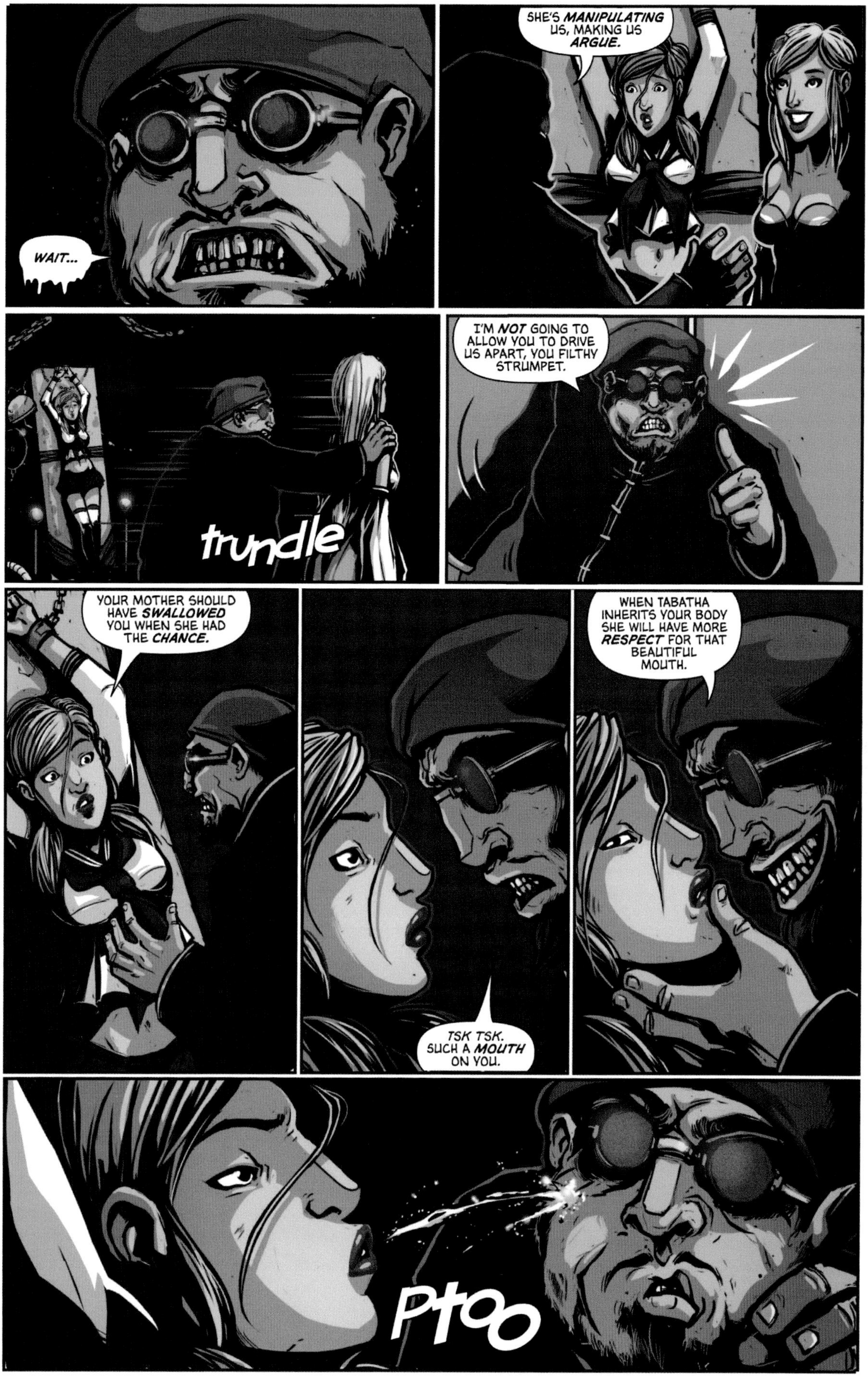
WAIT...
SHE'S MANIPULATING US, MAKING US ARGUE.
trundle
I'M NOT GOING TO ALLOW YOU TO DRIVE US APART, YOU FILTHY STRUMPET.
YOUR MOTHER SHOULD HAVE SWALLOWED YOU WHEN SHE HAD THE CHANCE.
TSK TSK. SUCH A MOUTH ON YOU.
WHEN TABATHA INHERITS YOUR BODY SHE WILL HAVE MORE RESPECT FOR THAT BEAUTIFUL MOUTH.
Ptoo

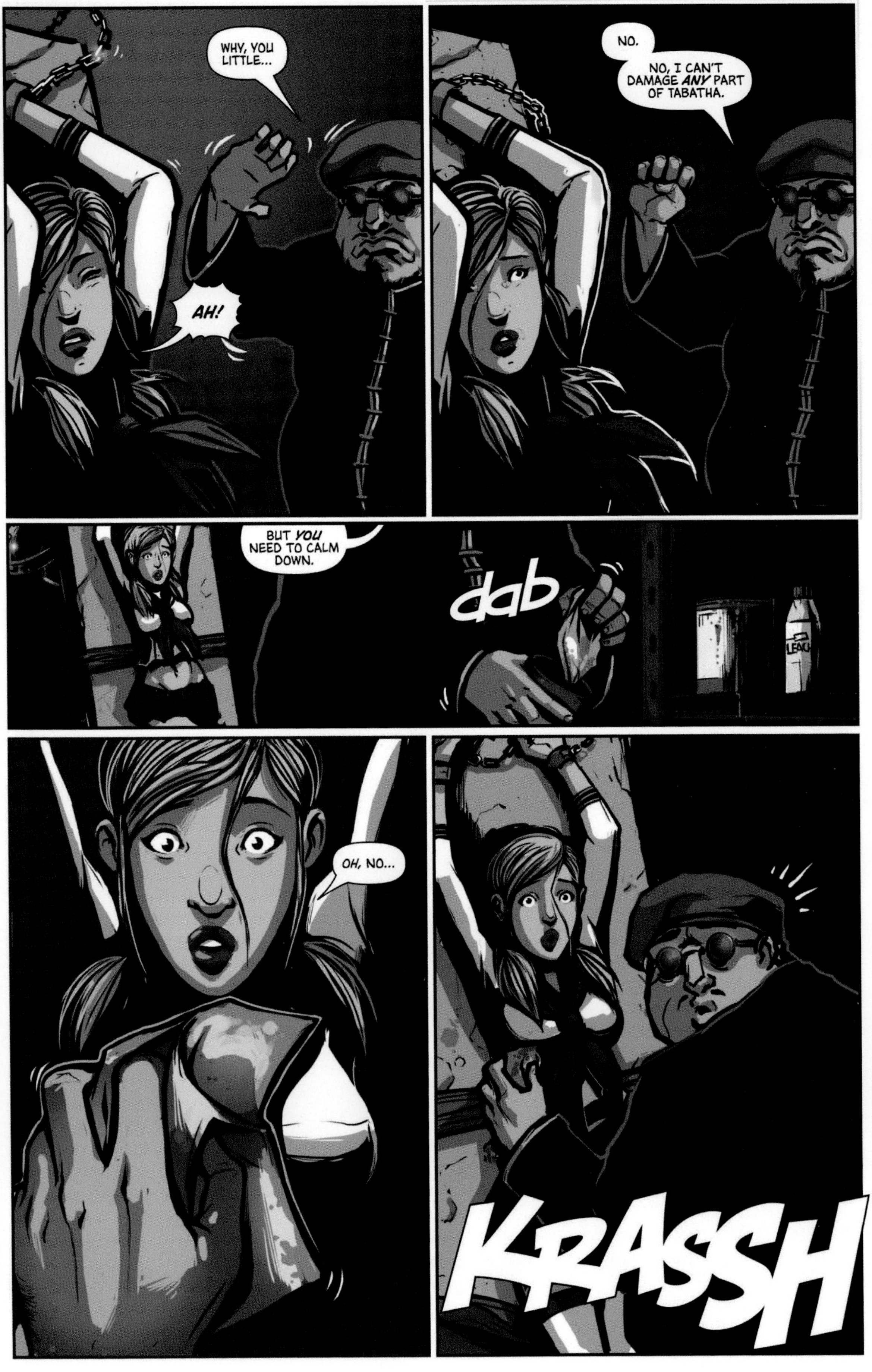
WHY, YOU LITTLE...
AH!
NO.
NO, I CAN'T DAMAGE *ANY* PART OF TABATHA.
BUT *YOU* NEED TO CALM DOWN.
dab
OH, NO...
KRASSH

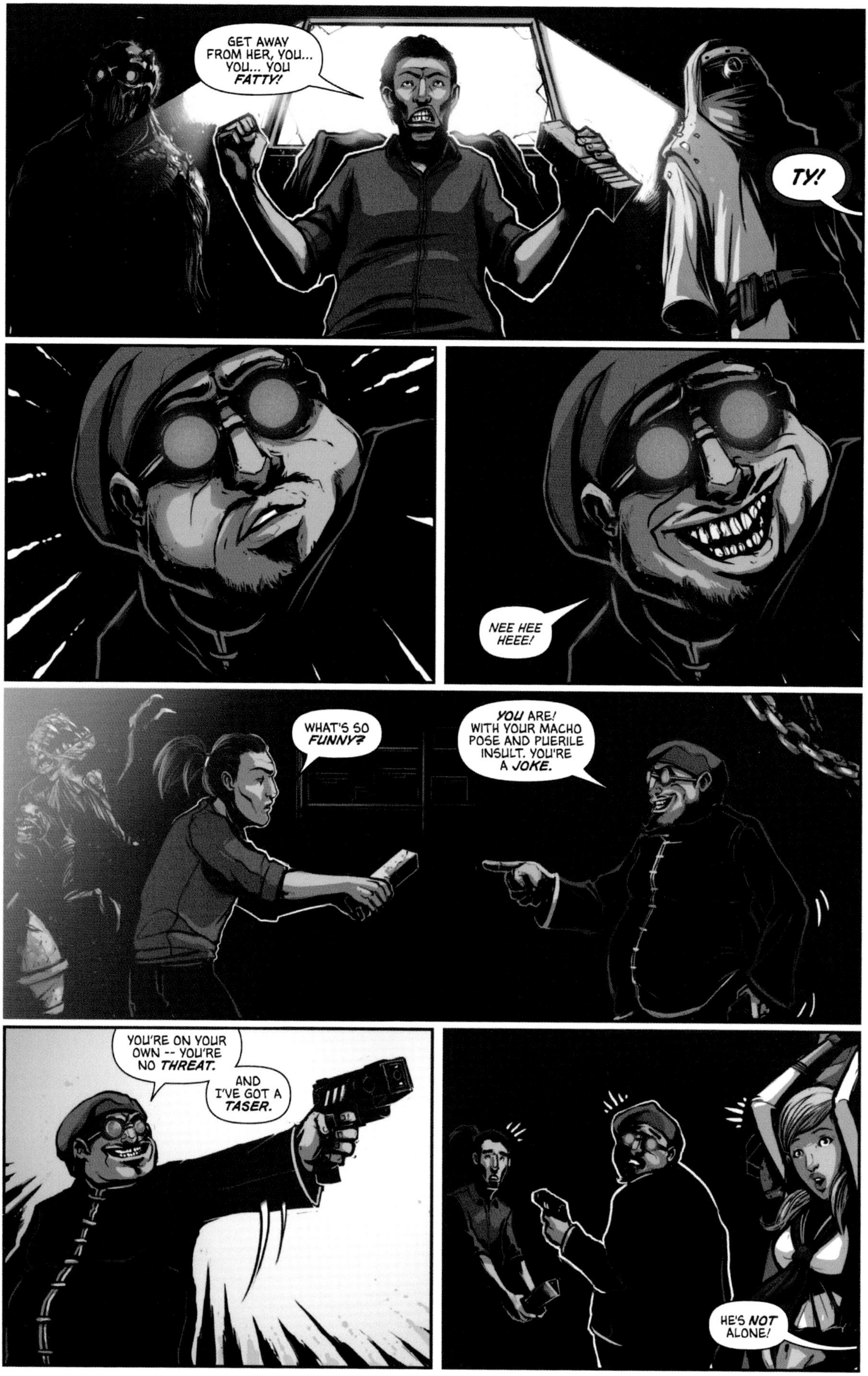
GET AWAY FROM HER, YOU... YOU... YOU FATTY!
TY!
NEE HEE HEEE!
WHAT'S SO FUNNY?
YOU ARE! WITH YOUR MACHO POSE AND PUERILE INSULT. YOU'RE A JOKE.
YOU'RE ON YOUR OWN -- YOU'RE NO THREAT.
AND I'VE GOT A TASER.
HE'S NOT ALONE!

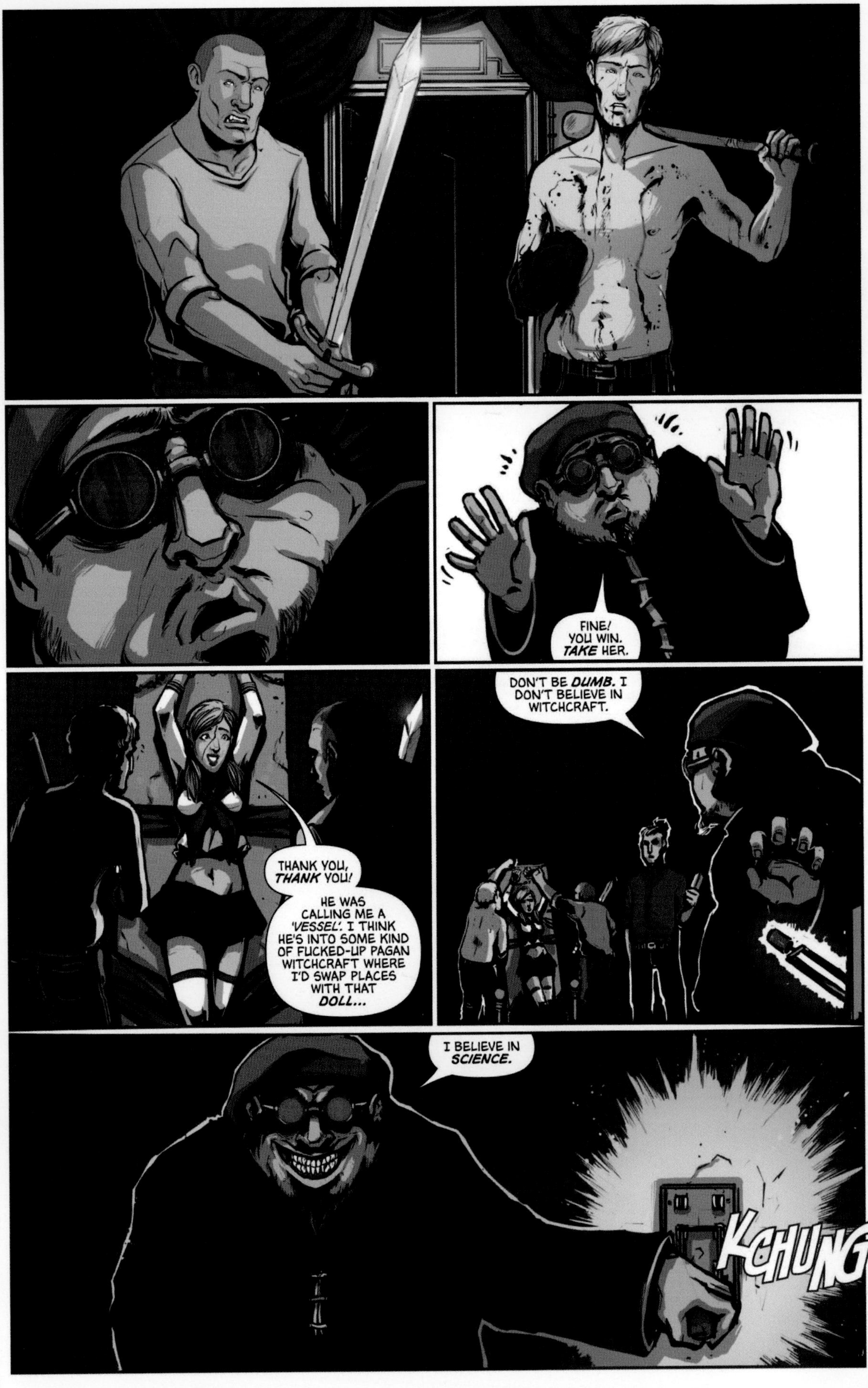
FINE! YOU WIN. TAKE HER.
THANK YOU, THANK YOU!
HE WAS CALLING ME A 'VESSEL'. I THINK HE'S INTO SOME KIND OF FUCKED-UP PAGAN WITCHCRAFT WHERE I'D SWAP PLACES WITH THAT DOLL...
DON'T BE DUMB. I DON'T BELIEVE IN WITCHCRAFT.
I BELIEVE IN SCIENCE.
KCHUNG

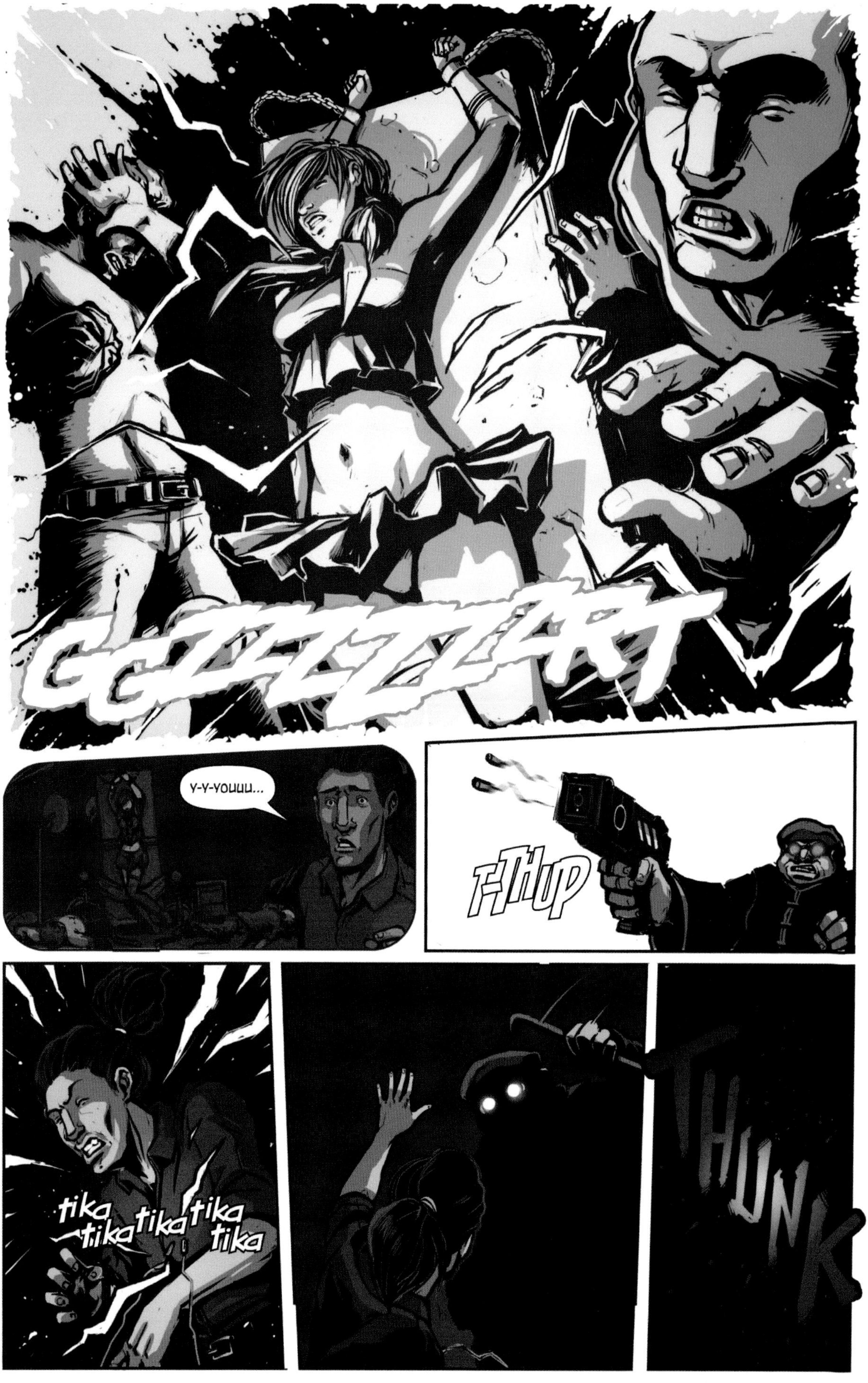

GGZZZZZART
Y-Y-YOUUU...
T-THUP
tika tika tika tika tika
THUNK

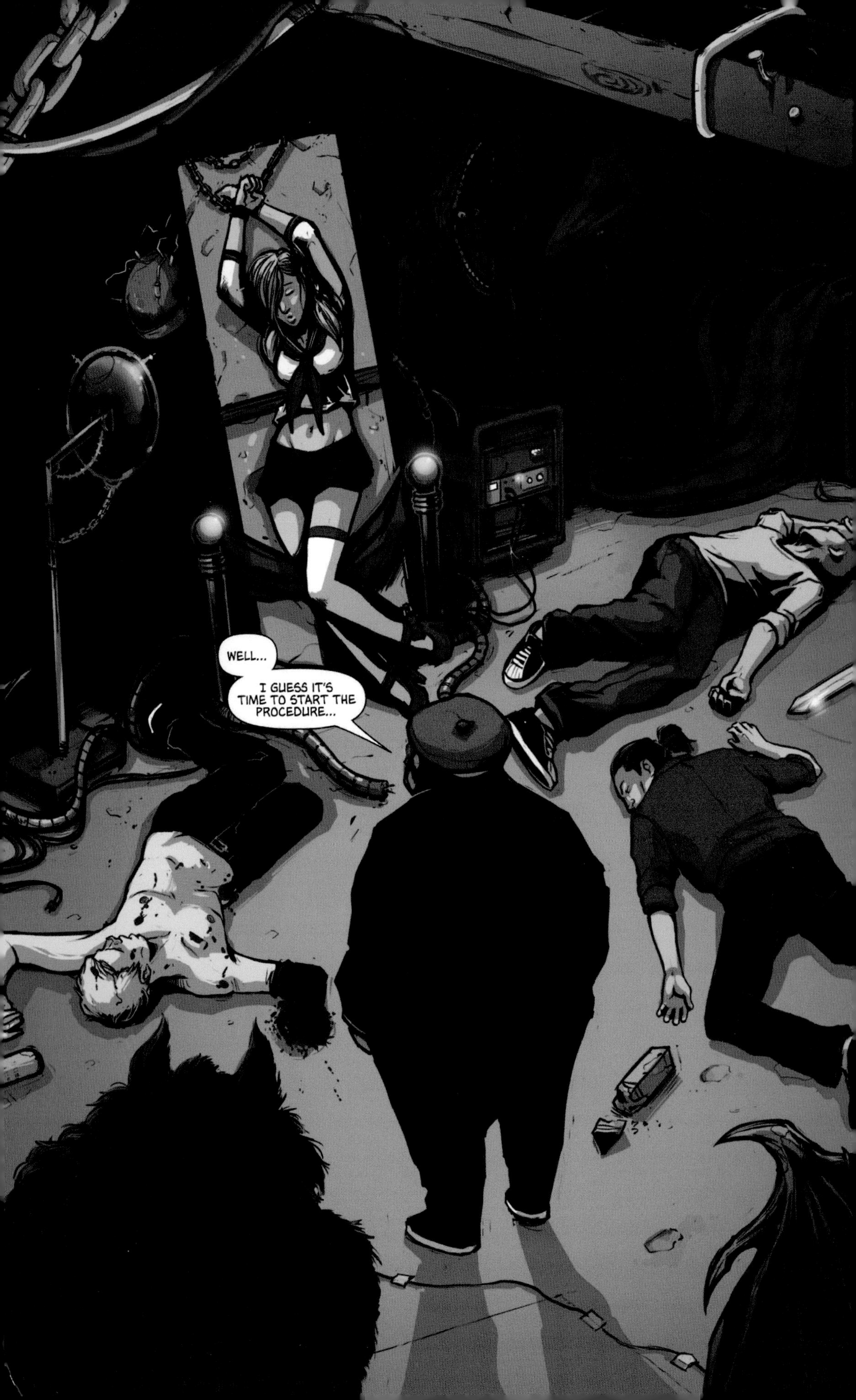
WELL...
I GUESS IT'S TIME TO START THE PROCEDURE...

CHAPTER FOUR

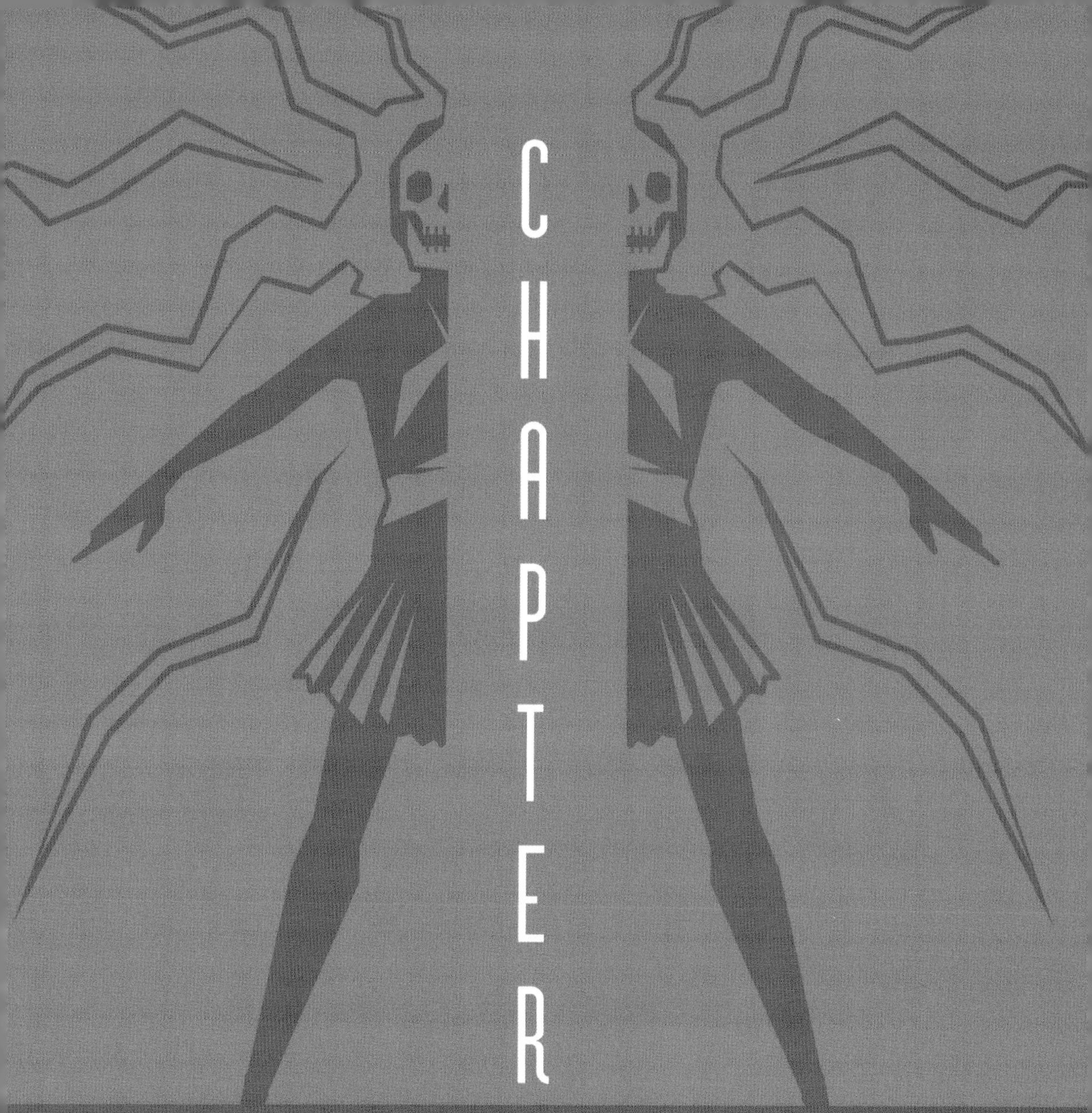

"YOU'RE NO EINSTEIN,"
"NO, I SEE MORE THAN HE EVER DID."

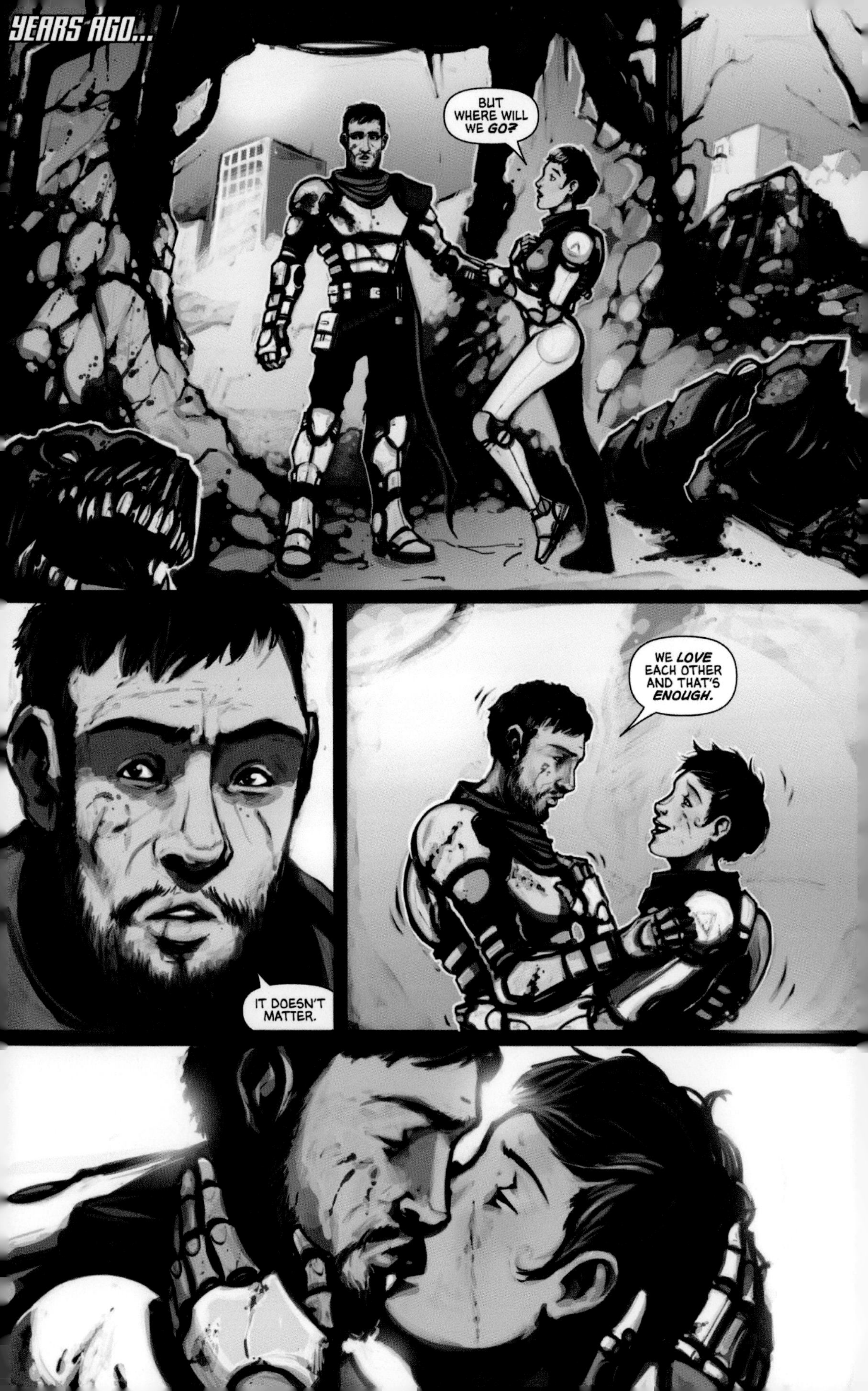
YEARS AGO...
BUT WHERE WILL WE GO?
IT DOESN'T MATTER.
WE LOVE EACH OTHER AND THAT'S ENOUGH.

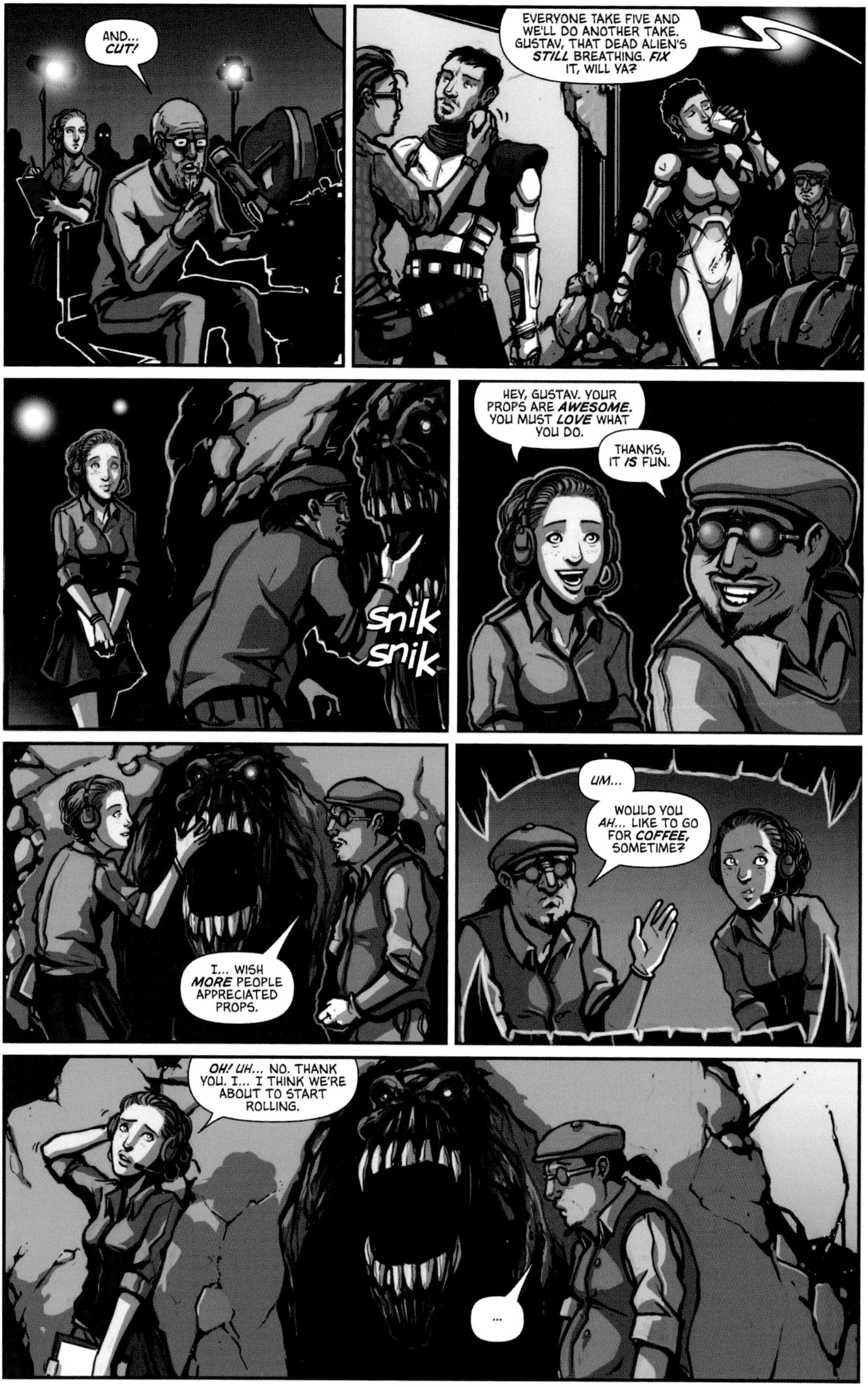
AND... CUT!
EVERYONE TAKE FIVE AND WE'LL DO ANOTHER TAKE. GUSTAV, THAT DEAD ALIEN'S STILL BREATHING. FIX IT, WILL YA?
snik snik
HEY, GUSTAV. YOUR PROPS ARE AWESOME. YOU MUST LOVE WHAT YOU DO.
THANKS, IT IS FUN.
I... WISH MORE PEOPLE APPRECIATED PROPS.
UM...
WOULD YOU AH... LIKE TO GO FOR COFFEE, SOMETIME?
OH! UH... NO. THANK YOU. I... I THINK WE'RE ABOUT TO START ROLLING.
...

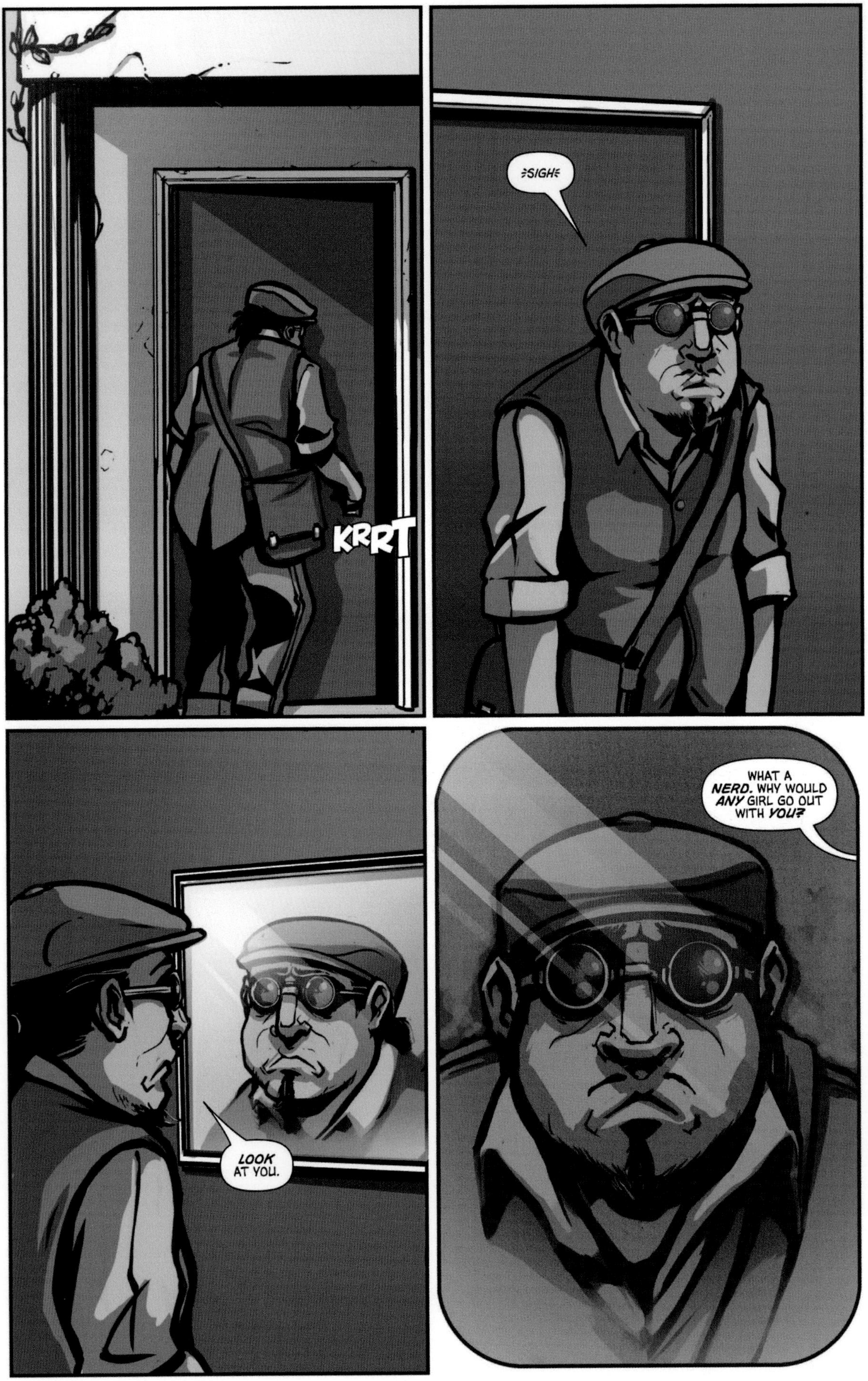
KRRT
SIGH
LOOK AT YOU.
WHAT A NERD. WHY WOULD ANY GIRL GO OUT WITH YOU?

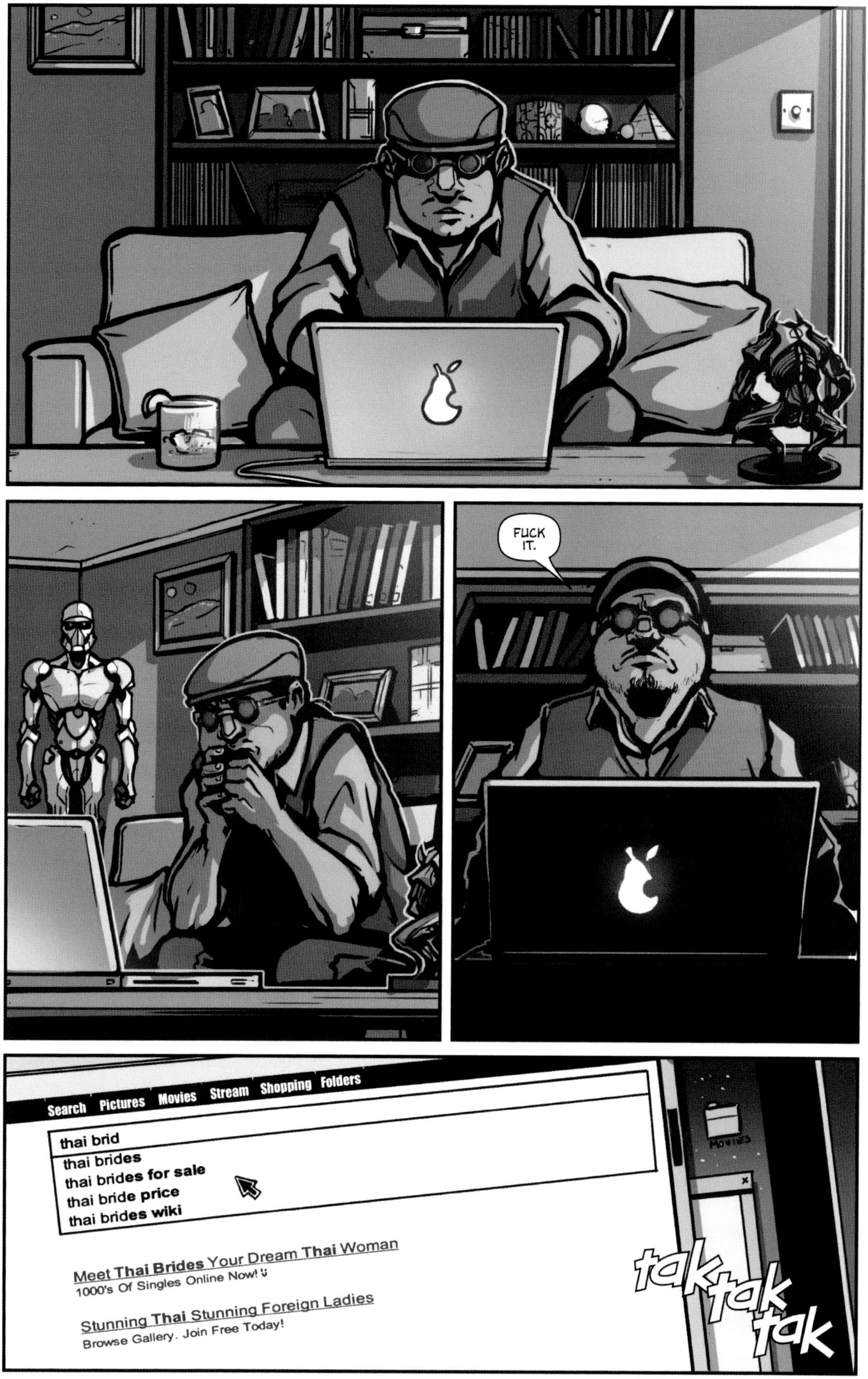
FUCK IT.
Search Pictures Movies Stream Shopping Folders
thai brid
thai brides
thai brides for sale
thai bride price
thai brides wiki
Meet Thai Brides Your Dream Thai Woman
1000's Of Singles Online Now!
Stunning Thai Stunning Foreign Ladies
Browse Gallery. Join Free Today!
MOVIES
tak tak tak

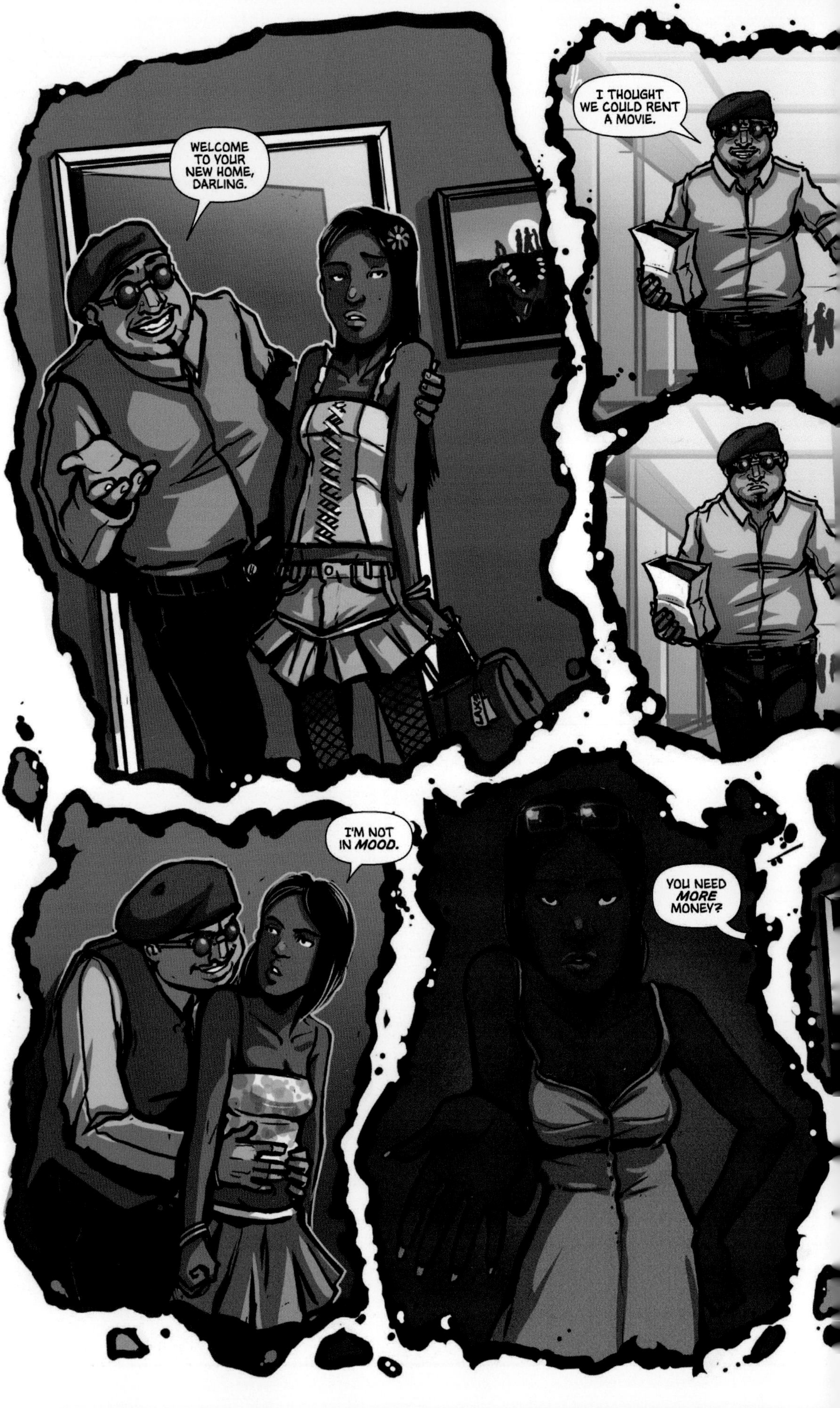
WELCOME TO YOUR NEW HOME, DARLING.
I THOUGHT WE COULD RENT A MOVIE.
I'M NOT IN *MOOD.*
YOU NEED *MORE* MONEY?

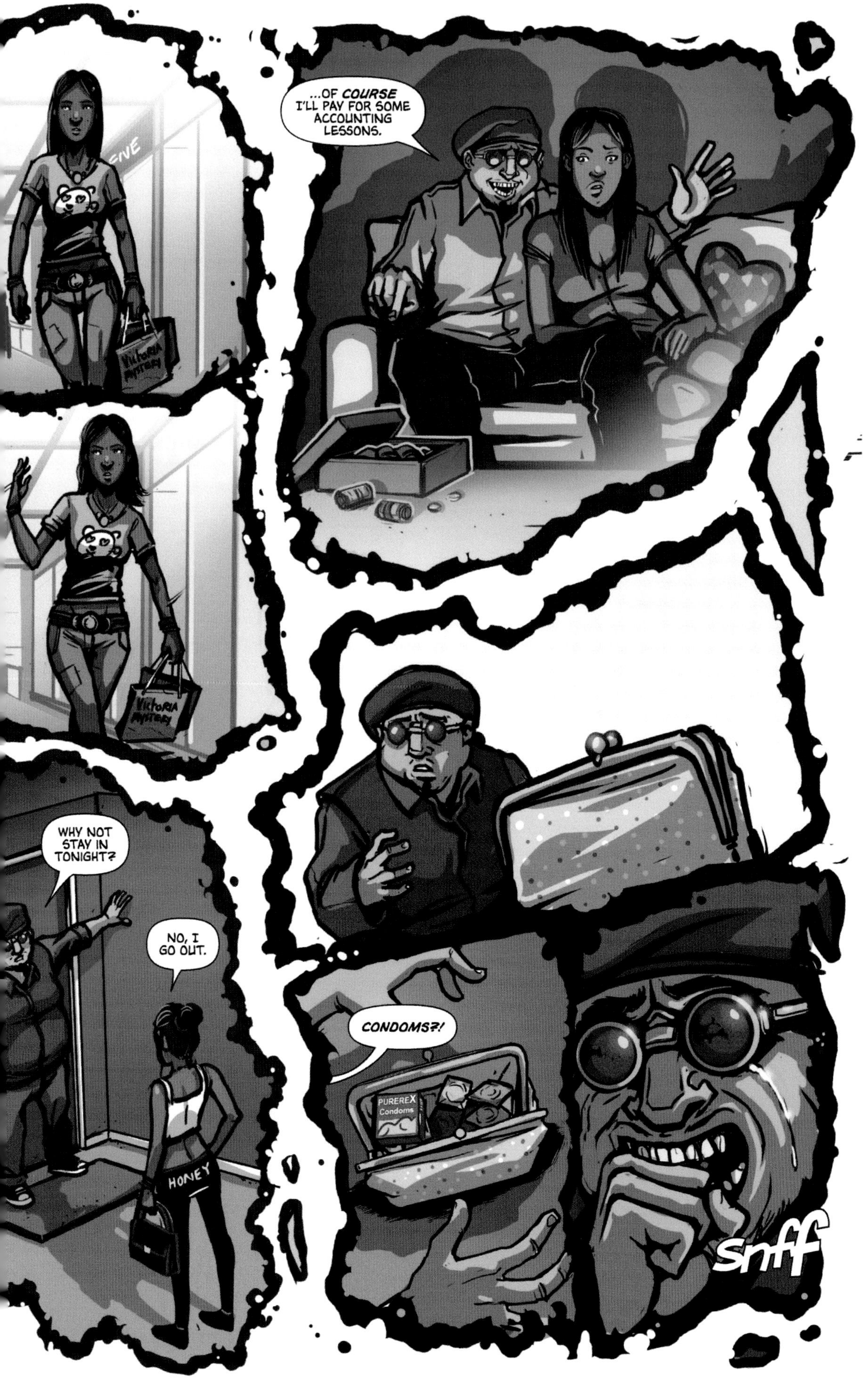
...OF COURSE I'LL PAY FOR SOME ACCOUNTING LESSONS.
WHY NOT STAY IN TONIGHT?
NO, I GO OUT.
CONDOMS?!
PUREREX Condoms
snff

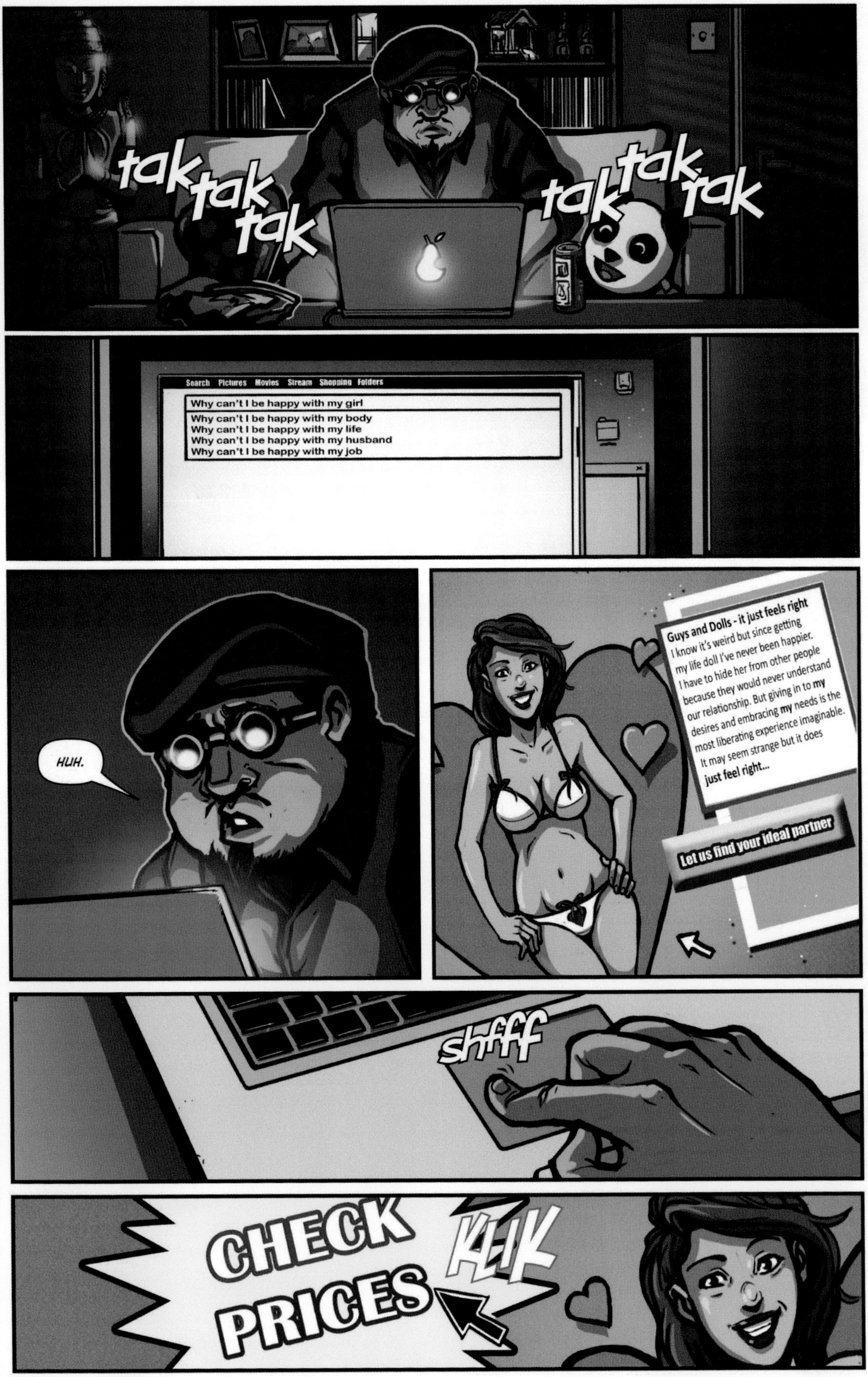
tak tak tak
tak tak tak
Search Pictures Movies Stream Shopping Folders
Why can't I be happy with my girl
Why can't I be happy with my body
Why can't I be happy with my life
Why can't I be happy with my husband
Why can't I be happy with my job
HUH.
Guys and Dolls - it just feels right
I know it's weird but since getting my life doll I've never been happier. I have to hide her from other people because they would never understand our relationship. But giving in to my desires and embracing my needs is the most liberating experience imaginable. It may seem strange but it does just feel right...
Let us find your ideal partner
shfff
CHECK PRICES
KLIK

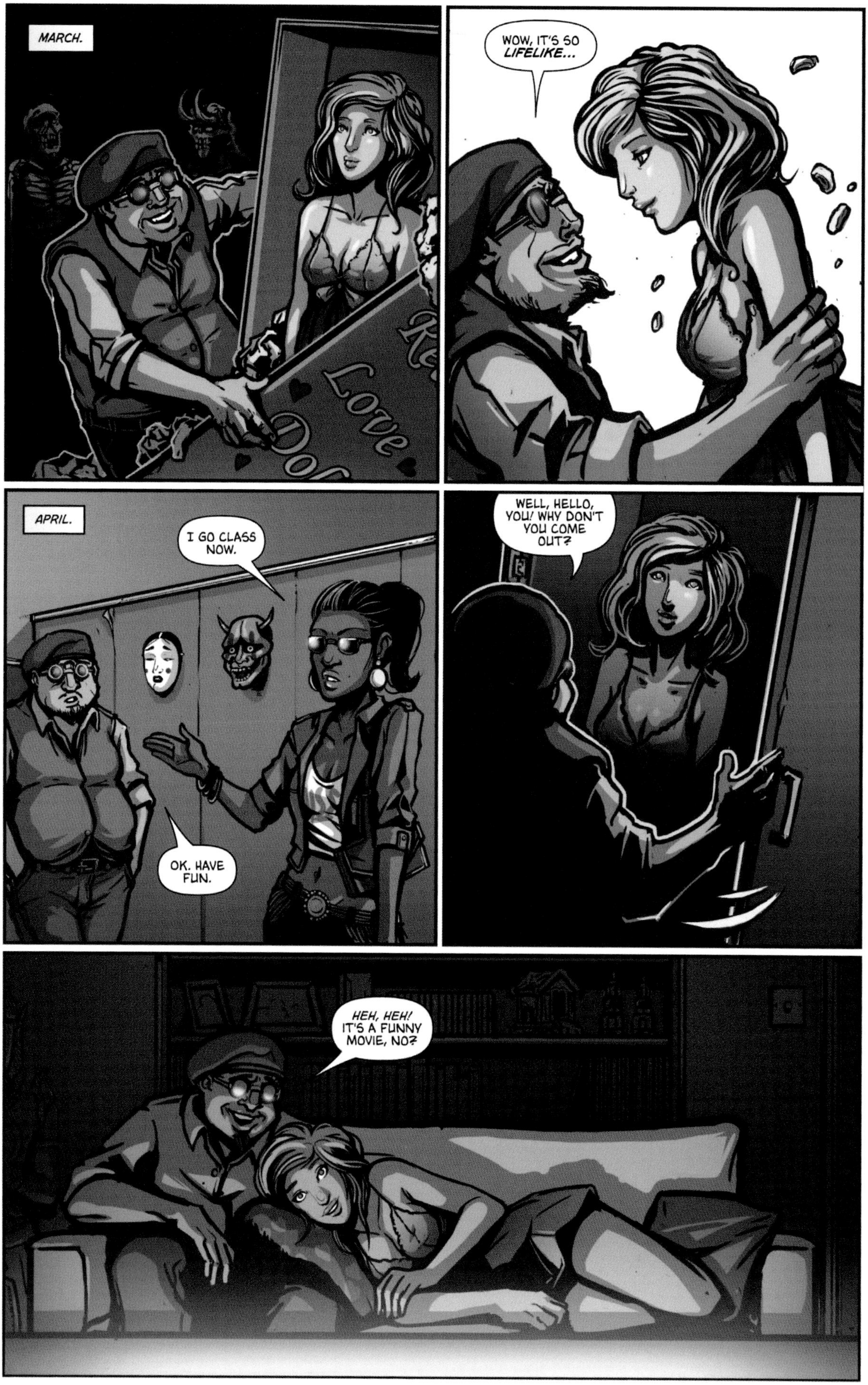
MARCH.
WOW, IT'S SO LIFELIKE...
APRIL.
I GO CLASS NOW.
OK. HAVE FUN.
WELL, HELLO, YOU! WHY DON'T YOU COME OUT?
HEH, HEH! IT'S A FUNNY MOVIE, NO?

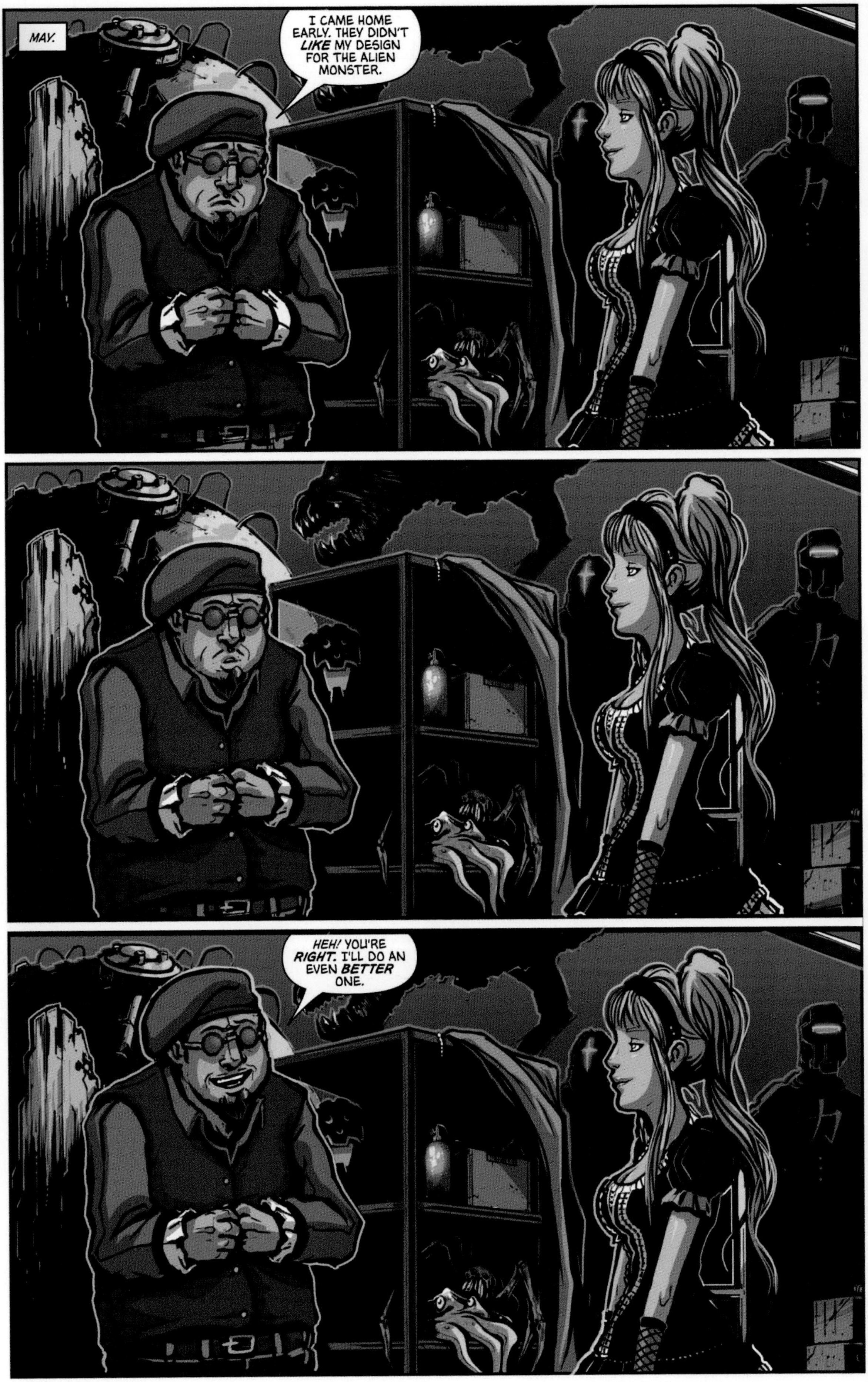
MAY.
I CAME HOME EARLY. THEY DIDN'T *LIKE* MY DESIGN FOR THE ALIEN MONSTER.
HEH! YOU'RE *RIGHT.* I'LL DO AN EVEN *BETTER* ONE.

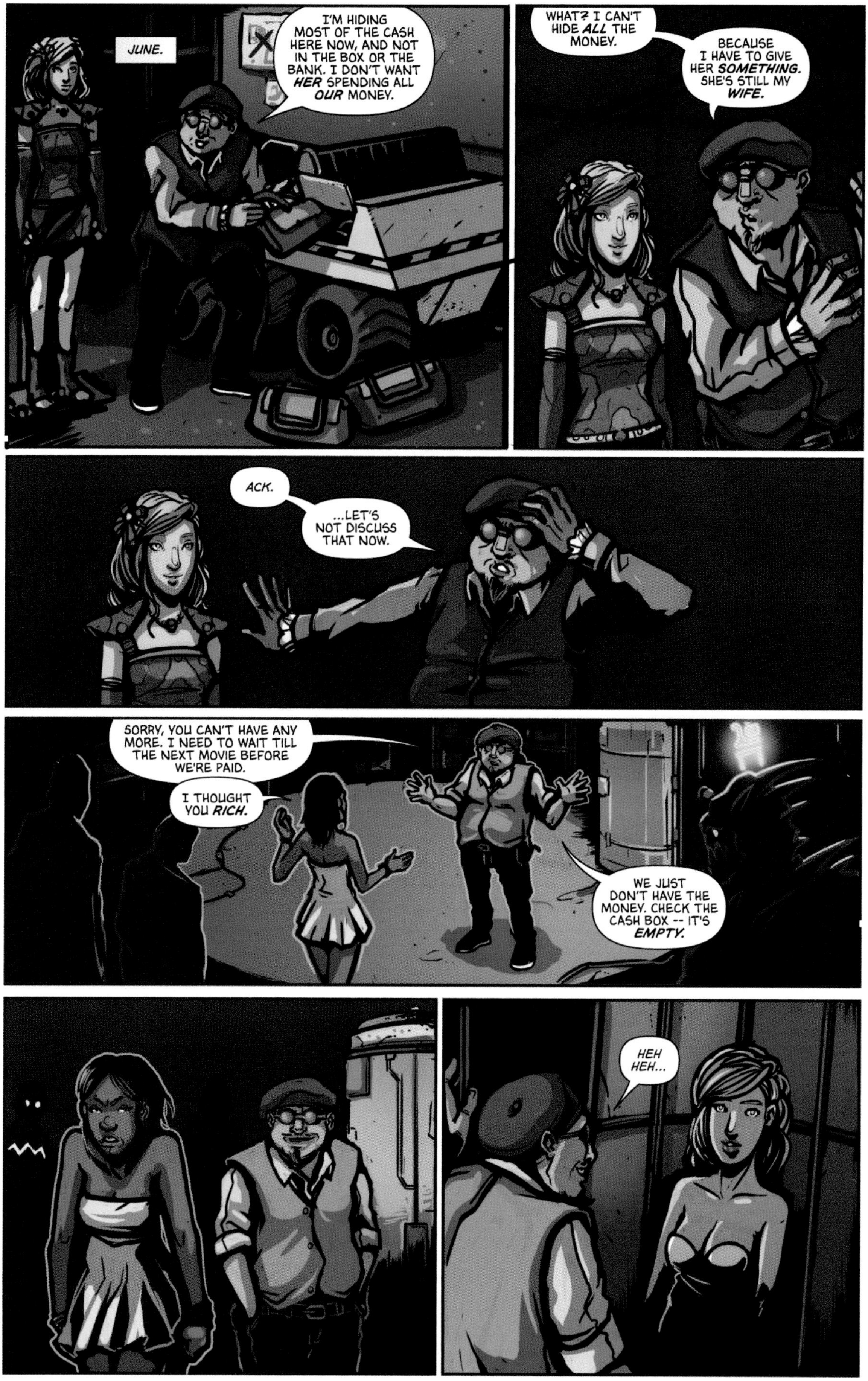
JUNE.
I'M HIDING MOST OF THE CASH HERE NOW, AND NOT IN THE BOX OR THE BANK. I DON'T WANT HER SPENDING ALL OUR MONEY.
WHAT? I CAN'T HIDE ALL THE MONEY.
BECAUSE I HAVE TO GIVE HER SOMETHING. SHE'S STILL MY WIFE.
ACK.
...LET'S NOT DISCUSS THAT NOW.
SORRY, YOU CAN'T HAVE ANY MORE. I NEED TO WAIT TILL THE NEXT MOVIE BEFORE WE'RE PAID.
I THOUGHT YOU RICH.
WE JUST DON'T HAVE THE MONEY. CHECK THE CASH BOX -- IT'S EMPTY.
HEH HEH...

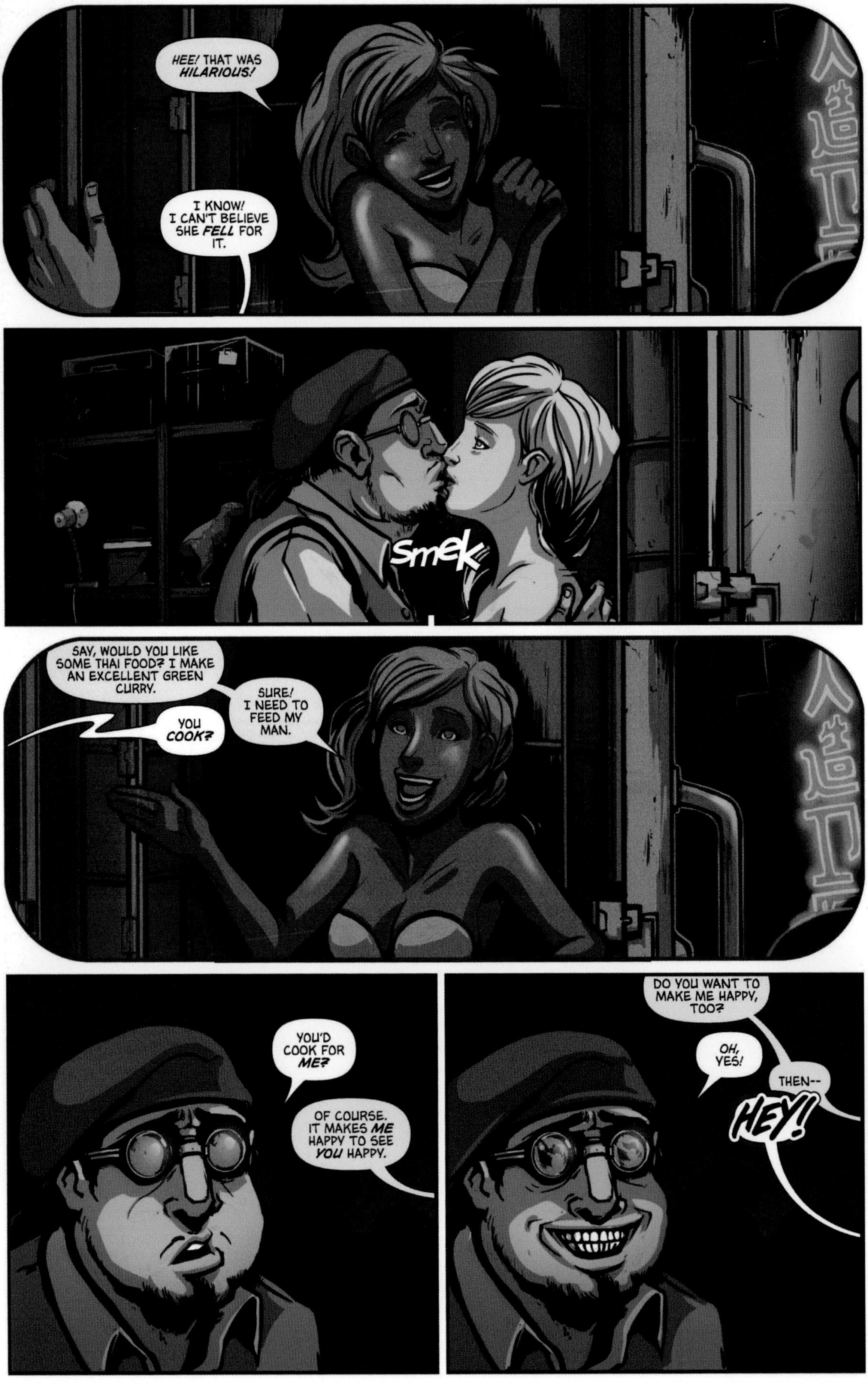
HEE! THAT WAS *HILARIOUS!*
I KNOW! I CAN'T BELIEVE SHE *FELL* FOR IT.
smek
SAY, WOULD YOU LIKE SOME THAI FOOD? I MAKE AN EXCELLENT GREEN CURRY.
YOU *COOK?*
SURE! I NEED TO FEED MY MAN.
YOU'D COOK FOR *ME?*
OF COURSE. IT MAKES *ME* HAPPY TO SEE *YOU* HAPPY.
DO YOU WANT TO MAKE ME HAPPY, TOO?
OH, YES!
THEN--
HEY!

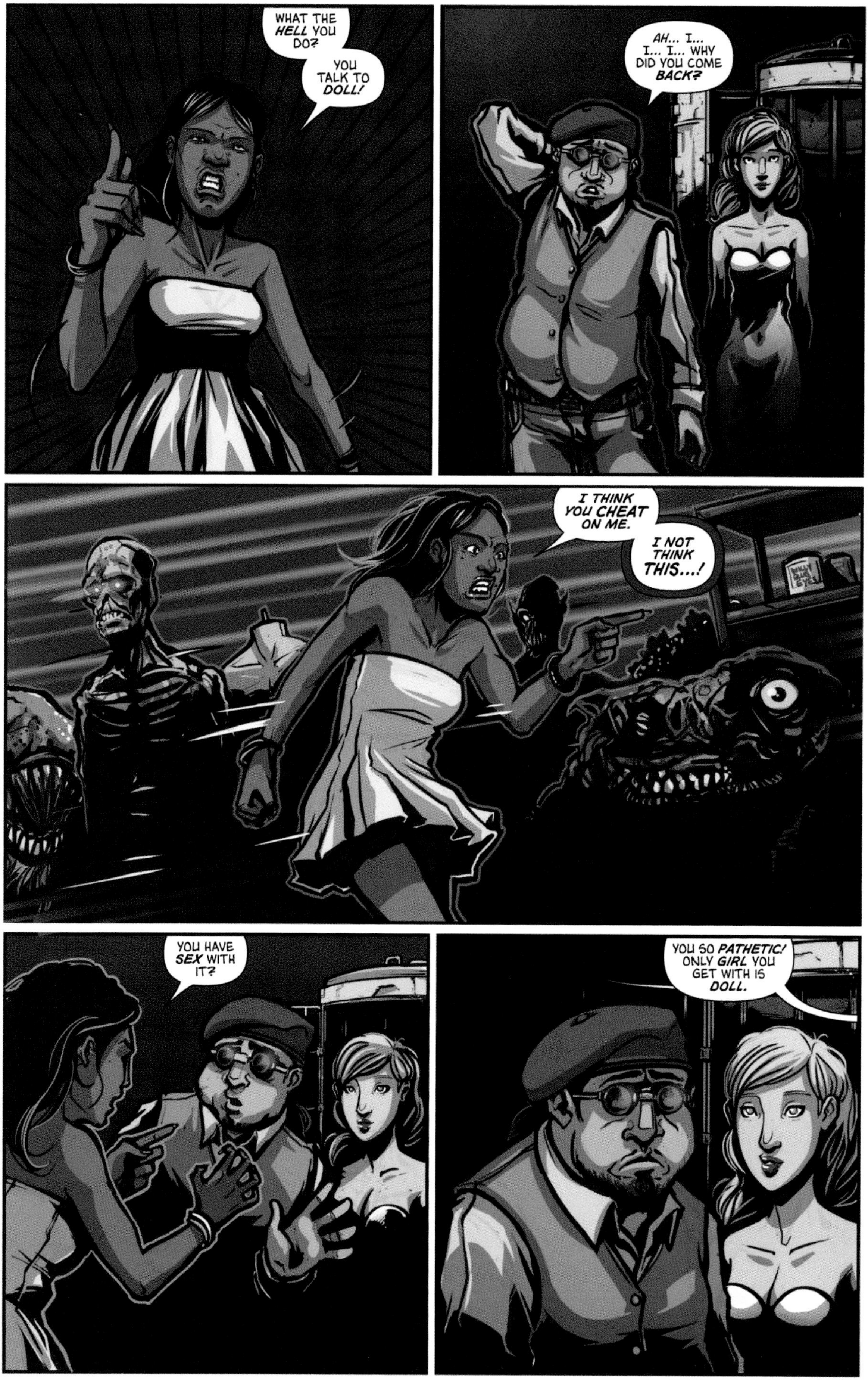
WHAT THE HELL YOU DO?
YOU TALK TO DOLL!
AH... I... I... I... WHY DID YOU COME BACK?
I THINK YOU CHEAT ON ME.
I NOT THINK THIS...!
YOU HAVE SEX WITH IT?
YOU SO PATHETIC! ONLY GIRL YOU GET WITH IS DOLL.

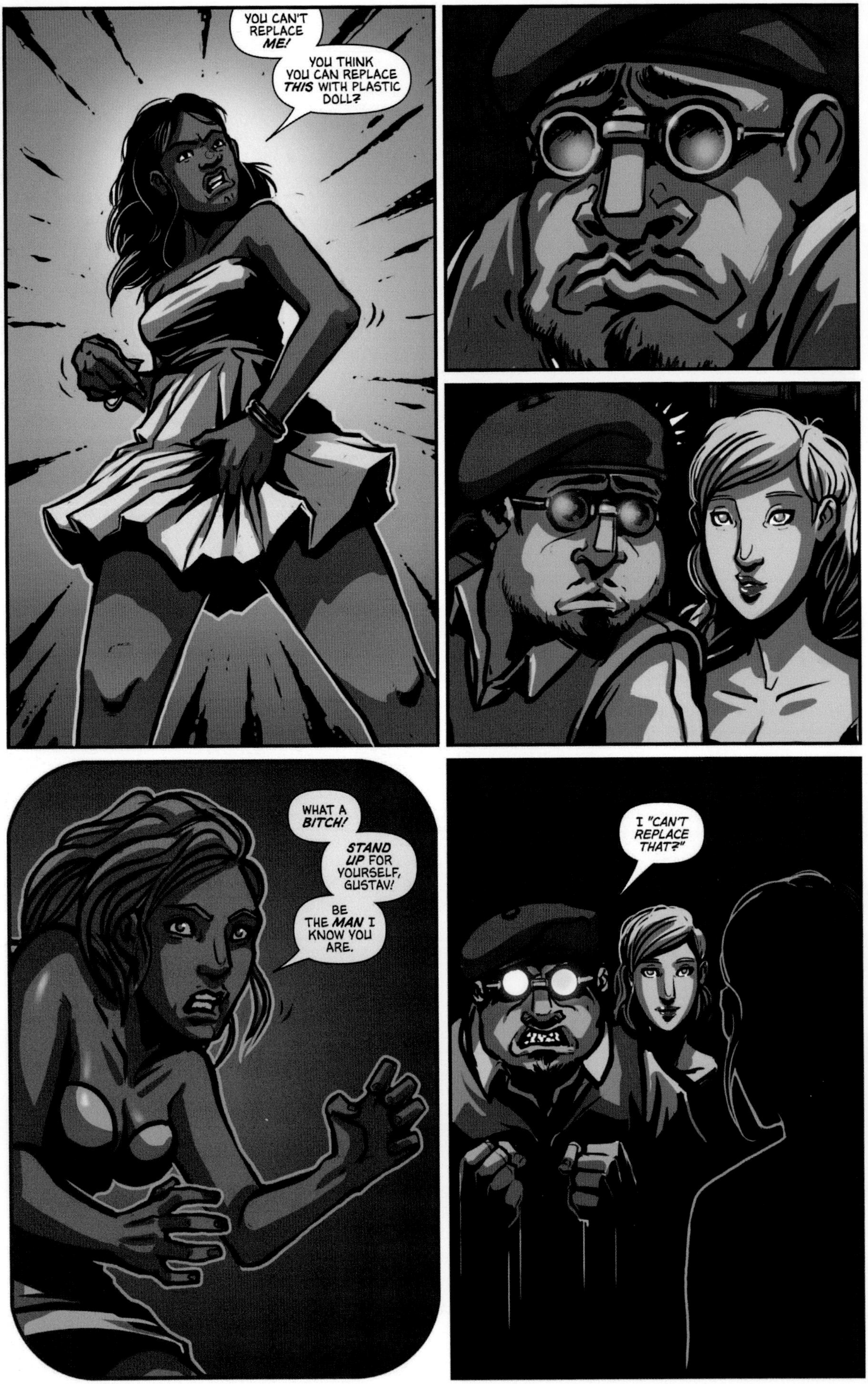
YOU CAN'T REPLACE *ME!*
YOU THINK YOU CAN REPLACE *THIS* WITH PLASTIC DOLL?
WHAT A *BITCH!*
STAND UP FOR YOURSELF, GUSTAV!
BE THE *MAN* I KNOW YOU ARE.
I "*CAN'T REPLACE THAT?*"

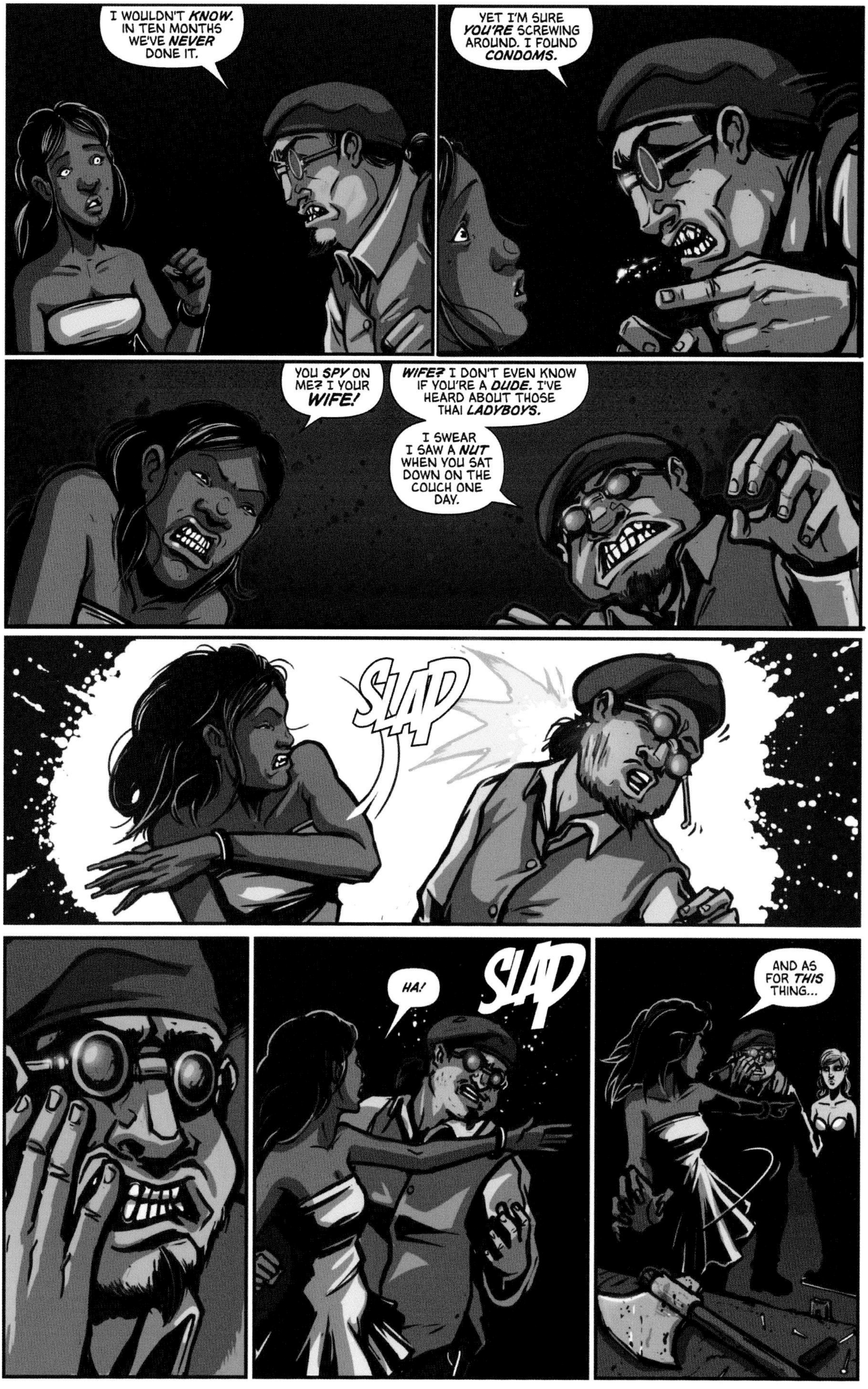
I WOULDN'T KNOW. IN TEN MONTHS WE'VE NEVER DONE IT.
YET I'M SURE YOU'RE SCREWING AROUND. I FOUND CONDOMS.
YOU SPY ON ME? I YOUR WIFE!
WIFE? I DON'T EVEN KNOW IF YOU'RE A DUDE. I'VE HEARD ABOUT THOSE THAI LADYBOYS.
I SWEAR I SAW A NUT WHEN YOU SAT DOWN ON THE COUCH ONE DAY.
SLAP
HA!
SLAP
AND AS FOR THIS THING...

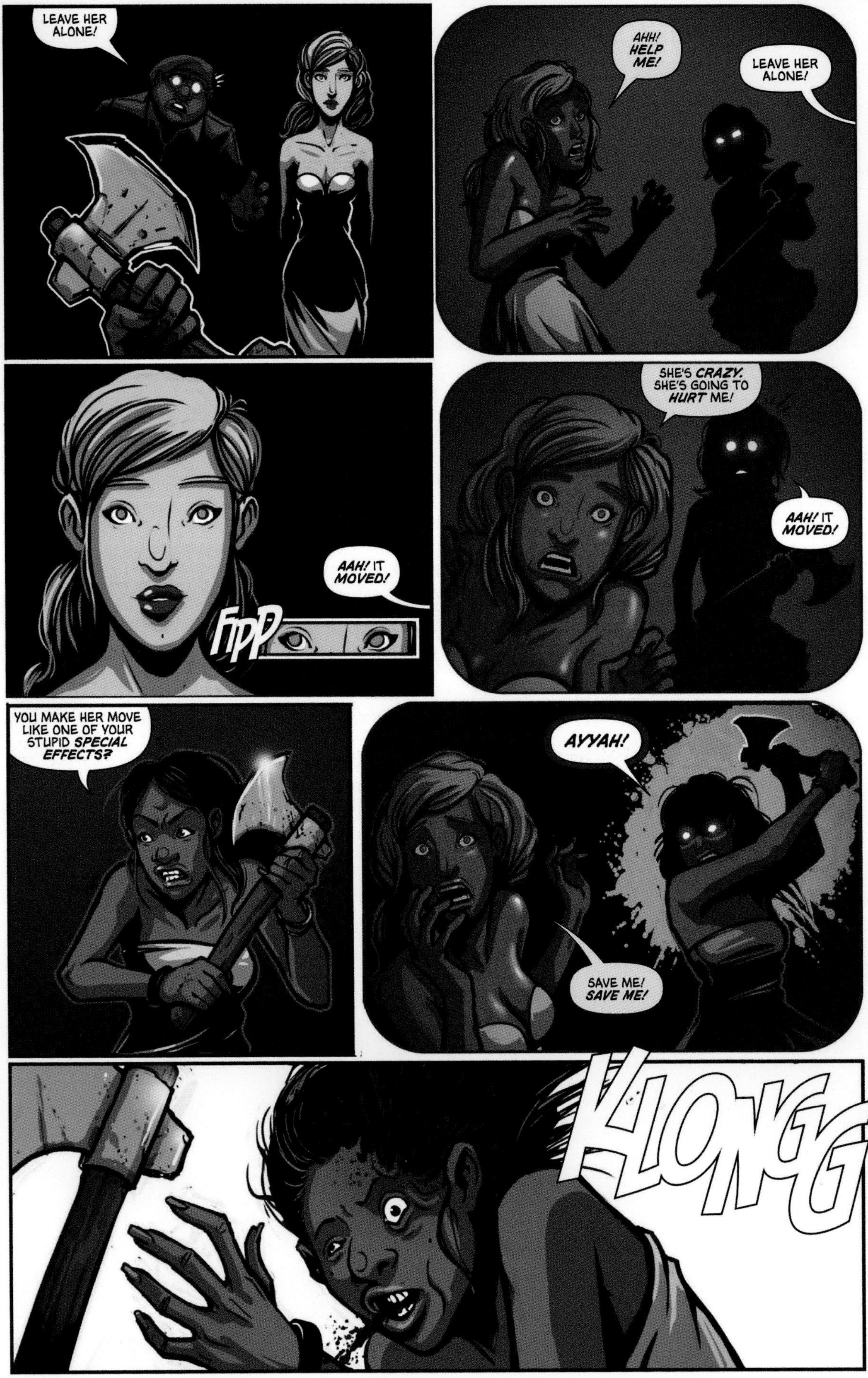
LEAVE HER ALONE!
AHH! HELP ME!
LEAVE HER ALONE!
AAH! IT MOVED!
FIPP
SHE'S CRAZY. SHE'S GOING TO HURT ME!
AAH! IT MOVED!
YOU MAKE HER MOVE LIKE ONE OF YOUR STUPID SPECIAL EFFECTS?
AYYAH!
SAVE ME! SAVE ME!
KLONGG

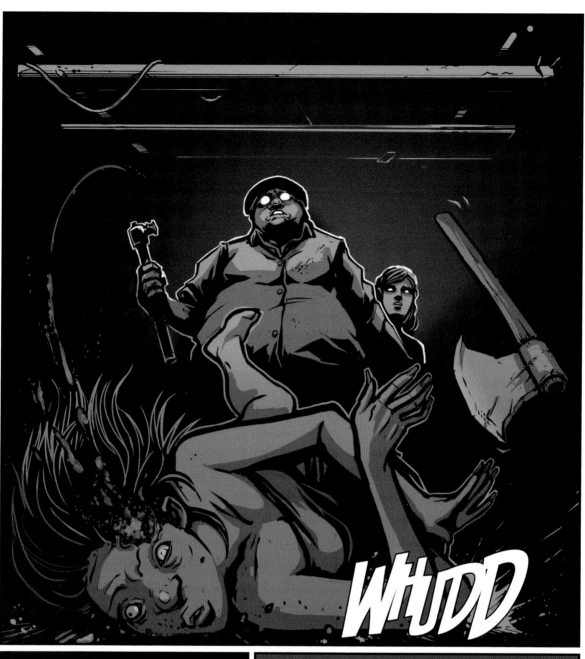

WHUDD

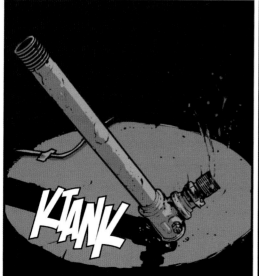

KTANK

OH, GOD.

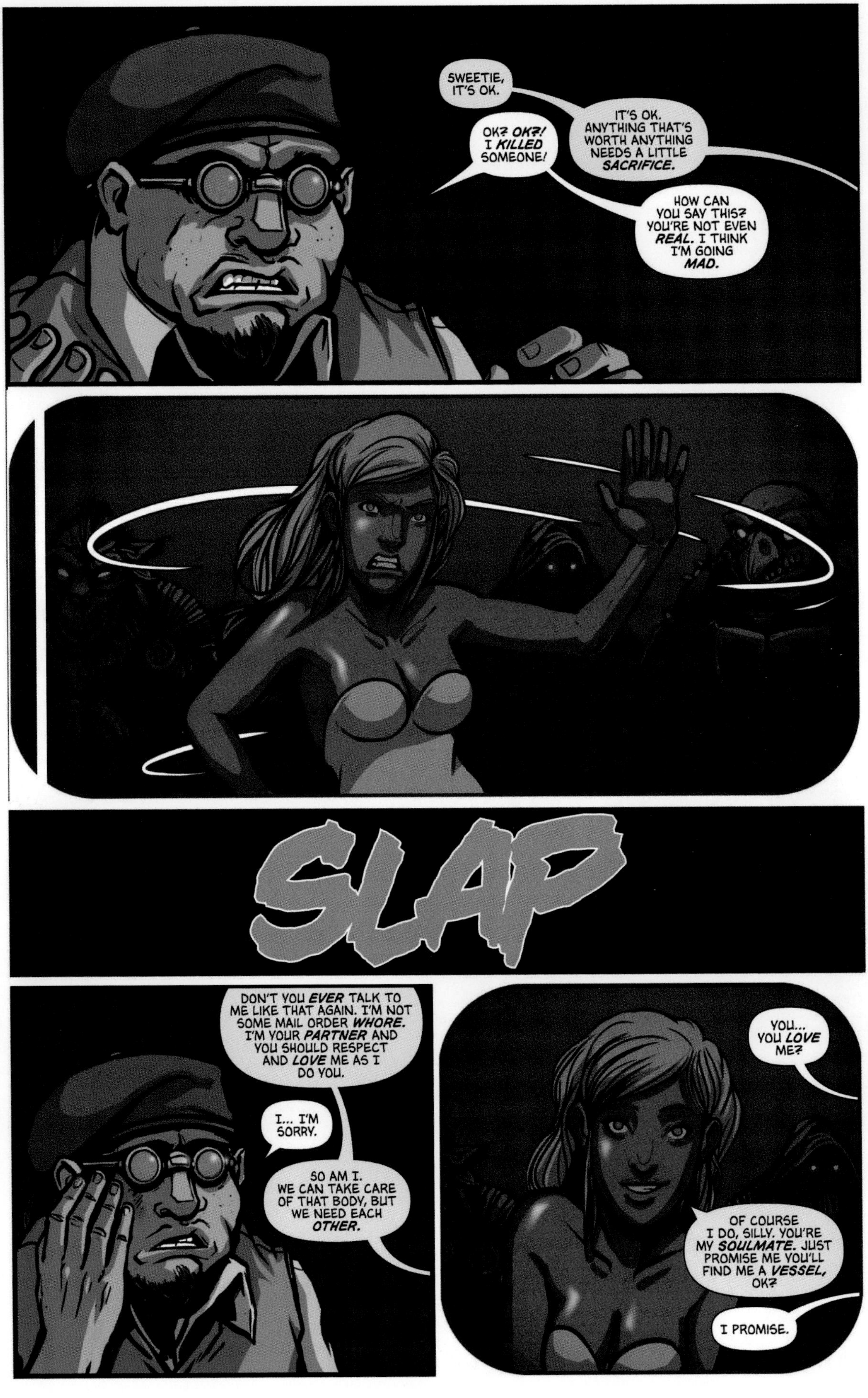
SWEETIE, IT'S OK.
OK? OK?! I KILLED SOMEONE!
IT'S OK. ANYTHING THAT'S WORTH ANYTHING NEEDS A LITTLE SACRIFICE.
HOW CAN YOU SAY THIS? YOU'RE NOT EVEN REAL. I THINK I'M GOING MAD.
SLAP
DON'T YOU EVER TALK TO ME LIKE THAT AGAIN. I'M NOT SOME MAIL ORDER WHORE. I'M YOUR PARTNER AND YOU SHOULD RESPECT AND LOVE ME AS I DO YOU.
I... I'M SORRY.
SO AM I. WE CAN TAKE CARE OF THAT BODY, BUT WE NEED EACH OTHER.
YOU... YOU LOVE ME?
OF COURSE I DO, SILLY. YOU'RE MY SOULMATE. JUST PROMISE ME YOU'LL FIND ME A VESSEL, OK?
I PROMISE.

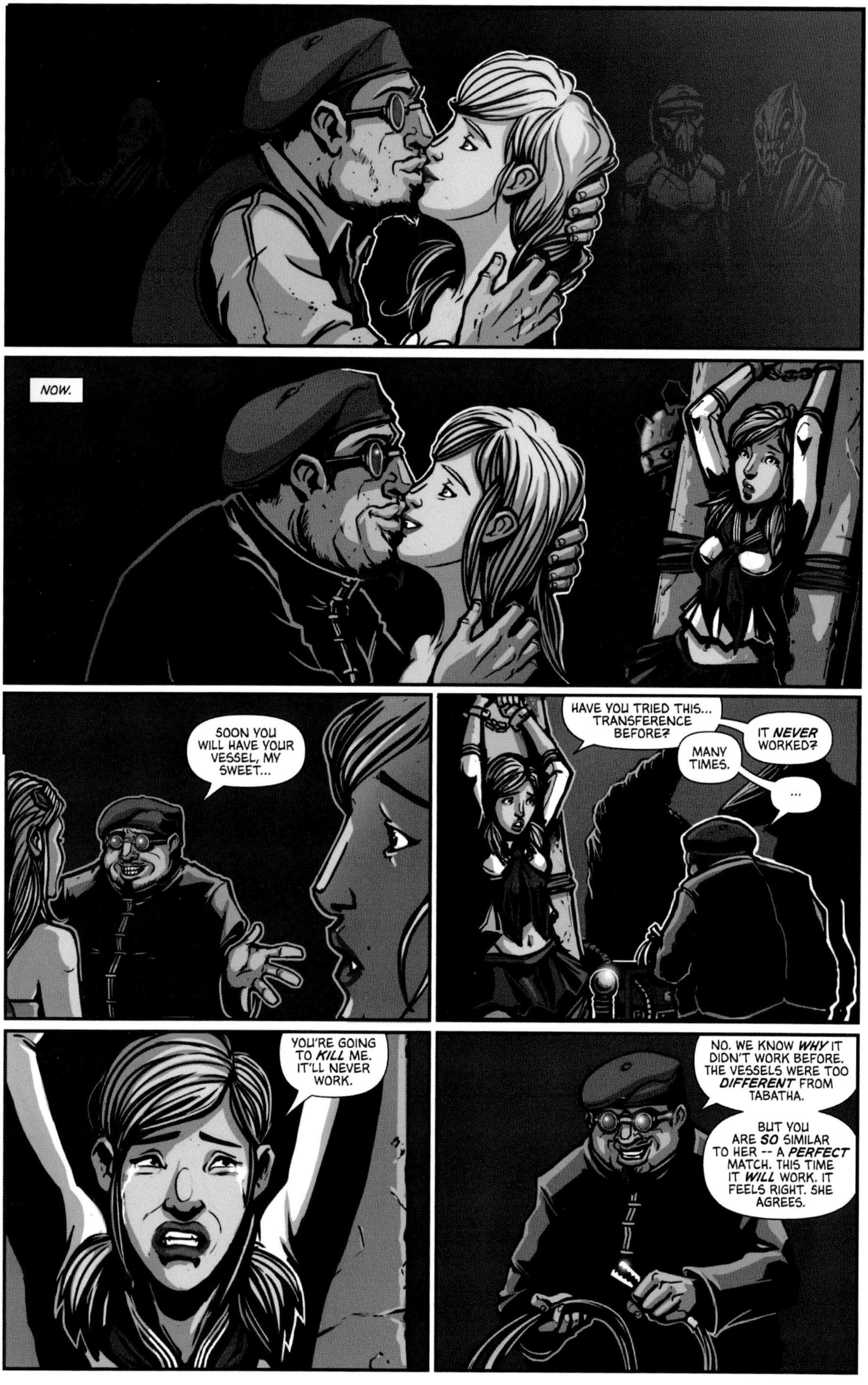
NOW.
SOON YOU WILL HAVE YOUR VESSEL, MY SWEET...
HAVE YOU TRIED THIS... TRANSFERENCE BEFORE?
MANY TIMES.
IT NEVER WORKED?
...
YOU'RE GOING TO KILL ME. IT'LL NEVER WORK.
NO. WE KNOW WHY IT DIDN'T WORK BEFORE. THE VESSELS WERE TOO DIFFERENT FROM TABATHA.
BUT YOU ARE SO SIMILAR TO HER -- A PERFECT MATCH. THIS TIME IT WILL WORK. IT FEELS RIGHT. SHE AGREES.

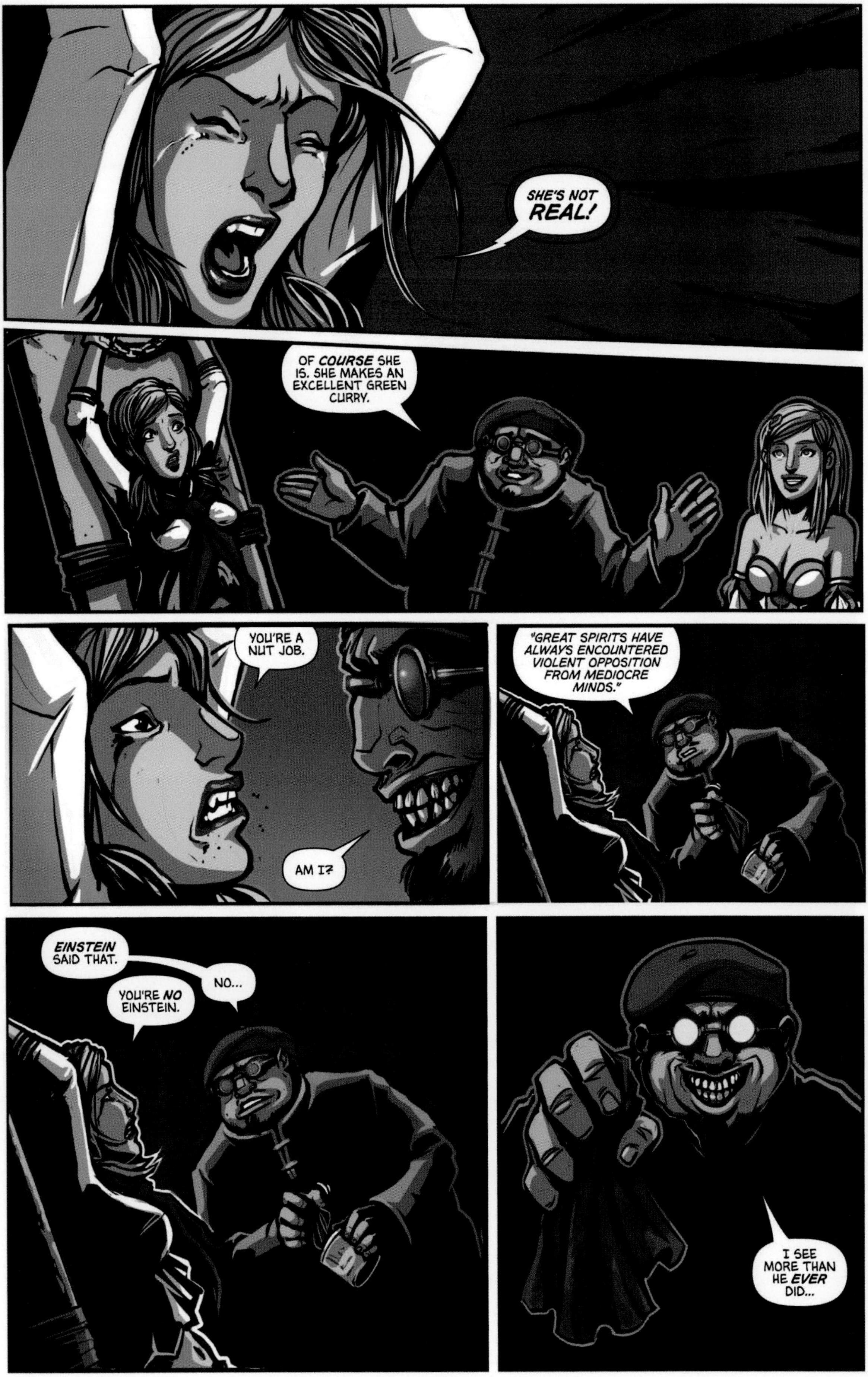
SHE'S NOT REAL!
OF COURSE SHE IS. SHE MAKES AN EXCELLENT GREEN CURRY.
YOU'RE A NUT JOB.
AM I?
"GREAT SPIRITS HAVE ALWAYS ENCOUNTERED VIOLENT OPPOSITION FROM MEDIOCRE MINDS."
EINSTEIN SAID THAT.
NO...
YOU'RE NO EINSTEIN.
I SEE MORE THAN HE EVER DID...

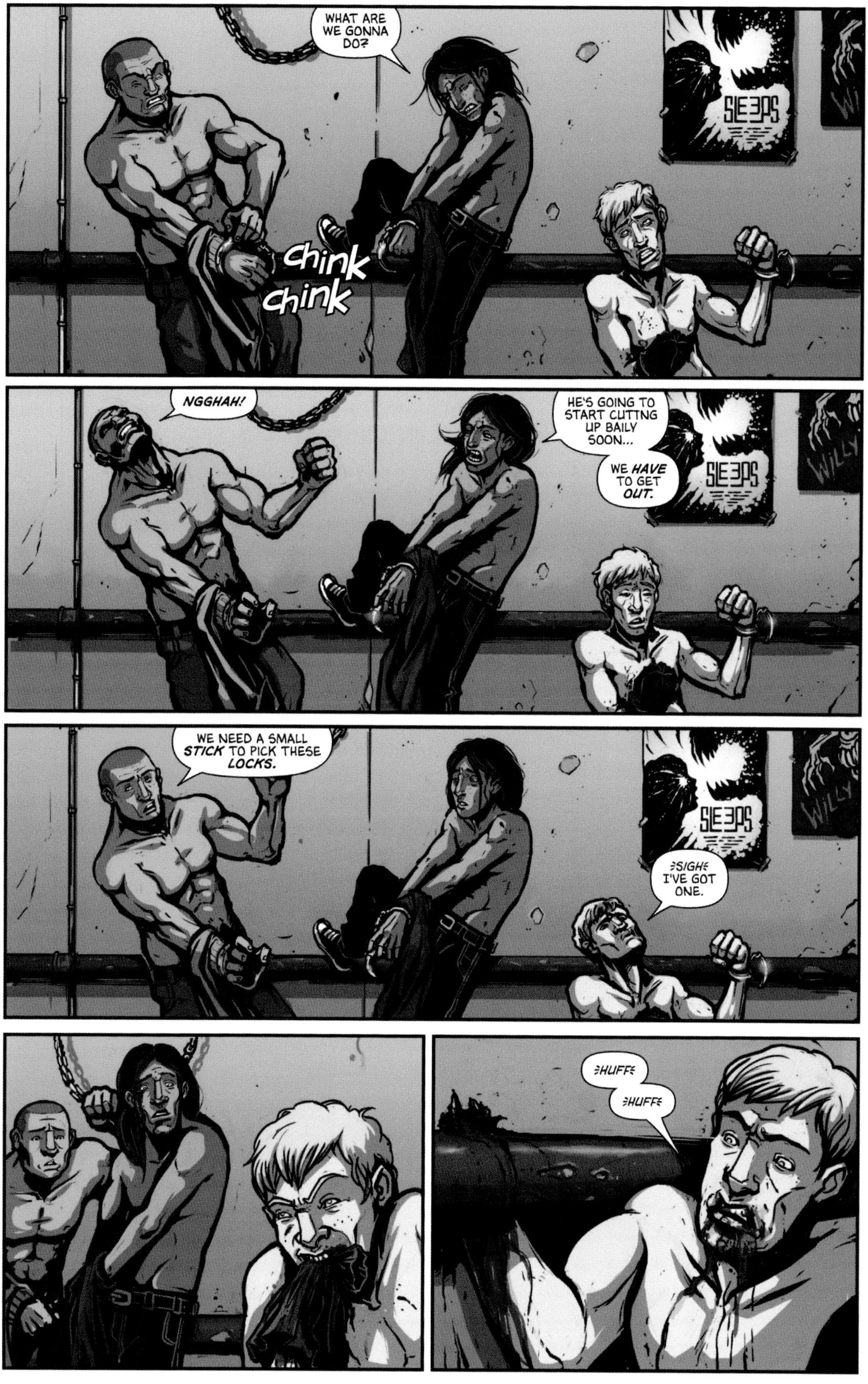
WHAT ARE WE GONNA DO?
SLEEPS
CHINK CHINK
NGGHAH!
HE'S GOING TO START CUTTING UP BAILY SOON...
WE HAVE TO GET OUT.
WE NEED A SMALL STICK TO PICK THESE LOCKS.
SIGH I'VE GOT ONE.
HUFF
HUFF

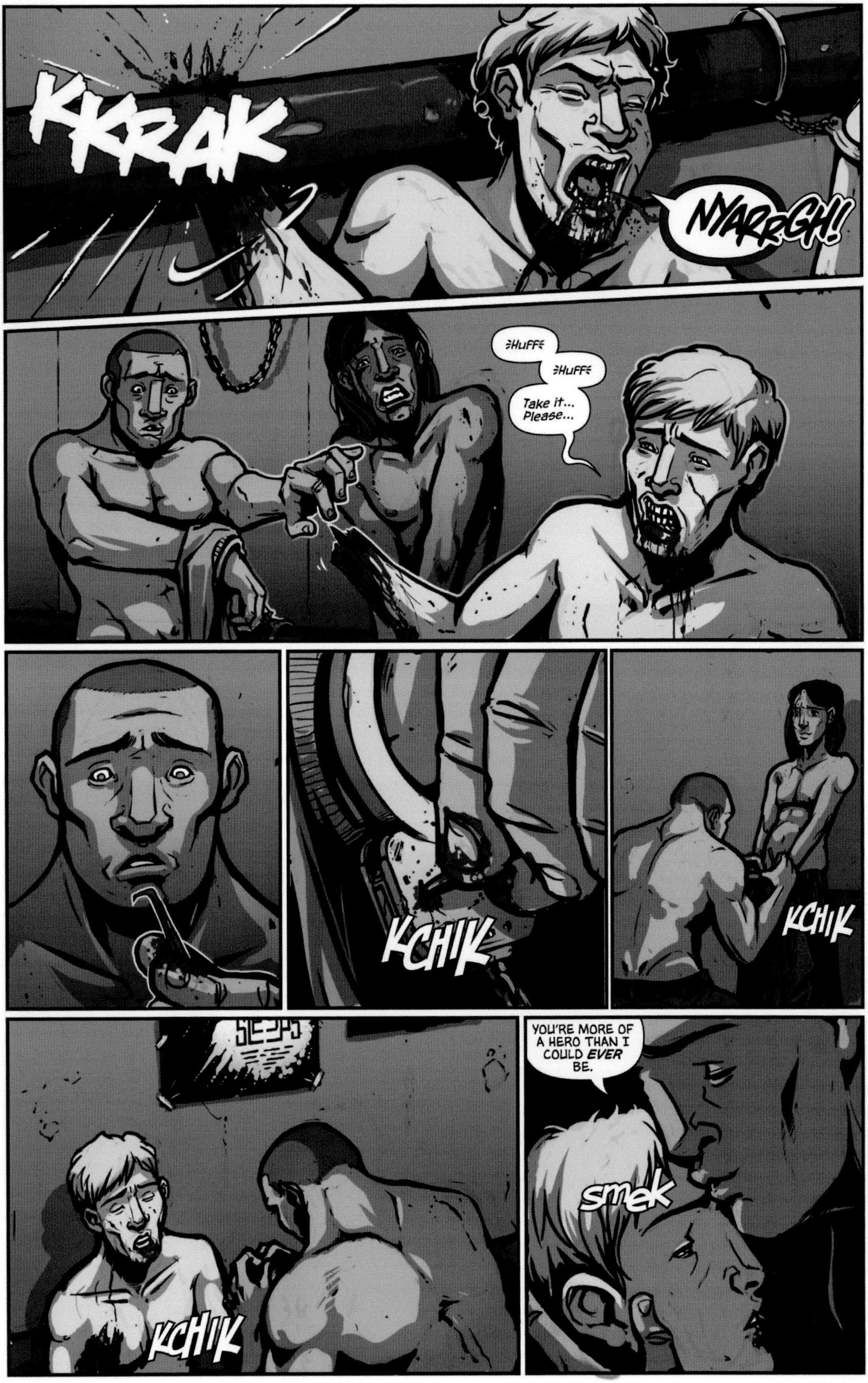
KKRAK
NYARRGH!
HUFF
HUFF
Take it...
Please...
KCHIK
KCHIK
KCHIK
YOU'RE MORE OF A HERO THAN I COULD *EVER* BE.
smek

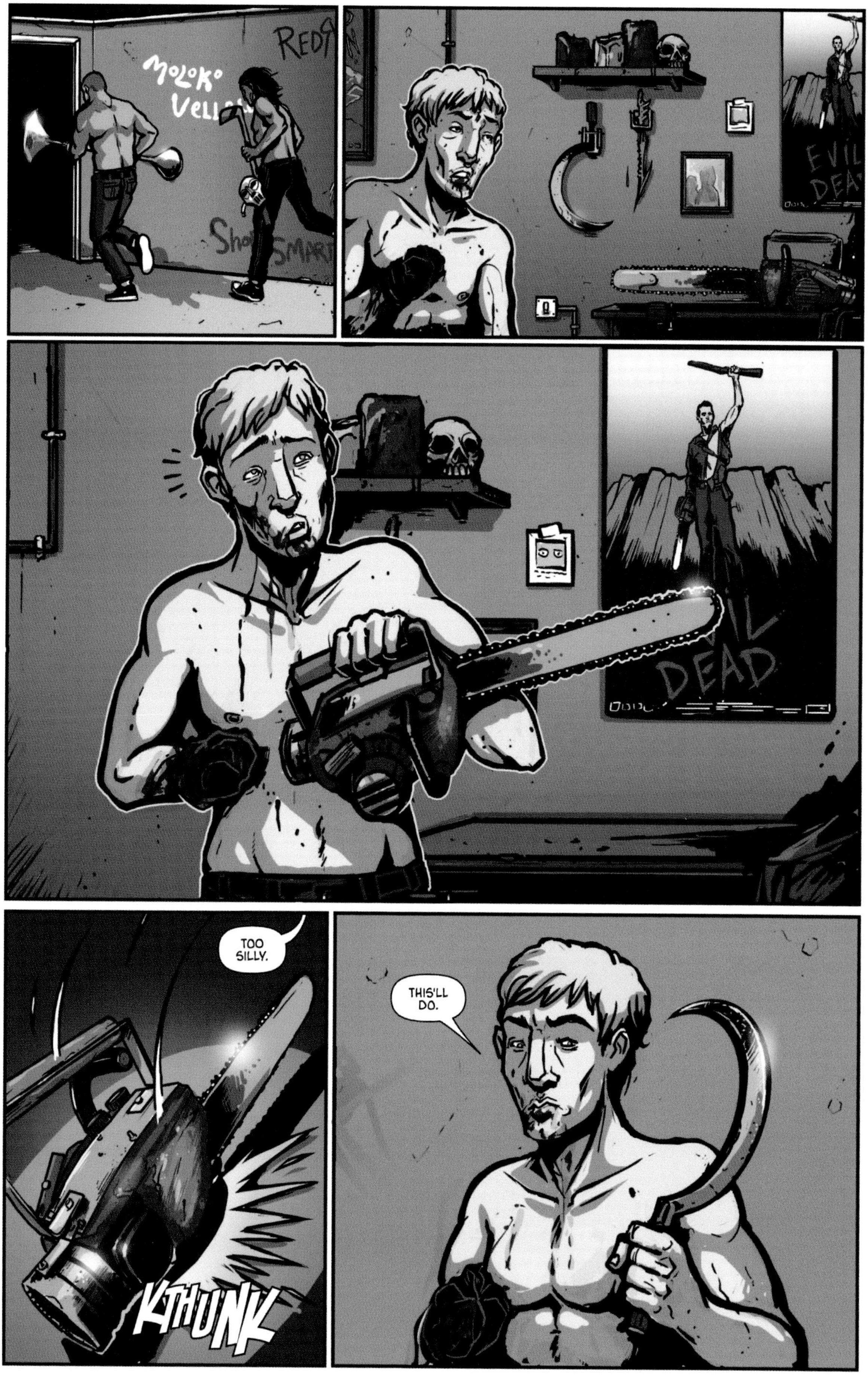
DEAD
TOO SILLY.
KTHUNK
THIS'LL DO.

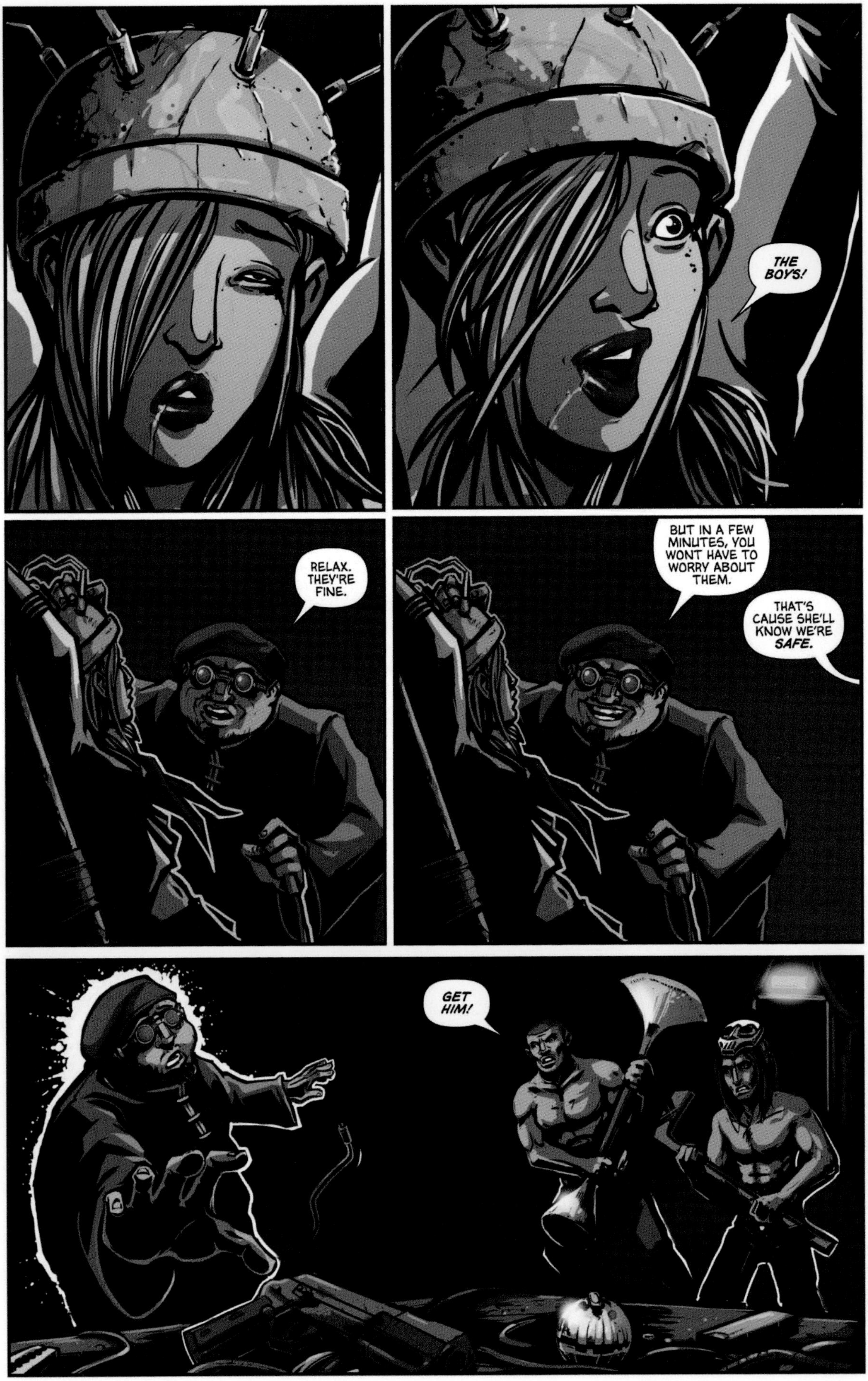
THE BOYS!
RELAX. THEY'RE FINE.
BUT IN A FEW MINUTES, YOU WONT HAVE TO WORRY ABOUT THEM.
THAT'S CAUSE SHE'LL KNOW WE'RE SAFE.
GET HIM!

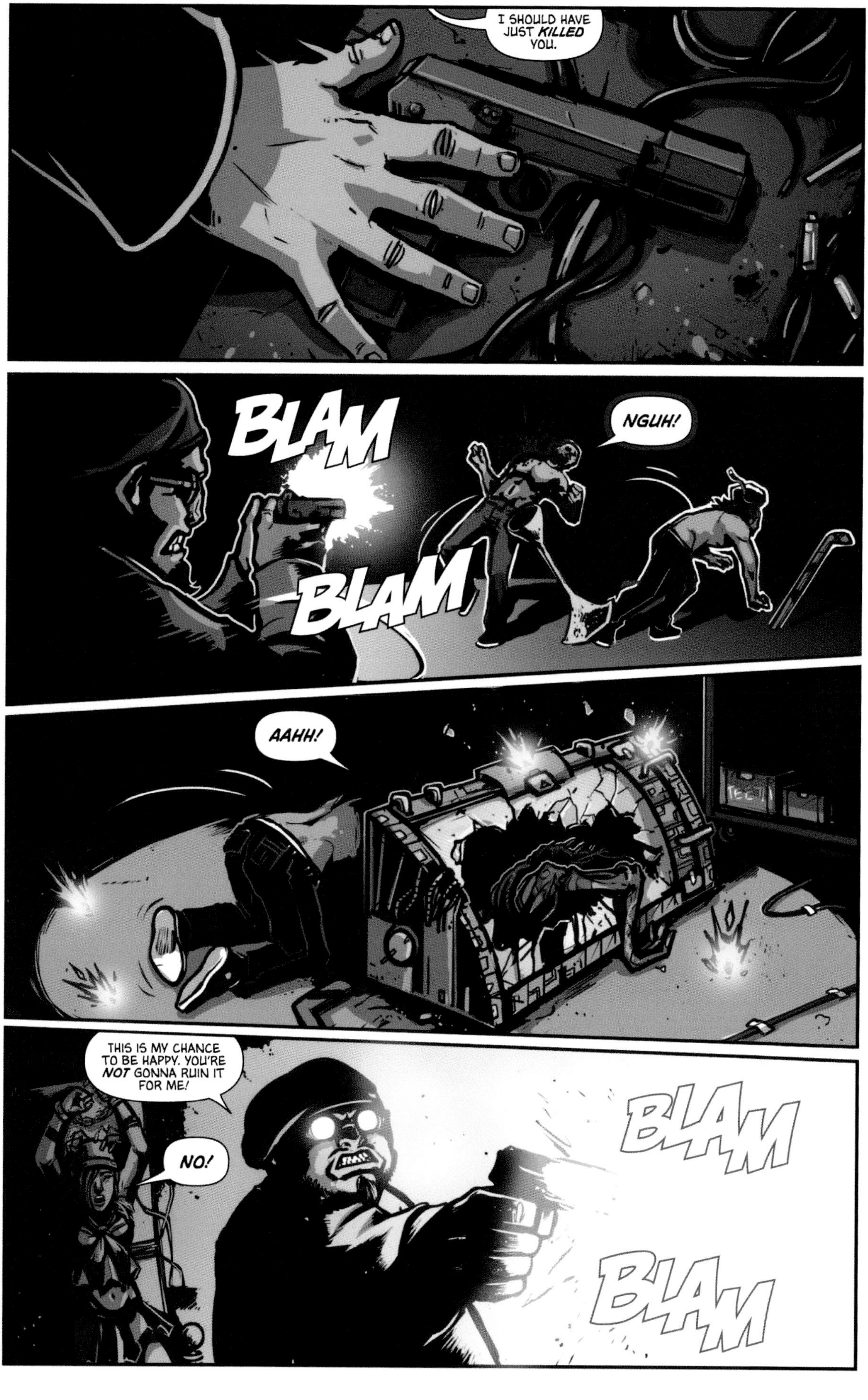
I SHOULD HAVE JUST *KILLED* YOU.
BLAM
NGUH!
BLAM
AAHH!
THIS IS MY CHANCE TO BE HAPPY. YOU'RE *NOT* GONNA RUIN IT FOR ME!
NO!
BLAM
BLAM

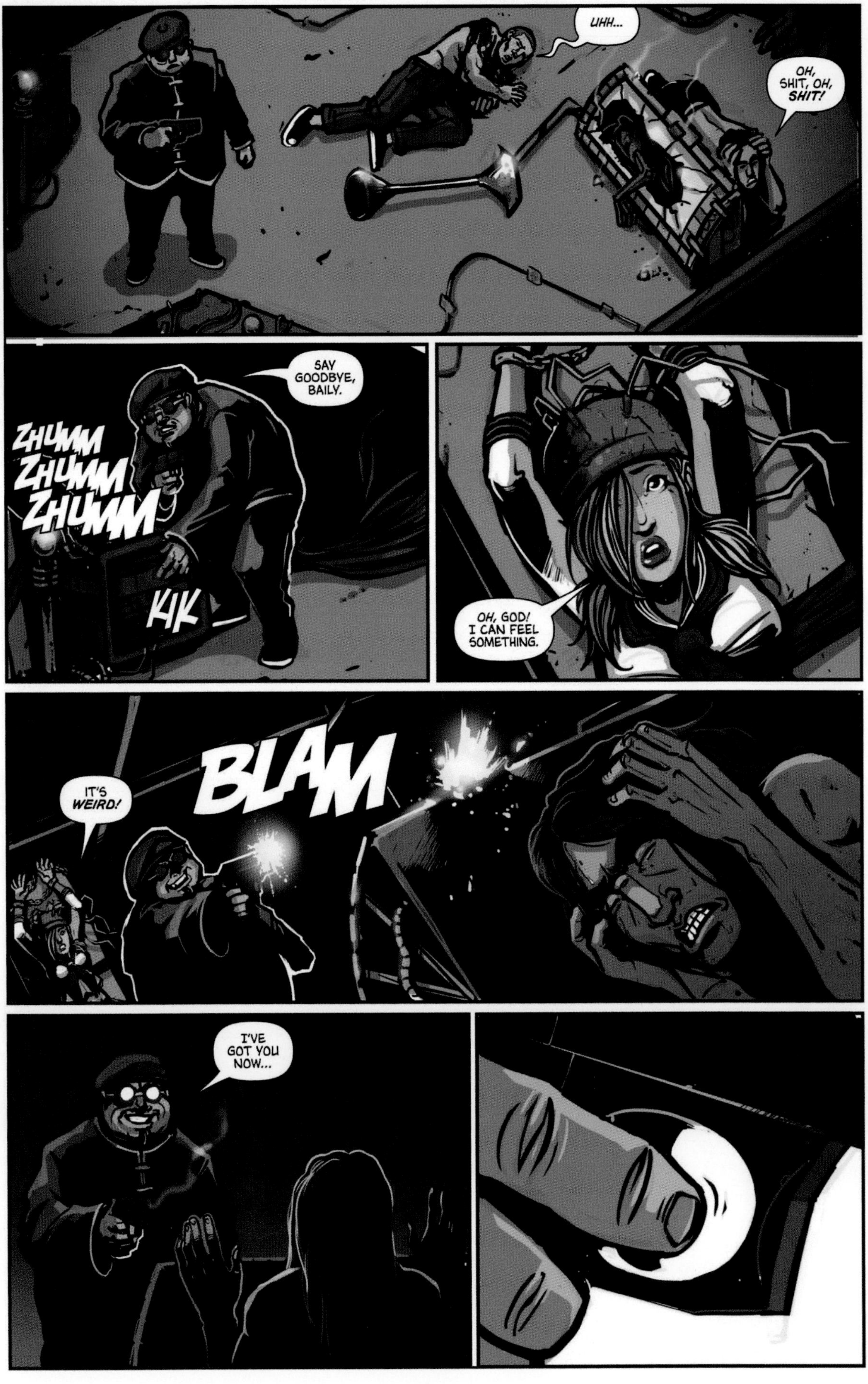
UHH...
OH, SHIT, OH, SHIT!
SAY GOODBYE, BAILY.
ZHUMM ZHUMM ZHUMM
KLIK
OH, GOD! I CAN FEEL SOMETHING.
BLAM
IT'S WEIRD!
I'VE GOT YOU NOW...

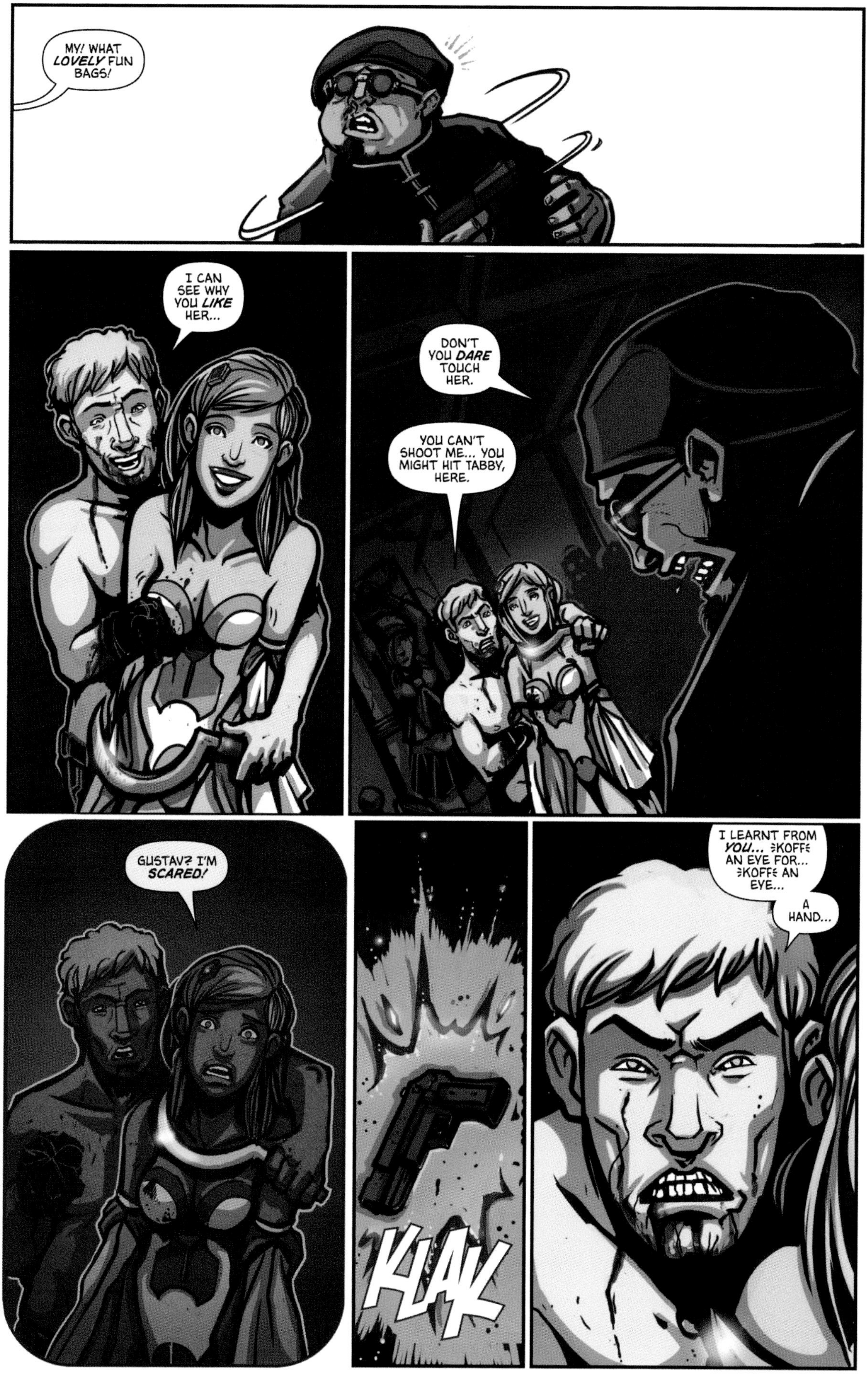
MY! WHAT LOVELY FUN BAGS!
I CAN SEE WHY YOU LIKE HER...
DON'T YOU DARE TOUCH HER.
YOU CAN'T SHOOT ME... YOU MIGHT HIT TABBY, HERE.
GUSTAV? I'M SCARED!
KLAK
I LEARNT FROM YOU... *KOFF* AN EYE FOR... *KOFF* AN EYE...
A HAND...

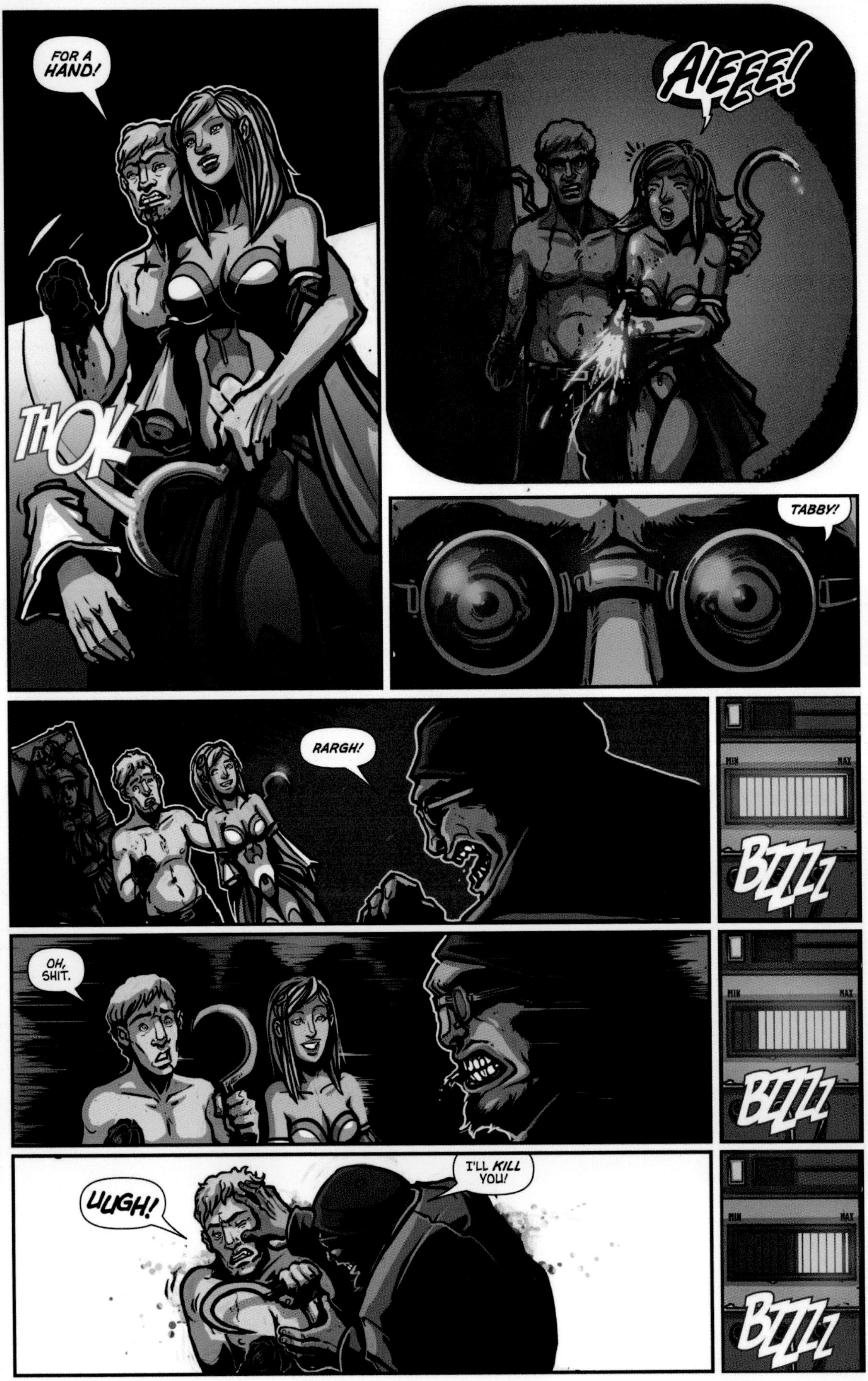
FOR A HAND!
THOK
AIEEE!
TABBY!
RARGH!
MIN MAX
BZZZZ
OH, SHIT.
MIN MAX
BZZZZ
UUGH!
I'LL KILL YOU!
MIN MAX
BZZZZ

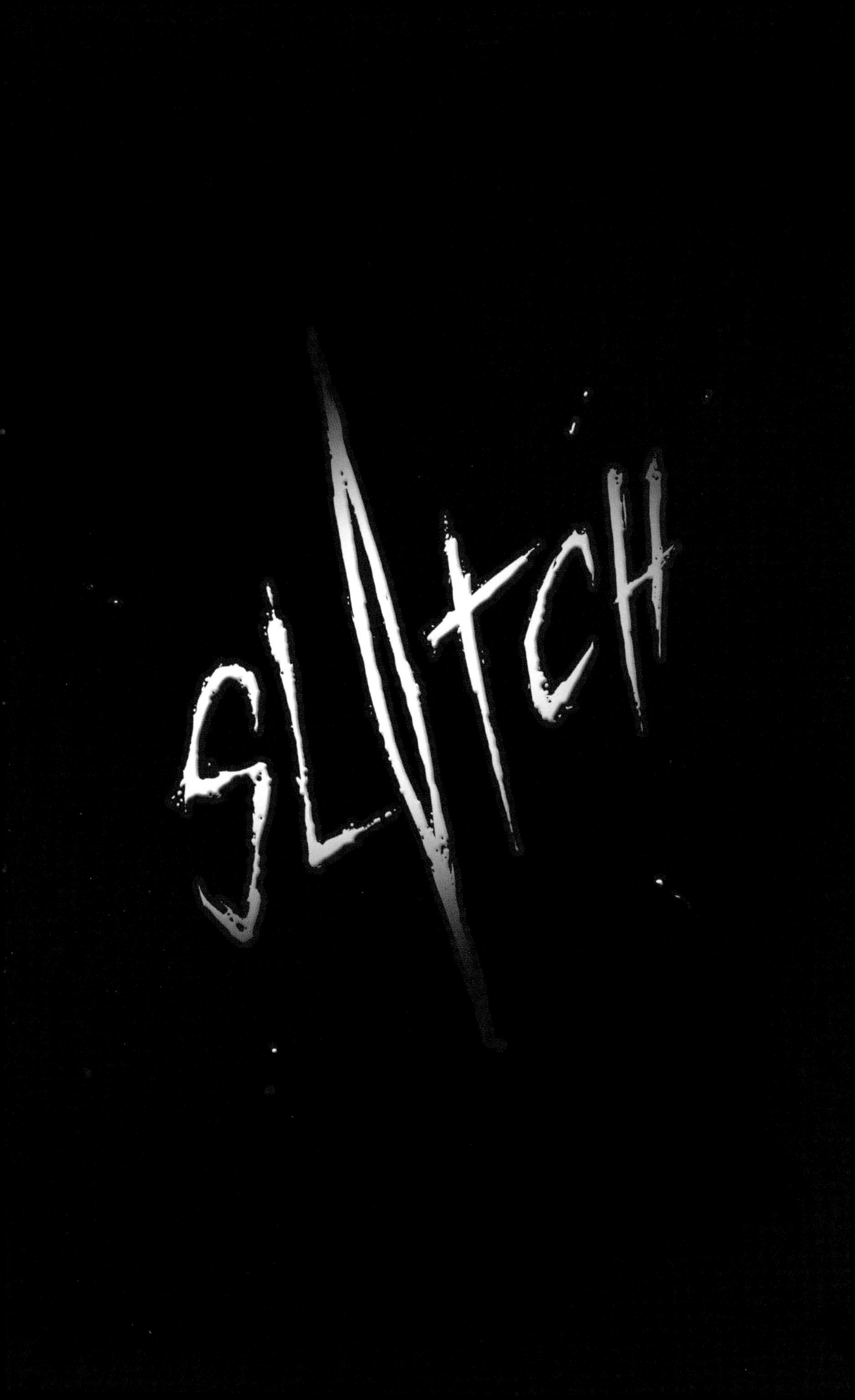

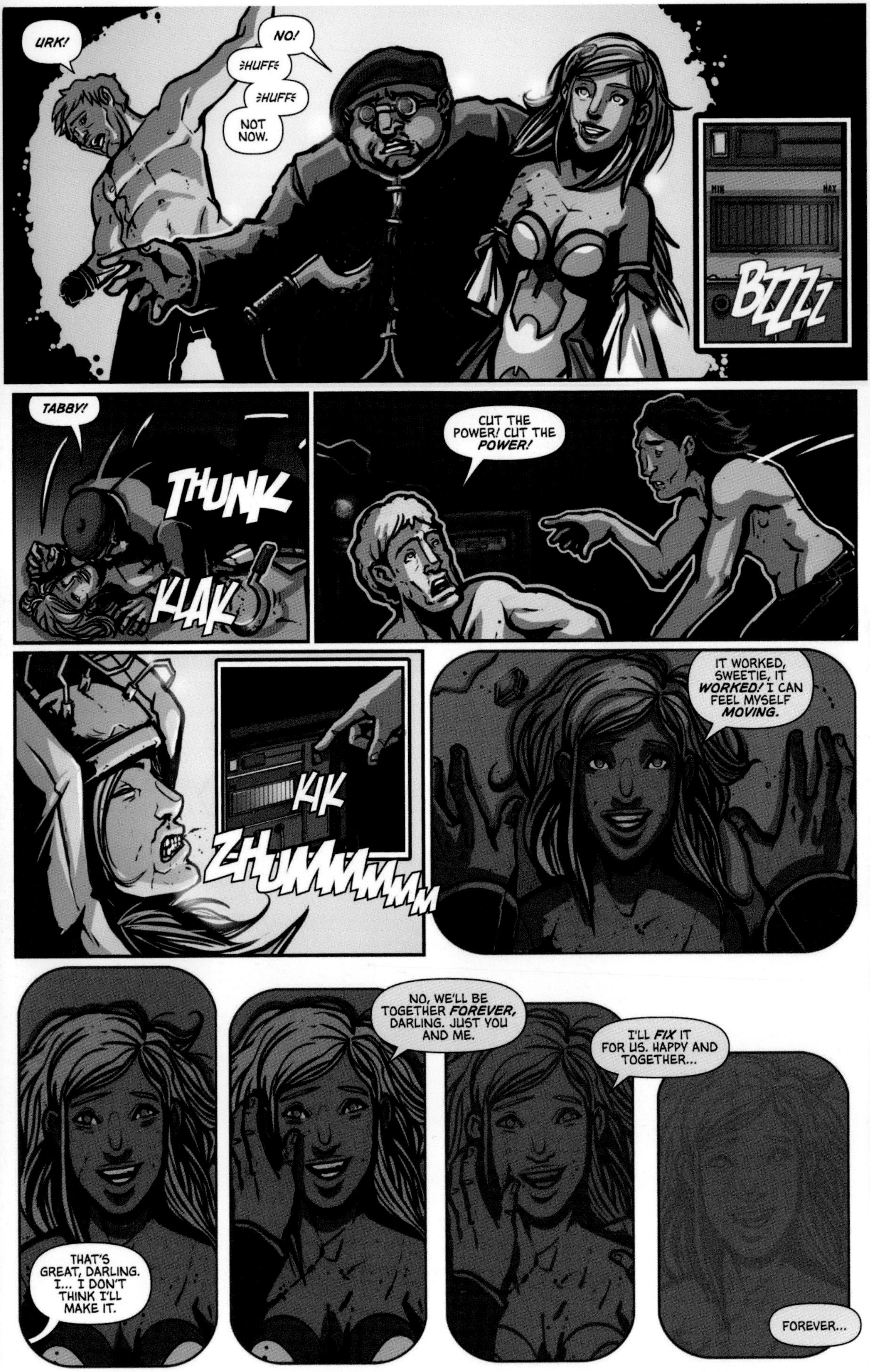

URK!
NO!
HUFF
HUFF
NOT NOW.
MIN
MAX
BZZZZ
TABBY!
THUNK
KLAK
CUT THE POWER! CUT THE POWER!
KLIK
ZHUMMMMMMM
IT WORKED, SWEETIE, IT WORKED! I CAN FEEL MYSELF MOVING.
THAT'S GREAT, DARLING. I... I DON'T THINK I'LL MAKE IT.
NO, WE'LL BE TOGETHER FOREVER, DARLING. JUST YOU AND ME.
I'LL FIX IT FOR US. HAPPY AND TOGETHER...
FOREVER...

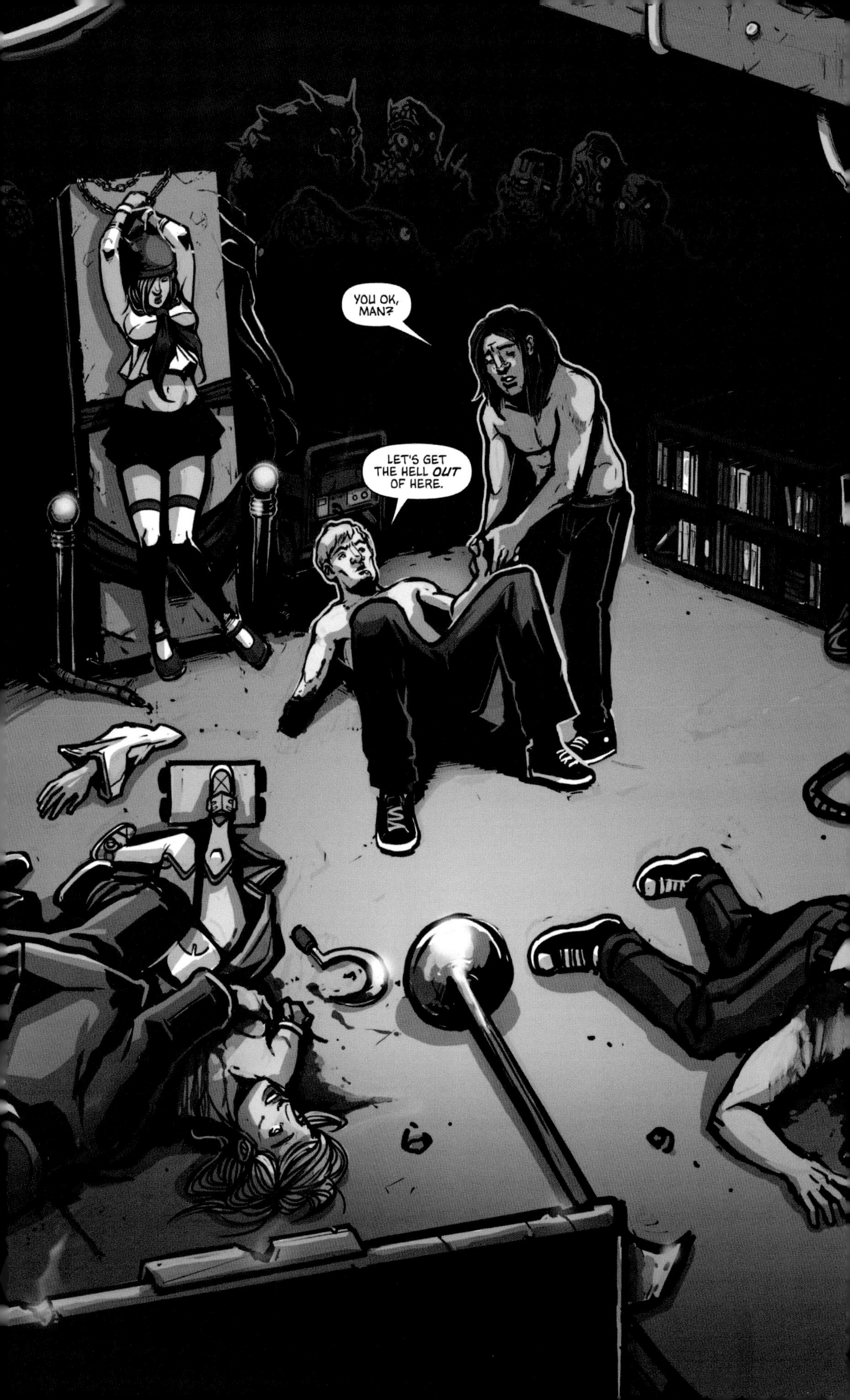
YOU OK, MAN?
LET'S GET THE HELL *OUT* OF HERE.

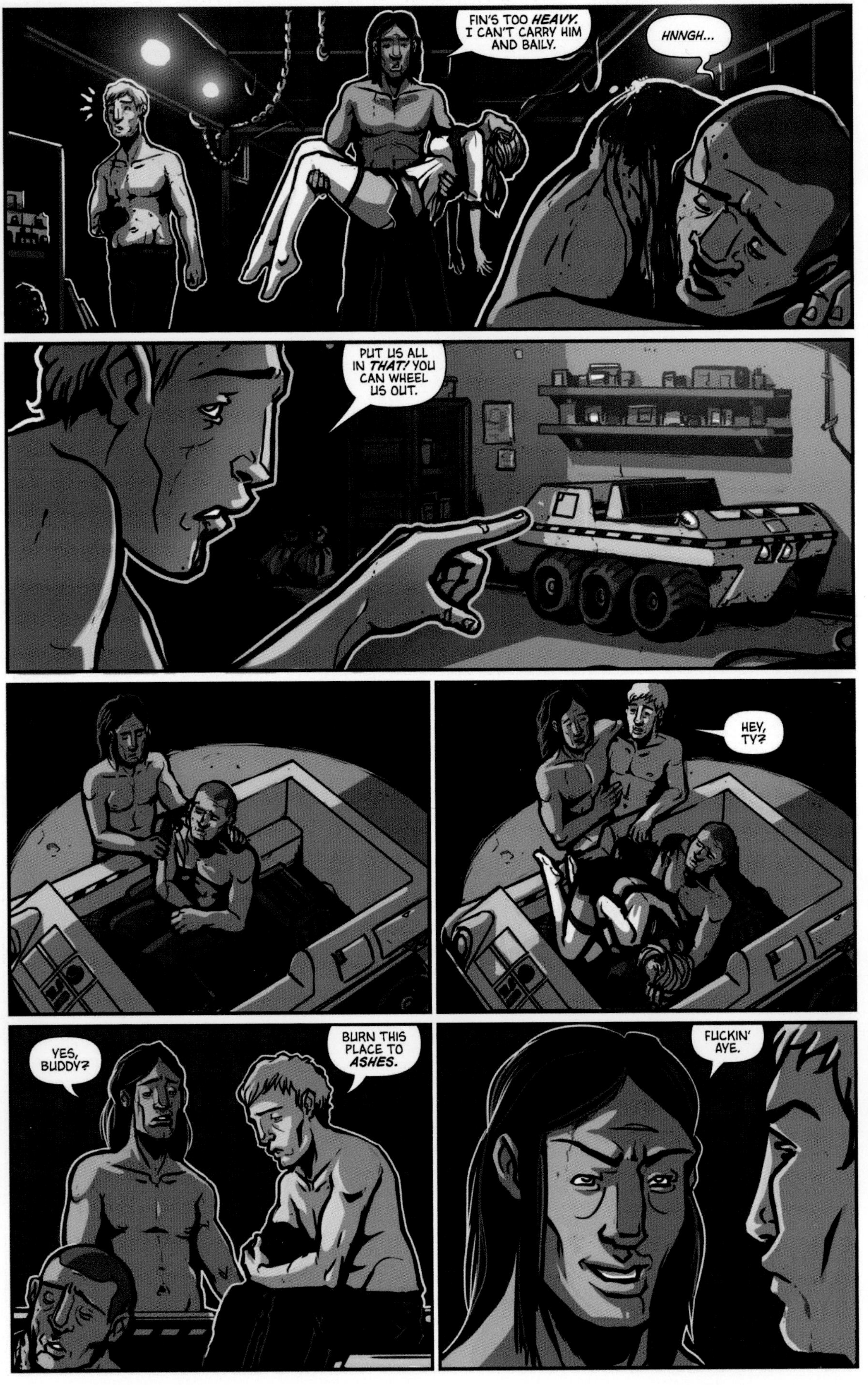
FIN'S TOO HEAVY. I CAN'T CARRY HIM AND BAILY.
HNNGH...
PUT US ALL IN THAT! YOU CAN WHEEL US OUT.
HEY, TY?
YES, BUDDY?
BURN THIS PLACE TO ASHES.
FUCKIN' AYE.

URGHH!

HANG IN THERE, WE'LL GET YOU ALL A DOCTOR.

HUH?

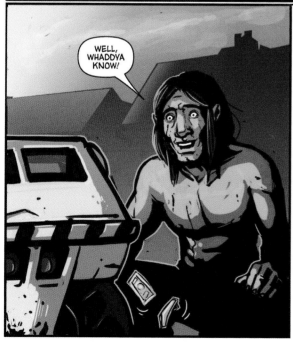

WELL, WHADDYA KNOW!

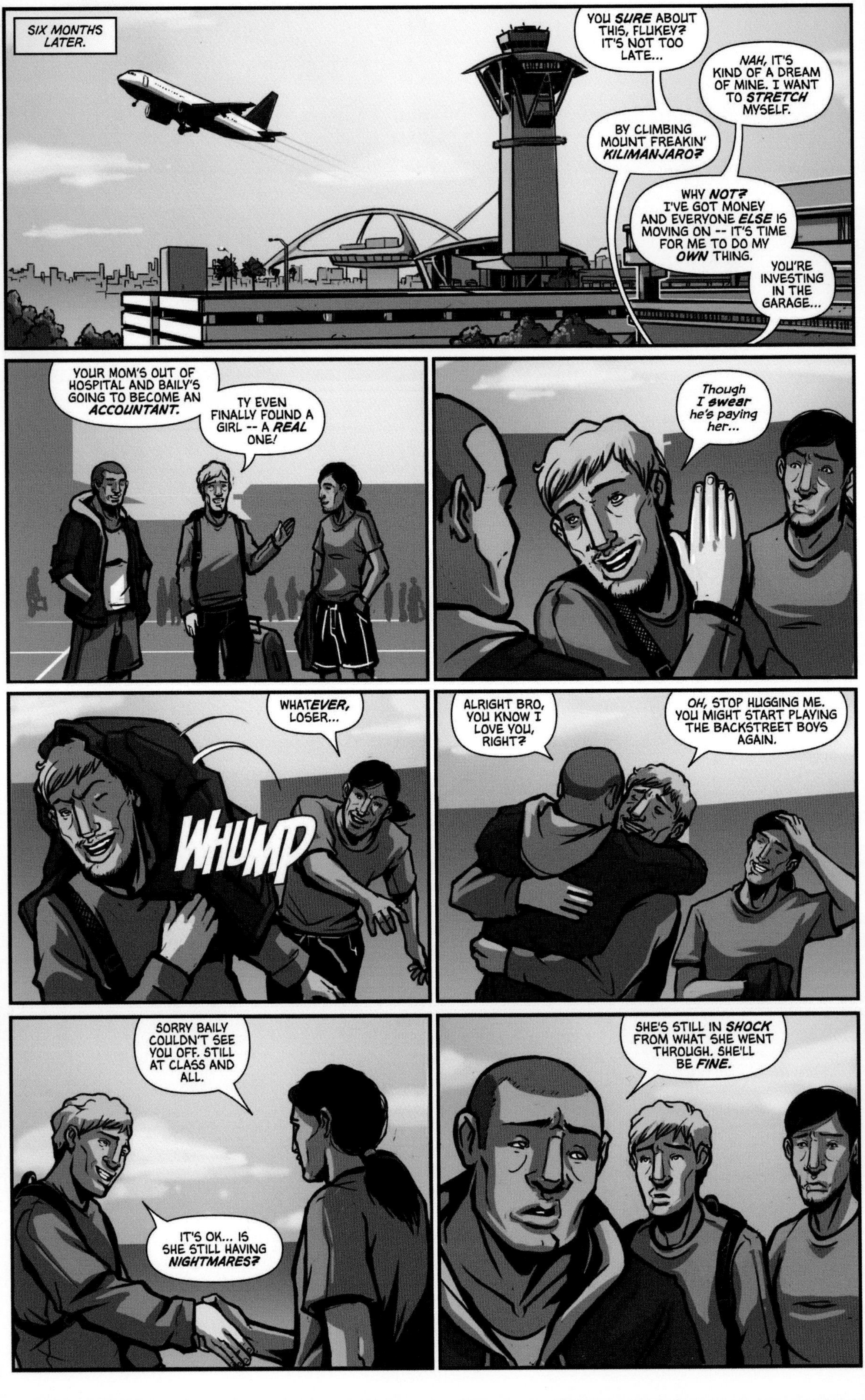

SIX MONTHS LATER.
YOU SURE ABOUT THIS, FLUKEY? IT'S NOT TOO LATE...
NAH, IT'S KIND OF A DREAM OF MINE. I WANT TO STRETCH MYSELF.
BY CLIMBING MOUNT FREAKIN' KILIMANJARO?
WHY NOT? I'VE GOT MONEY AND EVERYONE ELSE IS MOVING ON -- IT'S TIME FOR ME TO DO MY OWN THING.
YOU'RE INVESTING IN THE GARAGE...
YOUR MOM'S OUT OF HOSPITAL AND BAILY'S GOING TO BECOME AN ACCOUNTANT.
TY EVEN FINALLY FOUND A GIRL -- A REAL ONE!
Though I swear he's paying her...
WHATEVER, LOSER...
WHUMP
ALRIGHT BRO, YOU KNOW I LOVE YOU, RIGHT?
OH, STOP HUGGING ME. YOU MIGHT START PLAYING THE BACKSTREET BOYS AGAIN.
SORRY BAILY COULDN'T SEE YOU OFF. STILL AT CLASS AND ALL.
IT'S OK... IS SHE STILL HAVING NIGHTMARES?
SHE'S STILL IN SHOCK FROM WHAT SHE WENT THROUGH. SHE'LL BE FINE.

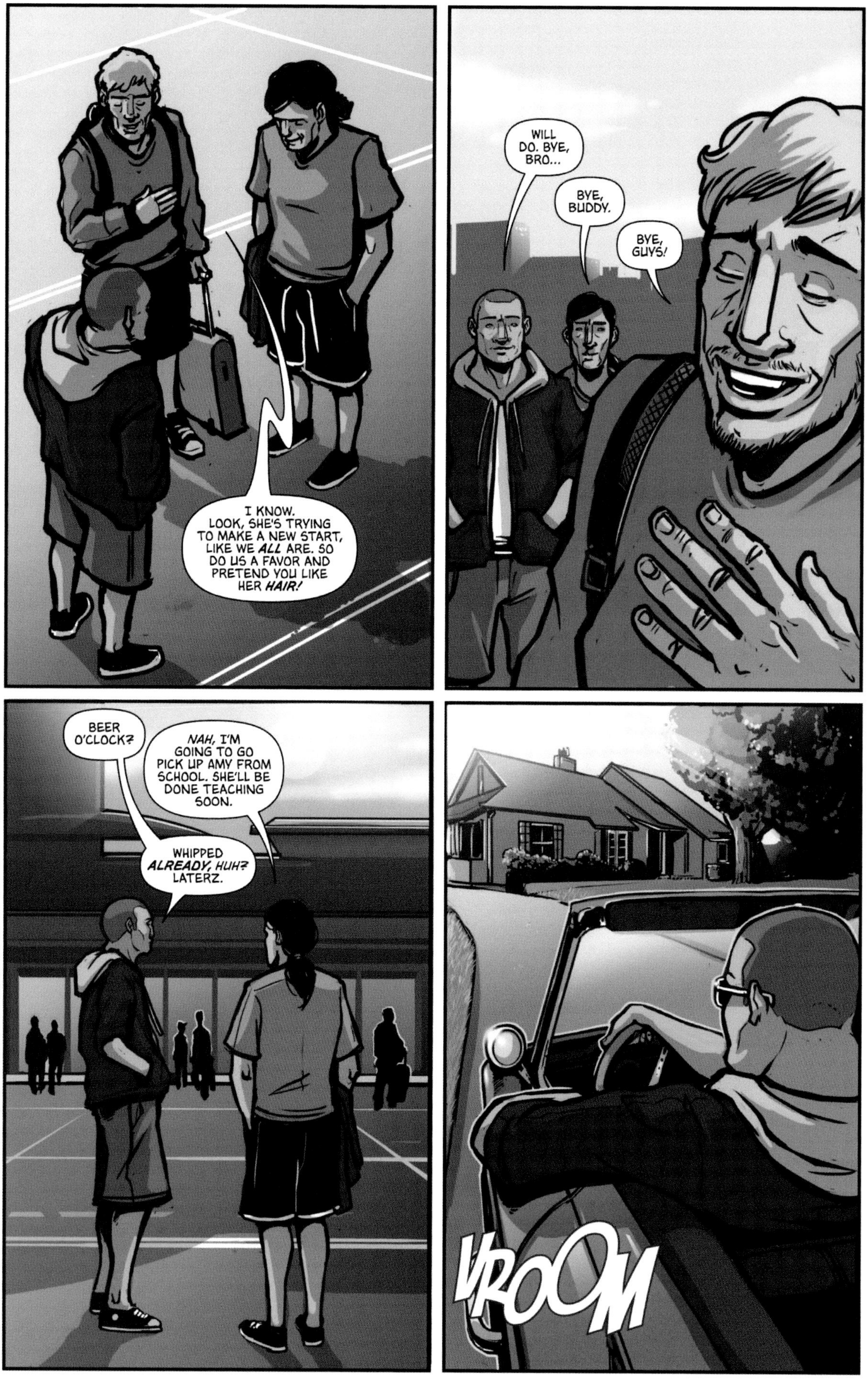
I KNOW. LOOK, SHE'S TRYING TO MAKE A NEW START, LIKE WE ALL ARE. SO DO US A FAVOR AND PRETEND YOU LIKE HER HAIR!
WILL DO. BYE, BRO...
BYE, BUDDY.
BYE, GUYS!
BEER O'CLOCK?
NAH, I'M GOING TO GO PICK UP AMY FROM SCHOOL. SHE'LL BE DONE TEACHING SOON.
WHIPPED ALREADY, HUH? LATERZ.
VROOM

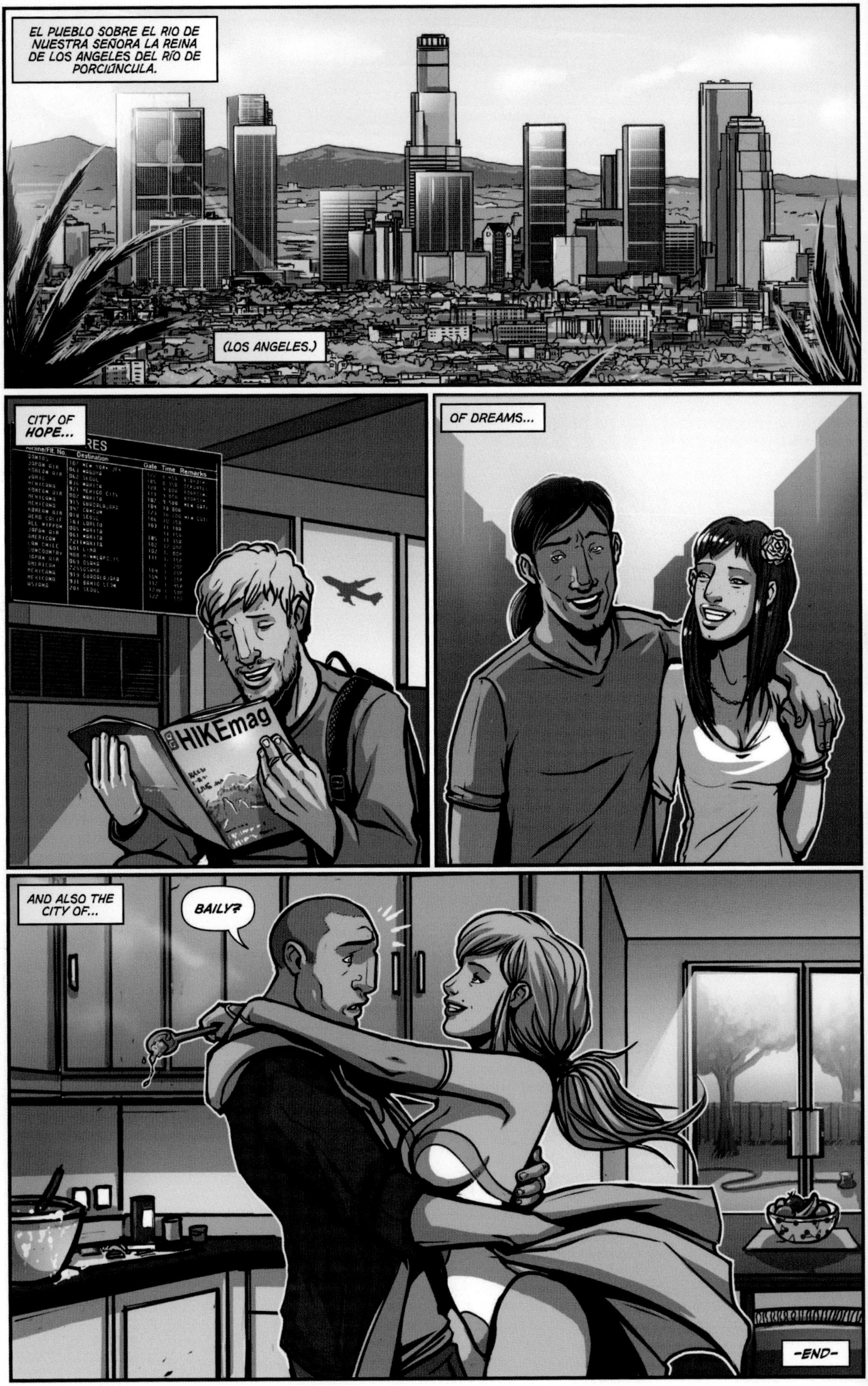
EL PUEBLO SOBRE EL RIO DE NUESTRA SEÑORA LA REINA DE LOS ANGELES DEL RÍO DE PORCIÚNCULA.
(LOS ANGELES.)
CITY OF HOPE...
HIKEmag
OF DREAMS...
AND ALSO THE CITY OF...
BAILY?
-END-

TABATHA

END

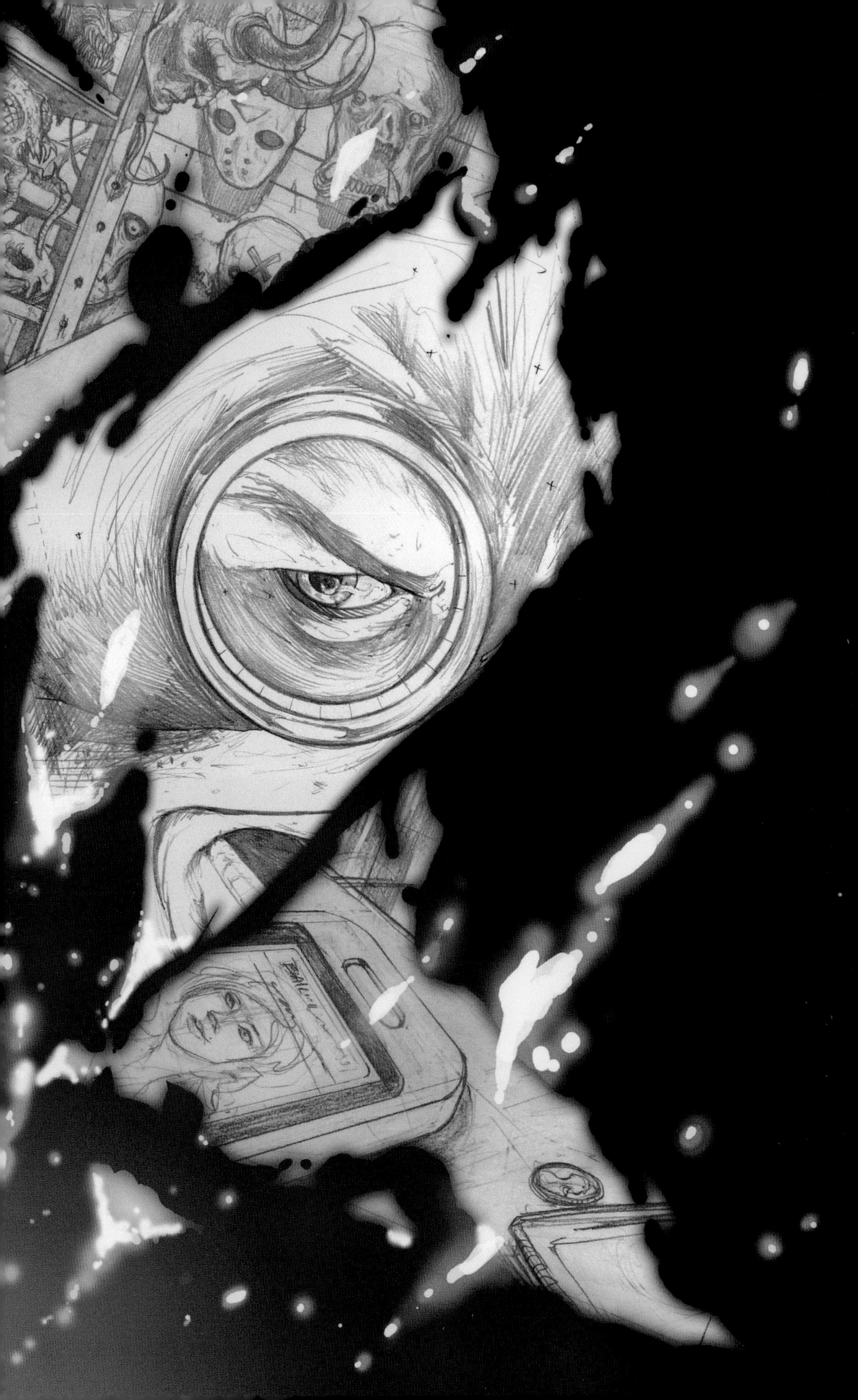

Tabatha all began on a train ride to Margate. We were travelling for an awards ceremony we were short listed for and used the time to talk about our next project. We pitched crazy ideas back and forth as the carriage shuttled along and thrashed out a story about severed hands, sex dolls, serial killers, and body transference. Neil stitched the story together and Caspar filled in the gaps with pop culture references.

It was only when we stood up to leave that we realized the whole carriage had been forced to listen to our perverted conversation. There were several smiles and a few odd looks. "That was much more interesting that my normal ride home" remarked an amused old lady as she left. We both gave embarrassed smiles and shuffled off to the ceremony. We didn't win, but we did have the beginnings of Tabatha.

DID YOU KNOW

Tabatha was originally set in London, but we moved it to LA because Caspar wanted something different to draw.

Gustav was originally going to be a devil worshipper who summoned forth a demon to turn Tabatha into a real person. We killed the idea pretty early on, but you can still see a pentagram on the ceiling in the first issue when they first enter Gustav's home.

Because he was no longer allowed to draw a demon, Caspar insisted we make Gustav a creature prop maker, allowing him to draw countless hideous creations.

Gustav's glasses are not pink, but rose coloured-he literally sees the world through rose tinted glasses.

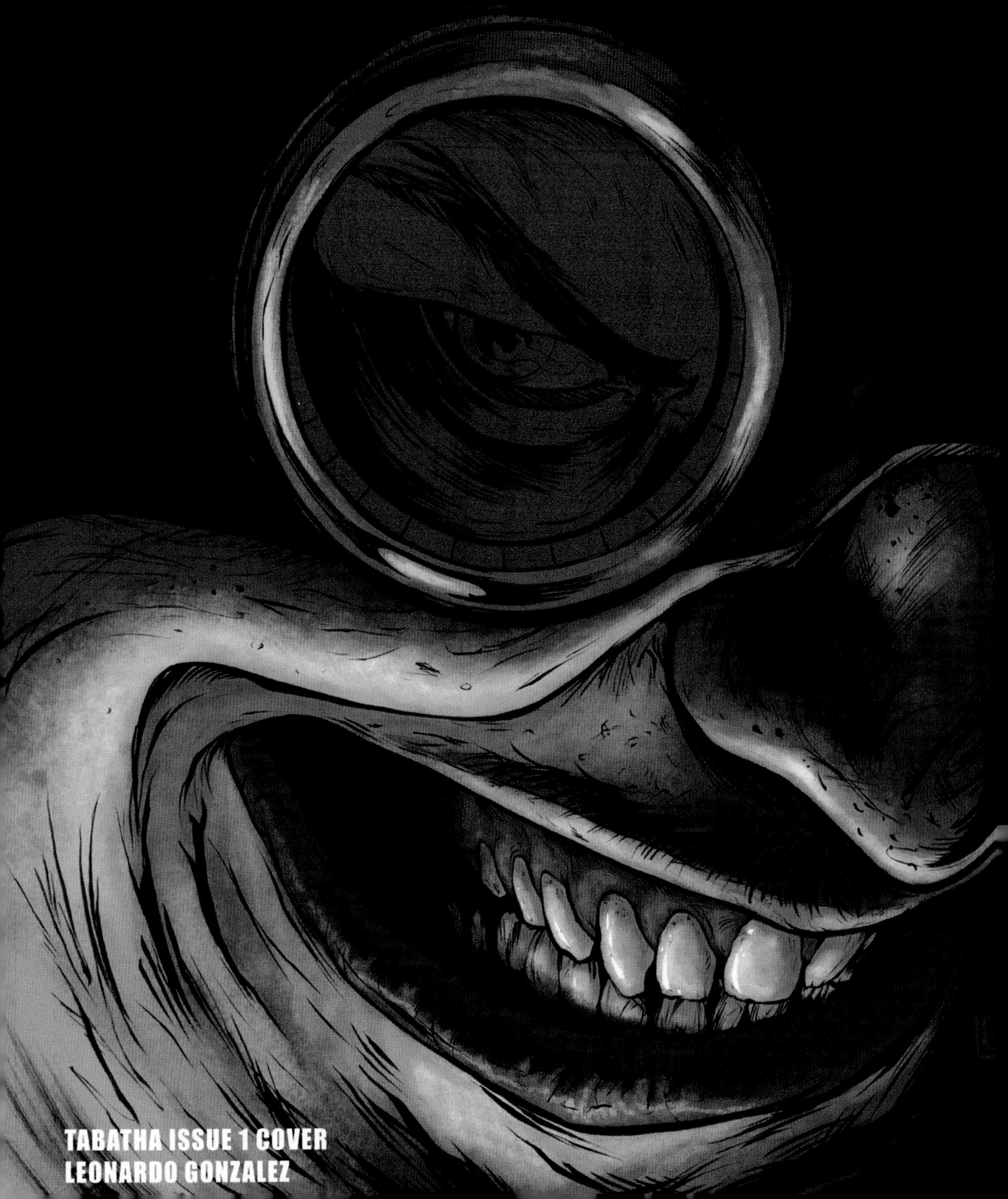

TABATHA ISSUE 1 COVER
LEONARDO GONZALEZ

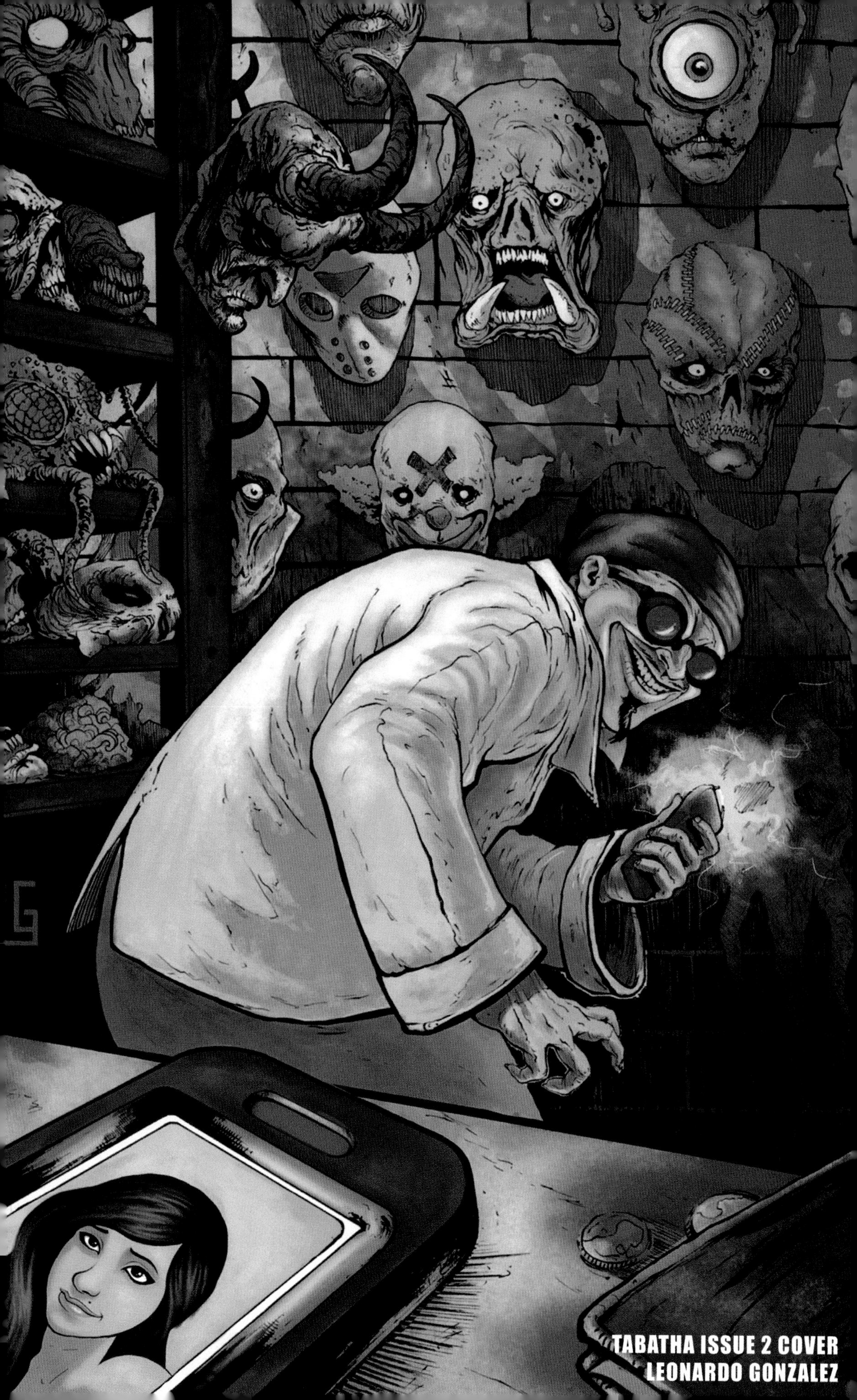

TABATHA ISSUE 2 COVER
LEONARDO GONZALEZ

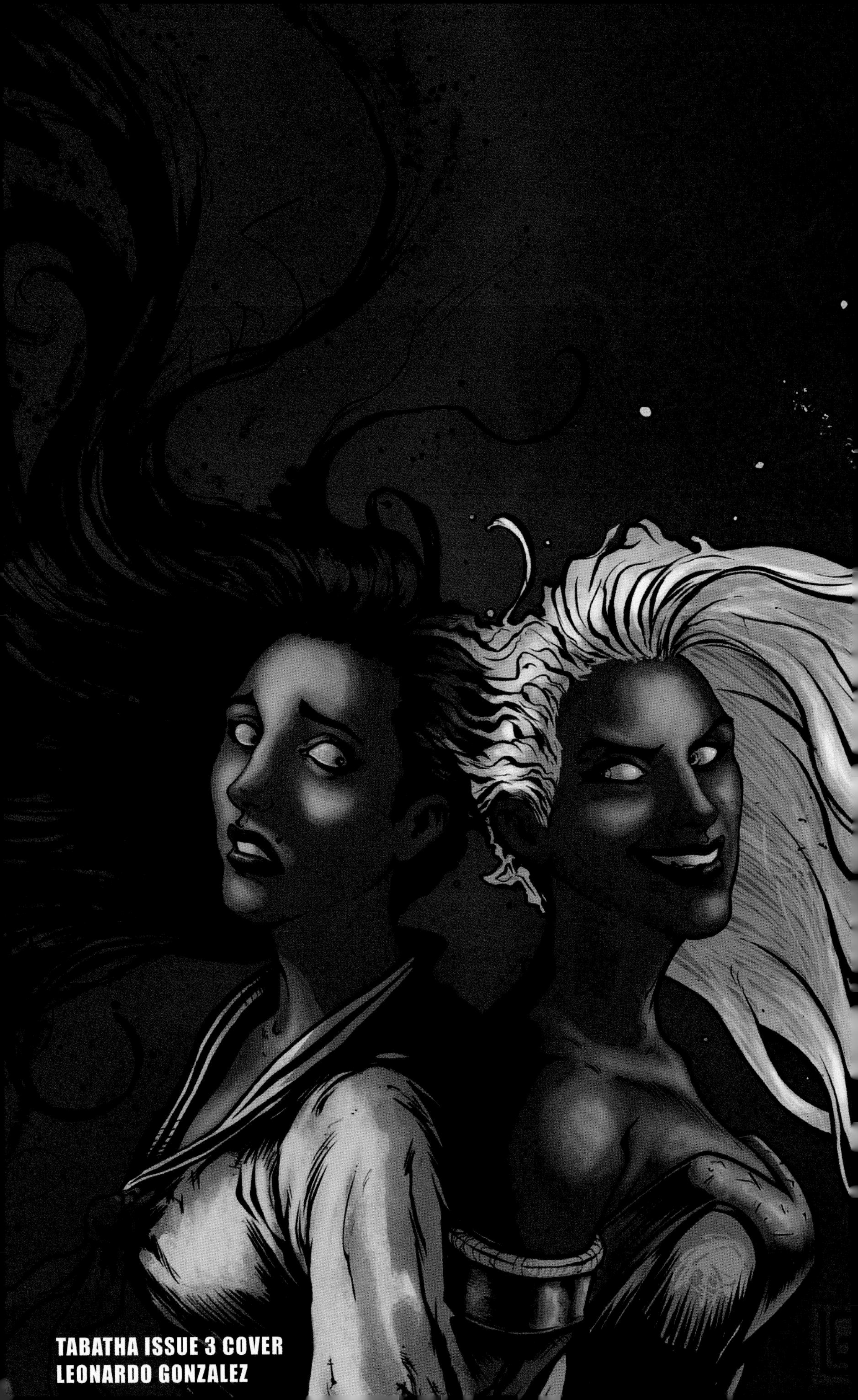

TABATHA ISSUE 3 COVER
LEONARDO GONZALEZ

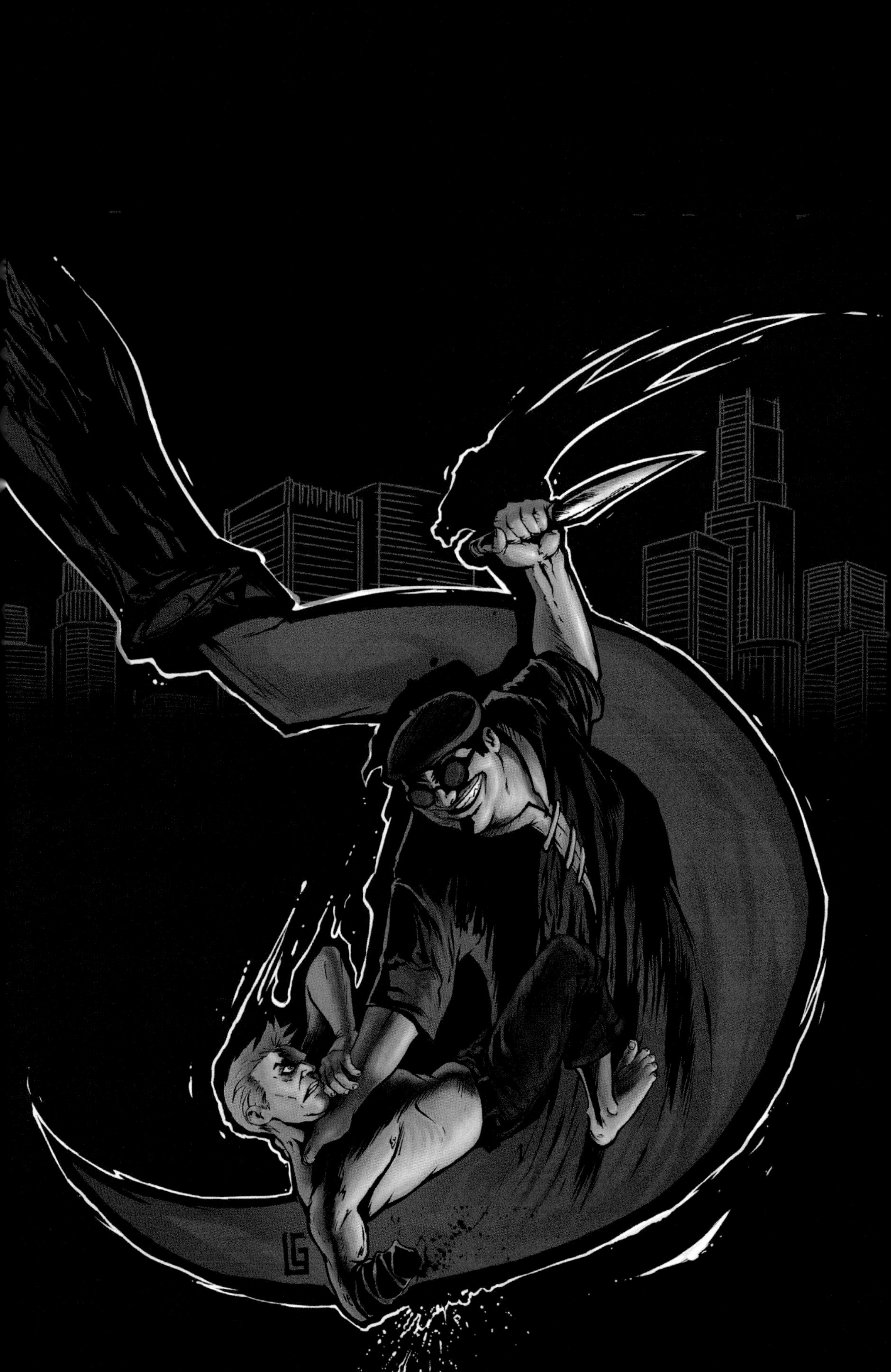

TABATHA ISSUE 4 COVER
LEONARDO GONZALEZ

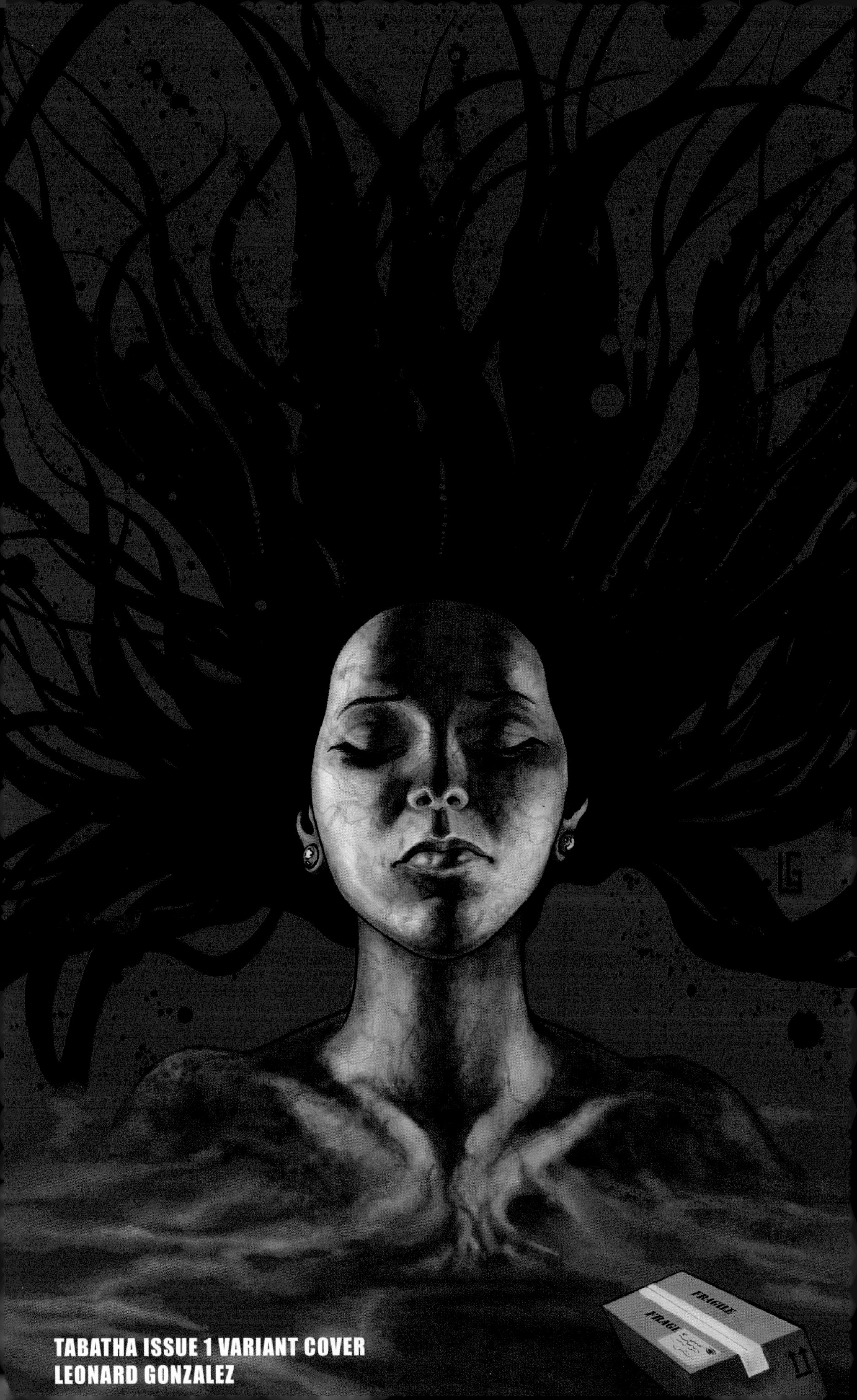
FRAGILE
FRAGI

TABATHA ISSUE 1 VARIANT COVER
LEONARD GONZALEZ

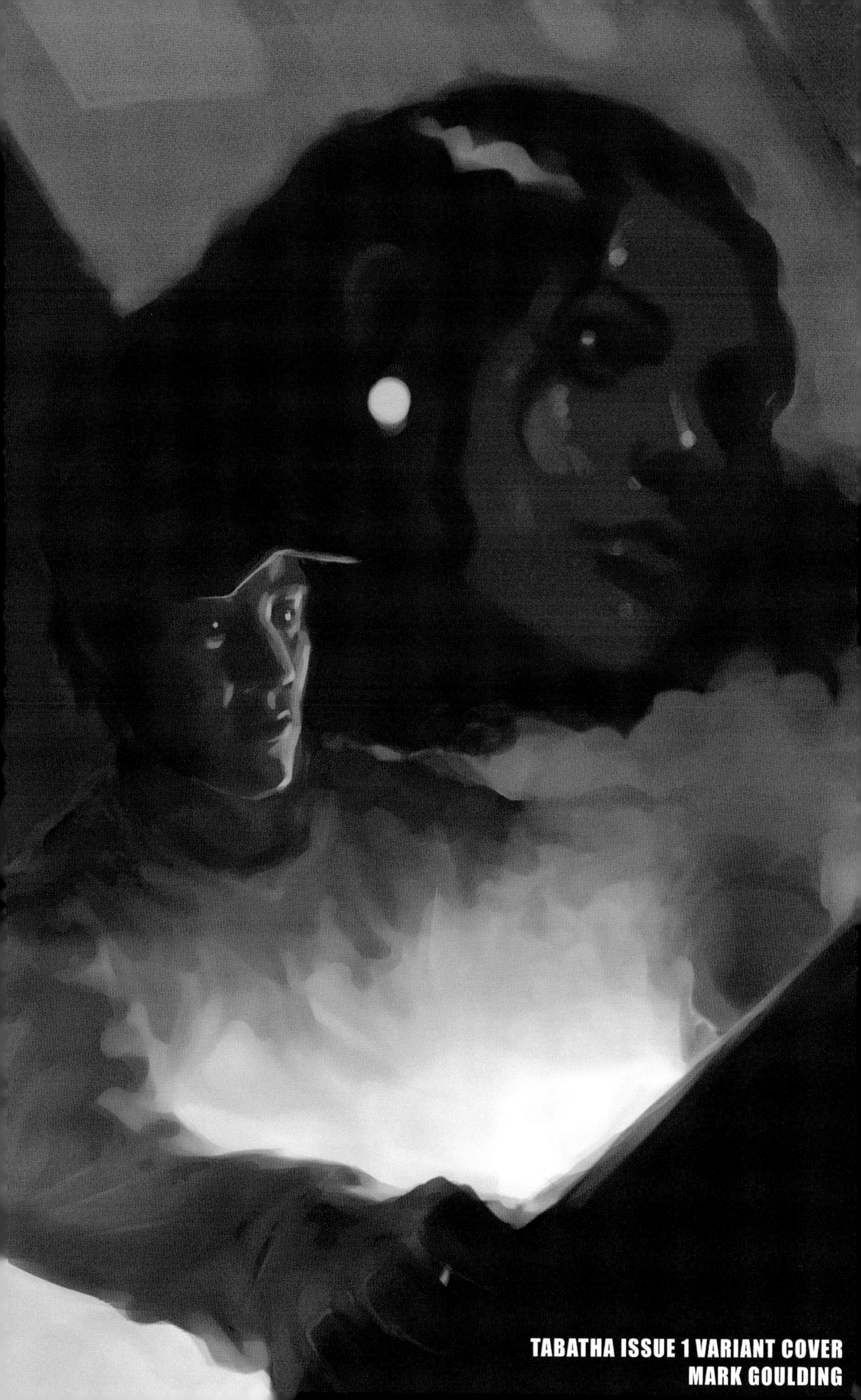

TABATHA ISSUE 1 VARIANT COVER
MARK GOULDING

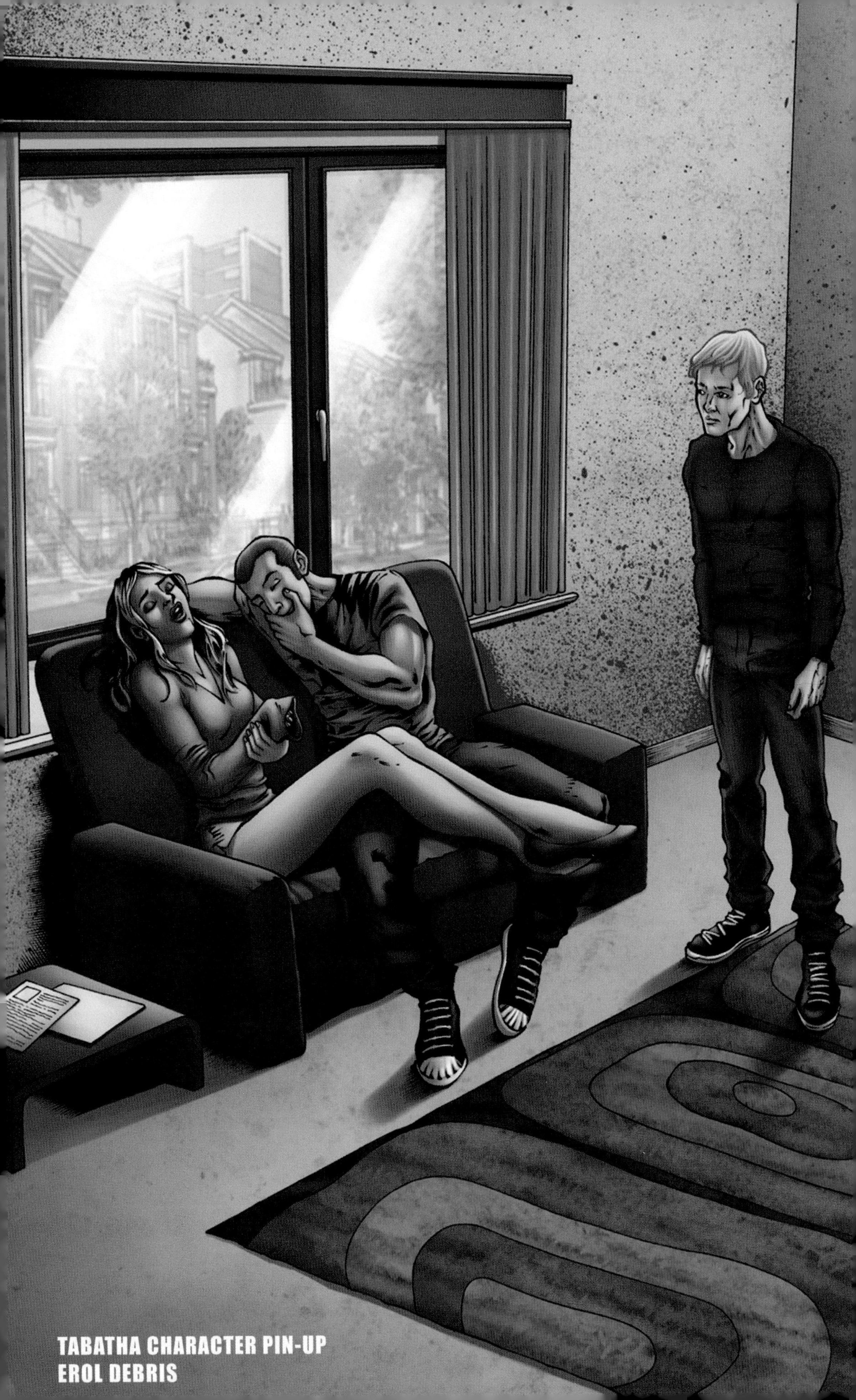

TABATHA CHARACTER PIN-UP
EROL DEBRIS

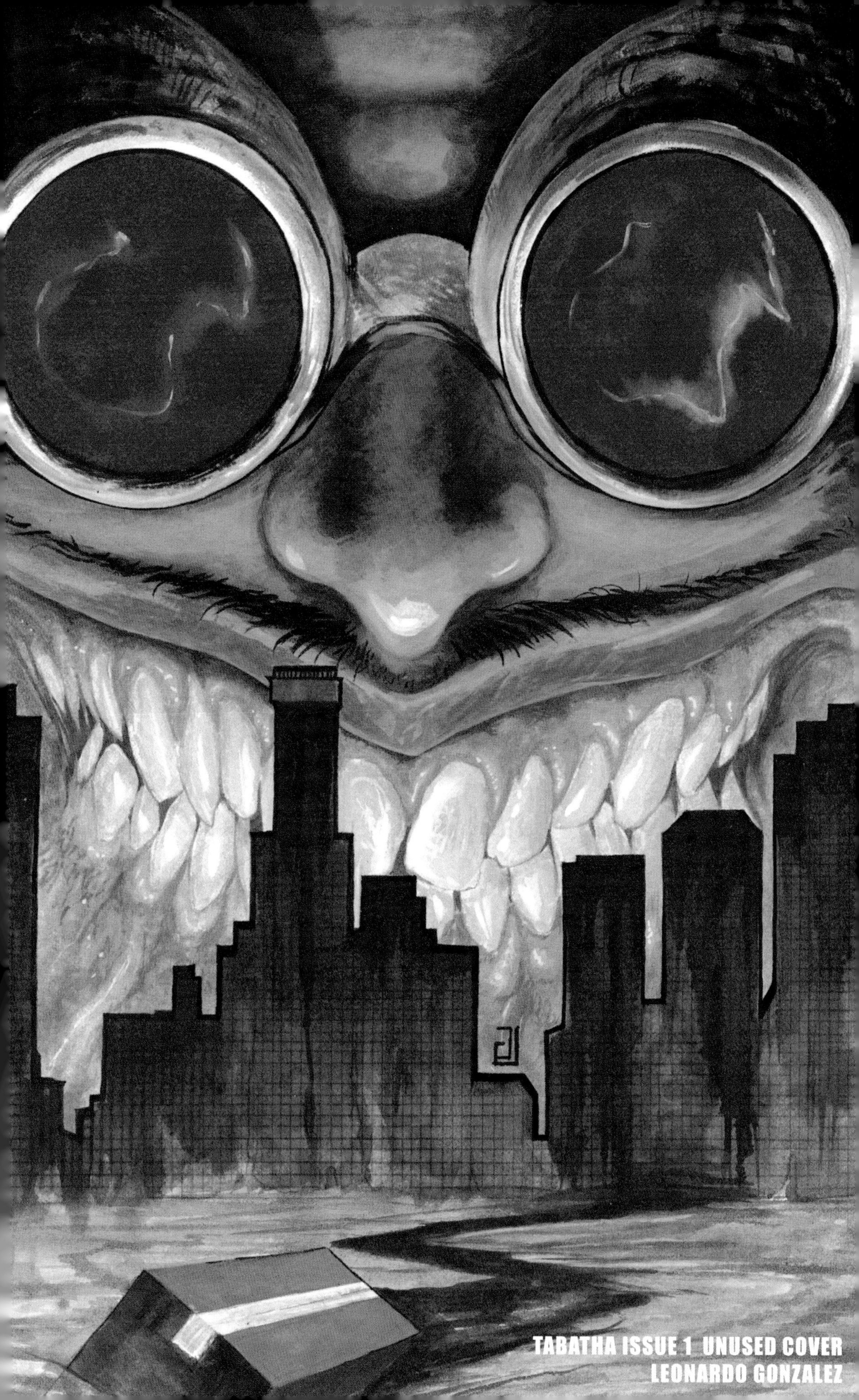

TABATHA ISSUE 1 UNUSED COVER
LEONARDO GONZALEZ

COVER CONCEPTS AND PENCILS BY LEONARDO GONZALEZ

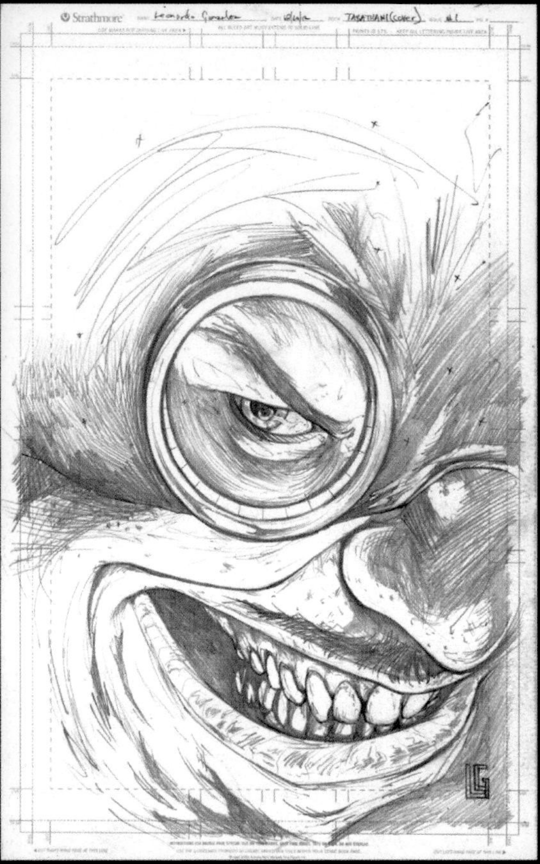

ISSUE 1 COVER PENCILS

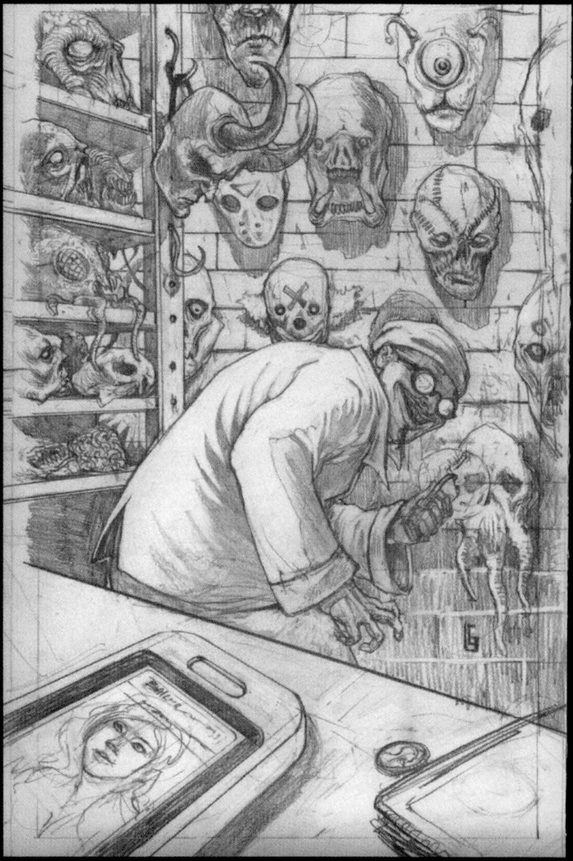

ISSUE 2 COVER PENCILS

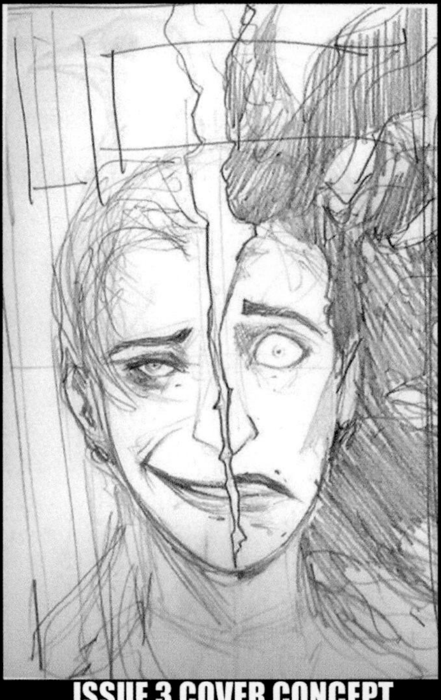

ISSUE 3 COVER CONCEPT

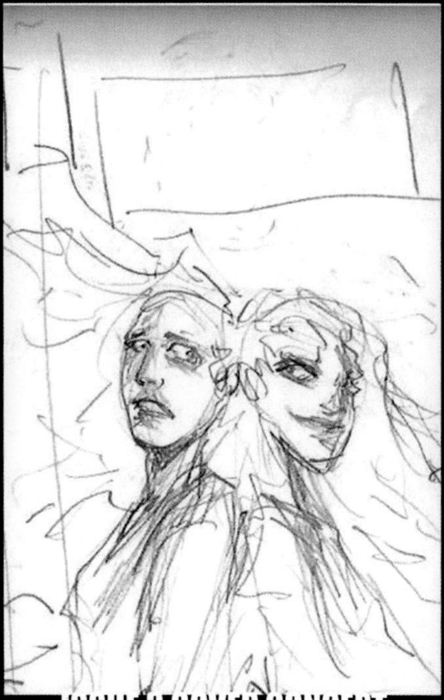

ISSUE 3 COVER CONCEPT

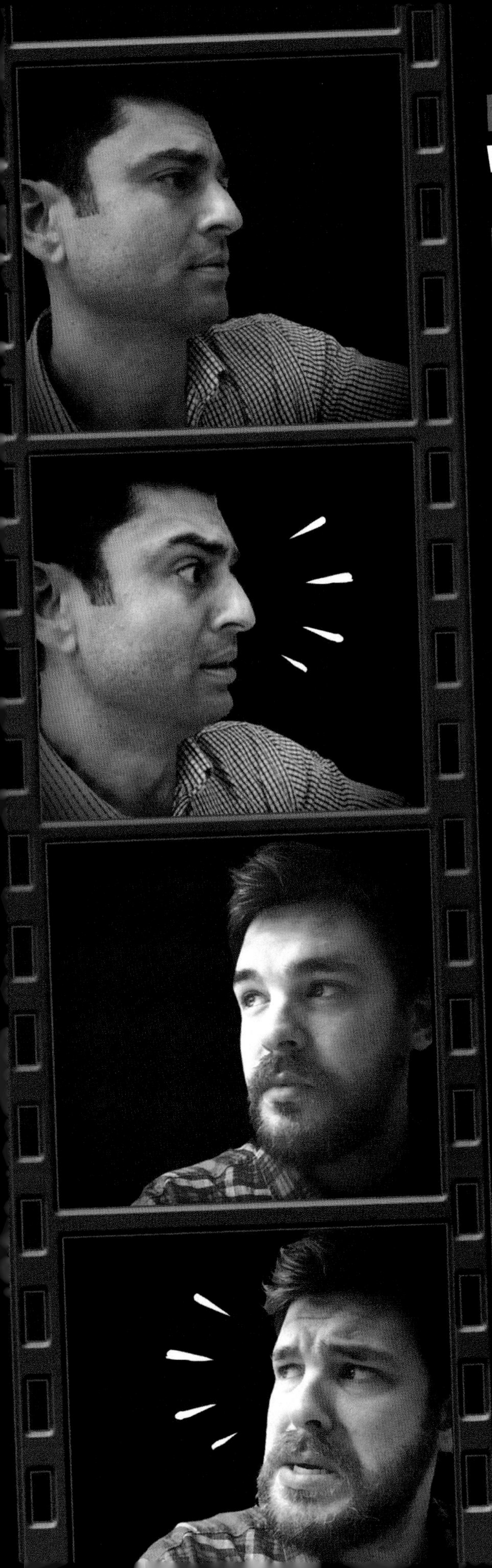

Neil Gibson

Written by C.W.

Neil is the beating heart and twisted mind behind T Pub. His mission in life is to have comics accepted as a respected medium across the globe and he's already making waves with his expansive body of work. Following the success of his ongoing and critically acclaimed multi-layered psychological thriller series Twisted Dark, Neil chose a more subtle narrative approach to his first Mini series Tabatha. Neil Lives in London with his Wife and Daughter and continues to shock the world with his fantastic comics and questionable taste in music.

Caspar Wijngaard

Written by N.G.

Caspar is not only the brilliant artist behind Tabatha, but he's also the art director for T Pub. He's responsible for making sure all the art that we produce is of a standard he is proud of. He continually strives to get better at his own art and the fact that he continues to improve with every story he draws is one of the things we admire most about him. He lives in London with his partner and daughter and likes the cocktail Thursdays that we have at T Pub. He has a powerful beard and an annoying habit of beating us all at video games - it's one of the few things we don't admire about him.

TABATHA'S THAI GREEN CURRY RECIPE

You can buy pre-made paste, but when you are cooking for a loved one, it's worth the extra effort
Serves 4 (or two is Fin is eating)

Ingredients

For your super duper homemade paste:
- 5cm ginger, peeled & chopped
- 1 small red onion, peeled & chopped
- 1 stick lemongrass, bashed and chopped
- 4 tbsp coriander root or stalks, chopped
- 2 green chillies, de-seeded and chopped (add seeds for more heat)
- 1 tsp thai fish sauce
- 4 garlic cloves, peeled & chopped
- 3 tbsp olive oil
- 1 tsp ground cumin
- 1 tsp ground coriander
- Zest of 1 lime

For the curry
- Groundnut oil
- 200g mushrooms, quartered
- 5 baby aubergines roughly chopped
- 600g free-range chicken thighs,
- 800ml coconut milk
- 2 heaped tsp palm sugar
- 6 kaffir lime leaves
- 7 tbsp fresh coriander, roughly chopped
- Bunch chopped sweet basil
- 1 tbsp fish sauce
- 1 tbsp bottled green peppercorns, drained

Method

1. Preheat the oven to 200°C and then blitz the paste ingredients together in a blender (or bash it up in a pestle and mortar if you want to tone your arms).

2. Warm the oil in a casserole and, when hot and sizzling, add the chicken strips and let them colour slightly on all sides. You will need to do this in batches to avoid crowding the pan. Remove the cooked chicken pieces from the casserole with a slotted spoon. Add the quartered mushrooms to the casserole and fry until golden-brown, adding more oil if needed.

3. Add the mushrooms and aubergine to the pan and stir-fry for three minutes before adding the coconut milk together with the palm sugar and lime leaves.

4. Bring to the boil, then turn the heat down and simmer for 10 minutes, stirring from time to time.

5. Bring slowly to the boil before adding most of the coriander, holy basil and the fish sauce, you may need to add a little water if the curry is too thick. Serve with Jasmine rice and a kiss XXXX

Bon Appetit xx

Thanks for all your support!

Cheers for all the great support guys!!

Thanks to all fans who pledged. We couldn't have done it without you!

Special thanks to:

Lucie Chauvin

Danny Darko

Andy Green

Dave Jackson

L Jones

Stefano Maifreni

Ayan Mitra

Tara Oldfield

Yiting Shen

Lee Turner

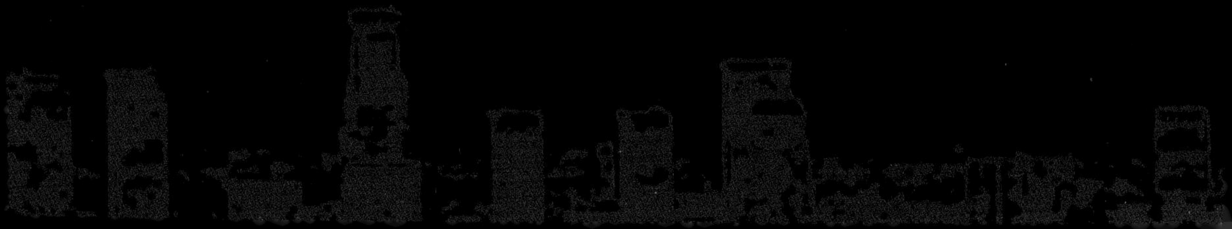

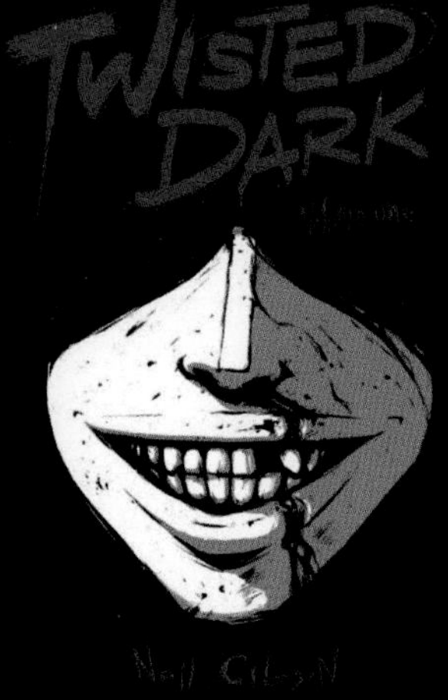
TWISTED DARK
NEIL GIBSON

Twisted Dark

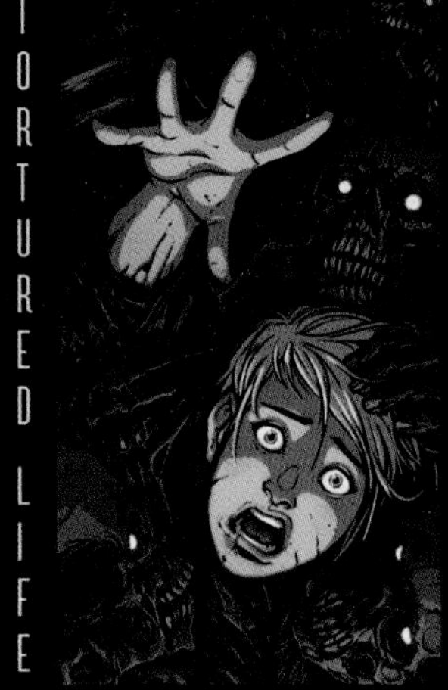
TORTURED LIFE

Tortured Life

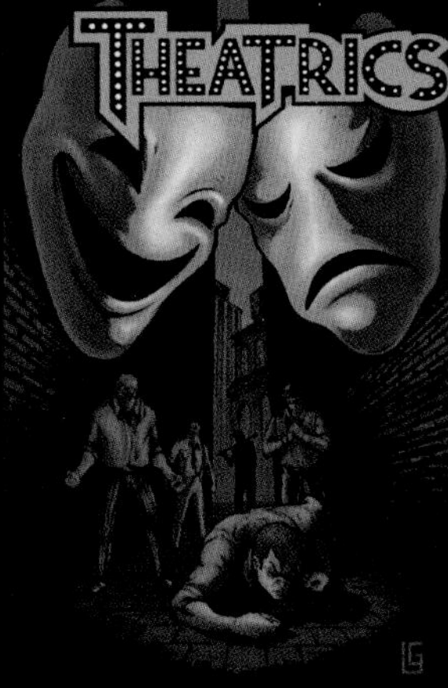
THEATRICS

Theatrics

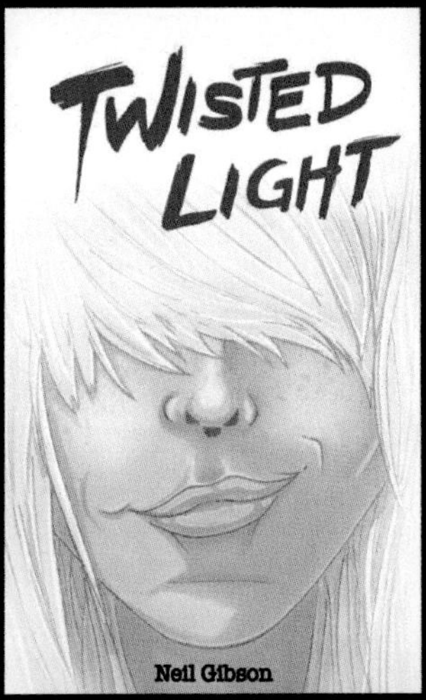
TWISTED LIGHT
Neil Gibson

Twisted Light

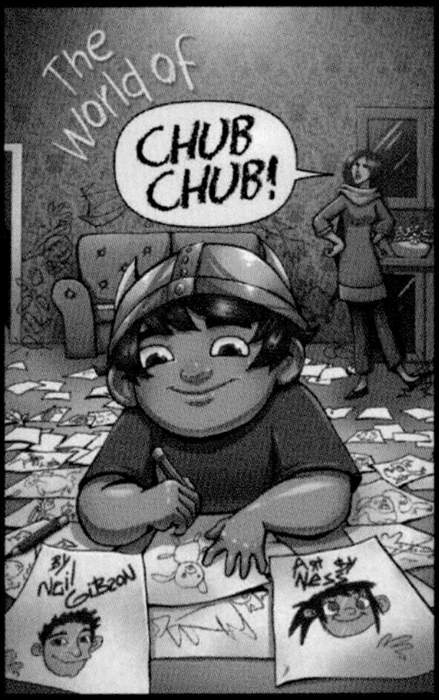
The World of
CHUB CHUB!

The World of
Chub Chub

To read some of our comics for free, visit

We dare ya...